Cultural Captives: The Beliefs and Behavior of American Young Adults

Stephen Cable

Library of Congress Cataloging-in-Publication Data

Cable, Stephen.

Cultural Captives: The Beliefs and Behavior of American Young Adults / Stephen Cable – 1st ed.

p. cm.

Includes bibliographical references

ISBN 978-0-945241-20-1

We hope you enjoy this book from Probe Ministries. For more information on this subject and related topics from a Christian worldview perspective, please visit us at www.probe.org .

Endorsements:

"Steve Cable has provided an invaluable service for Bible-believing Christians across America in *Cultural Captives*. He not only documents the alarming decline in a genuinely biblical worldview in America, but provides a powerful answer in a program for reversing that precipitous decline."

Dr. Richard Land,
President Ethics & Religious Liberty Commission
Southern Baptist Convention

"In this age of overabundant information, the challenge is sorting through it to find the core nuggets of truth. In this book, Probe Ministries has done just that. Cutting through the conflicting claims of various pundits, they have found that the data is unanimous in stating, "Born again Christians are more aligned with the cultural norms of our day than with the clear teaching of Jesus Christ." If you want to know what today's emerging adults are thinking and how we may be able to influence them with a biblical worldview, I recommend you take the time to read this new offering from Probe."

Josh McDowell,
Josh McDowell Ministry, a division of Cru

"To effectively minister within their culture, church leaders must have an accurate understanding of the actual religious beliefs and practices of the current generation. In this book, Steve Cable provides a comprehensive analysis of this issue drawing from multiple surveys including one commissioned by Probe Ministries specifically for this analysis. The conclusions drawn from this work are must reading for anyone who wants to help Christianity in America to a vibrant future."

Kerby Anderson,
President of Probe Ministries

Acknowledgements

Many people have been involved in writing this book beginning with my fellow Probe staff members. As a group, we began looking at related issues in 2008. Their interest and support have kept me focused on making some of our data and conclusions available through this book.

Thanks to the Barna Group for their timely work in preparing our survey questions and obtaining responses from born-again, 18 – 40 year olds. I particularly want to thank David Kinnaman and Lynn Hanacek for their leadership of the survey effort.

My daughter, Kristen was invaluable as an English proficient, proofreader of the material.

Finally, I want to thank Patti, my wife, for her support and understanding as I waded through the all of the survey data.

Cultural Captives: The Beliefs and Behavior of American Young Adults

Contents

Cultural Captives

Introduction

By the fall of 2009, the leaders of Probe Ministries were convinced the trajectory of Christian faith in America had moved into a critical wobble that could easily crash into irrelevancy. To better understand what was happening to Christian faith in this country, we began examining existing survey data on this topic. In addition to published reports from sociologists and others who commissioned relevant studies, we were able to delve into the raw survey results themselves for much of the data. We also commissioned our own survey to delve more deeply into the beliefs of born-again young adults and why they held them.

Helpful Information For Readers

This book provides a fairly comprehensive summary of what these surveys reveal about the state of Christianity among young adults in America. As such, the following chapters contain a large number of graphs and charts using data from the various surveys. For some of you, this type of data driven analysis is the type of work you love to dive into. Many others of you want to say, "I'm glad you did the analysis, but just give me the bottom line results." Recognizing this desire, a summary of key results is provided in this introductory chapter with references to where each item is discussed in later parts of this book.

Because the surveys utilized in this analysis cover different age groups and because sometimes it is informative to draw distinctions between different age groups, three different age groups are considered in this book. To clearly identify the age subset being discussed at a given time, the following nomenclature is utilized:

Ages 18 – 23	New Adults
Ages 18 – 29	Emerging Adults
Ages 18 – 40	Young Adults

In this book, we also distinguish between two primary groups of Protestants – Mainline Protestants and Evangelicals. Mainline Protestants have a greater focus on social issues than on evangelism and tend to be more liberal than other Protestants. In this report, we have determined the distinction based on a person's denomination following the breakdown used in the Pew Research surveys as shown in Appendix B. For example, United Methodists are classified as Mainline Protestants while Southern Baptists are classified as Evangelicals.

Much of the information in this book is presented in graphical, bar chart form. Some graphs include independent probabilities (where each item shown in the graph is treated independently) and other graphs include cumulative probabilities (where probabilities build cumulatively from left to right). A detailed description of these graphical structures is provided in Chapter 5 immediately preceding Figure 5-4.

Key Findings Regarding American Emerging Adults:

- **All Surveys Consistent**. All surveys evaluated are **consistent with one another**. For example, the Barna survey data is consistent with the GSS survey data in every respect. Some authors imply this is not the case, but our analysis leaves no doubt as to their consistency with one another. This result is excellent news as we do not have to try to reconcile disparate survey data. This fact also heightens our belief in the accuracy of the information presented herein. (Chapter 3)
- **Non-Christians Are Largest Group**. The percent of emerging adult Americans (i.e. those between the ages of 18 and 29) who **do not align themselves with any Christian denomination** (either Protestant or Catholic) was constant from 1970 through 1990. Since that time, it has increased by over 75% from 1995 through 2010. As of 2010, over 37% of emerging adults' fall into this non-Christian affiliation category. (Figure 1-1)
- **Born-again Protestants Steady at 25%**. Over the same forty years, **born-again, Protestant** believers have remained remarkably consistent at roughly 25% of all emerging adults. (Figure 1-2)
- **One Third of Born-agains Maintain a Biblical Worldview**. Averaging the results from four different surveys, about 1/3 of born-again (or Evangelical depending on the survey) Americans profess a set of beliefs about Christianity that are consistent with a biblical worldview. (Figure 4-5)
- **Only 14% of Born-agains Combine Biblical Worldview with Biblical Practices**. The percent of born-again, emerging adults

with a biblical worldview and who practice a minimally consistent set of religious practices (i.e. prayer, reading the Bible, attending church, involvement in a small group) is 14% (Figure 5-12). Since 36% of emerging adults are born again (Figure 4-1), we can combine these two figures to determine that only 5% (i.e. 14% x 36%) of American, emerging adults combine a basic set of biblical beliefs with a minimal set of religious practices.

- **<u>Less Than 2% of Born-agains Apply Biblical Worldview to Life Choices</u>**. The percent of born-again, emerging adults with a biblical worldview, at least a minimal biblical practice and biblical cultural beliefs (e.g. beliefs regarding abortion, sex outside of marriage, science and faith, etc.) is less than 2%.
- **<u>Evangelical Behavior Closer to Non-Evangelical than Biblical Standard</u>**. Throughout the book, charts are shown for both non-Evangelicals and Evangelical Christians. Time after time, comparing these charts shows: beliefs of Evangelicals are significantly different than non-Evangelicals **but much closer** to them than to any biblically defined standard. In other words, Evangelicals tend to have beliefs which follow closer to the beliefs of the population as a whole than to a set of beliefs consistent with the New Testament.
- **<u>Significant Change from Teenagers to New Adults</u>**. A significant change is apparent in the stated beliefs of American teenagers versus those of emerging adults. Much of the change is probably a result of no longer living in their parents' household (or at least not under the same rules in their parents' household). (Chapter 5)
- **<u>Parents Most Important Factor in Young Adult Beliefs</u>**. Most born again, young adults state that their parents were the single most important factor in establishing their current religious beliefs. However, of the born again, young adults surveyed only 28% had a biblical worldview and attended church regularly. Almost 67% of them did not have a biblical worldview. (Figure 10-2) Pastors and youth groups have little primary impact on the religious beliefs of young adults.
- **<u>College May Offset Negative Parental Influence</u>**. College has an interesting impact on today's emerging adults. A college graduate influenced by sources other than their family is 33% more likely to be a regular church attender with a biblical worldview than a college graduate whose primary influence is

their family and 110% more likely than a young adult who did not graduate from college. (Figure 11-6) This result probably comes from college students having their faith challenged and looking for answers from online sources such as www.probe.org.

- **Situation Warned About in New Testament**. The level of cultural captivity shown in these surveys is not a given, but it is not a surprise as well. It is consistent with the warnings in the New Testament encouraging believers to watch out for cultural captivity. (Chapters 2 & 9)
- **Church Response Must Be Proactive**. Doing nothing or continuing to do what we have been doing is not a good solution to the problems identified in this book. We must speak to this generation with a message that can clearly be understood within the context of this culture. (Chapter 14)

Summary of Methodology and Structure

The following sets of survey data were analyzed to help us understand the real state of Christian belief among young adults from age 18 to 40, with particular focus on emerging adults, age 18 to 30:

- **National Study of Youth and Religion**[1] – a five year study of about 3,000 young people beginning when they were 13 to 18 years old and concluding when the same group, now 'new adults', was 18 to 23 years old.[2]

- **Baylor Religion Survey**, 2005[1] and 2007 – a survey of 1,721 adults in 2005 and 1,648 adults in 2007 covering their religious values, practices and behaviors.[3]

- **General Social Survey**, 2008 [1] – a survey of 3,559 adults covering a number of social issues including questions on their religious beliefs and practices.[4] Some analysis was also done using the GSS survey data from 1976, 1988, 1990, 1994, 1996, 2000, 2006 and 2010.

- **Barna Group** summary of biblical worldview questions from 2009

- **Barna Group, The Buster Report** – based upon a series of nationwide tracking reports between 2002 and 2007 each of which used a sample of 1,000 plus adults[5]

- **Probe Ministries Culturally Captive Christian Study 2010** – a survey performed for Probe by the Barna Group of 813 born-again young adults from age 18 through 40 looking at the source of their religious beliefs and cultural practices[6]

In general, analysis of the data collected in these surveys added fuel to the fire of concern. When analyzed in a common fashion, all of the surveys resounded with a common theme. If one takes the view that historical, biblical evangelical thought is the desired goal, ***the state of American religion is not only faltering; it is worse than we thought!*** Although the percentage of young American adults identifying with an evangelical church has remained relatively constant over the last forty years, the religious and cultural beliefs of these young people are far removed from a biblical worldview.

In this book, we capture the results from multiple studies in a way that

- extracts the essence of the data as it relates to the trajectory of Christianity in America,
- adds to previously published data the results of Probe's survey of American, young adult born-agains, and
- encourages Evangelicals to take an active role in countering the mad dash away from a biblical worldview.

The first segment of the book examines the problems facing the church in America today. After a summary of the beliefs of Christians today and a comparison with the issues facing the 1st century church, we begin by attempting to make sense of the confusing array of conclusions offered in other commentators' analysis of the survey data. Although our conclusions may differ from others looking at the same data, a clear case is made upholding our conclusions. We discovered that all the sets of data give very similar results on similar questions. The key distinction between the differing analyses of the data was whether one simply looked at each question by itself or whether one looked at the composite beliefs and actions of the study group.

This discussion is followed by looking at what the data tells us about 1) the religious beliefs and religious practices of young, American adults, 2) their cultural beliefs and cultural practices, and 3) the impact of other factors (e.g. education levels, regions of the country, etc.) on the previous two topics. We will see how our culture trumps our religious teachings so that the majority of evangelical young adults have adopted a lifestyle that is carnal, confused, compromised and complacent.

The second segment of this book looks at the data to see if there is hope that we can restore these captives to freedom in Jesus Christ. We begin by looking at born-again, young adults to understand how they obtained their current beliefs and what might make them change those beliefs. Since most young adults acquired their religious beliefs from their parents, we will have a hard time influencing the beliefs of today's teenagers and younger children (and children to be) if we cannot make a dent in the faulty beliefs of their parents (or parents to be). Looking specifically at born-again young adults, we consider the religious beliefs being passed on to them and how, if at all, those beliefs are impacting their interaction with today's culture. We will also consider how different ethnic, education and income backgrounds work in defining their religious and cultural beliefs.

The focus of this book is primarily to understand what existing survey data reveals concerning the spiritual direction of our young adults. It strives to bring together data from different sources and different interpretations to see if there is a common message to be found. However, the results of this analysis cry out for proactive steps to change the projected future of faith in this country. Consequently, the final chapter lays out steps which may help to stem the flood of 'popular postmodernism' rapidly consuming traditional evangelical Christianity.

Part I Living as Captives of Our Culture

Chapter 1 Young Adults and Christian Belief in America 2010

If America continues on its current trend, the number of 18 – 29 year old Americans who state, "My religious preference is No Religion or a non-Christian religion" will grow to over 50% of the population by the year 2030. In other words, America will be undeniably a non-Christian nation. How can one say this beyond looking at the trends in society and guessing? The General Social Survey has been collecting data on this question since 1976. Figure 1-1 plots the percentage of young Americans who select a non-Christian religion or None when asked, "What is your religious preference?" Although, "None" does not mean an individual does not share some beliefs with Evangelical Christians, we can be confident that the vast majority of the "None" category do not hold to an evangelical worldview.

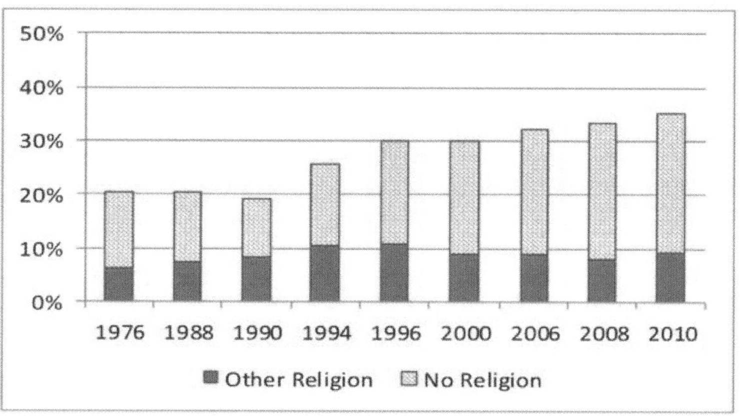

Figure 1-1 GSS Survey: Non-Christians

As you can see, from 1976 through 1990, the number remained basically constant at around 20%. From 1990 through 2010, it grew by 75% to just over one third of American emerging adults. Interestingly, it was not the percentage of other non-Christian religions (e.g. Islam, Hinduism, etc.) that grew. Instead, the percentage of those professing no religion grew from 10% of the emerging adult population in 2009 to over one quarter of them in 2010. If that linear rate of growth continues for the next twenty years, 50% of young Americans will not profess a Christian religion.

To get a fuller picture of what has happened over the last 35 years, let's add the rest of the population divided into Catholics, Protestants, and born-again Protestants. There are several aspects to take note of in Figure 1-2. First, notice that the percentage of Catholics is virtually constant over that period at about 27% of emerging adult Americans. However, this result is misleading because there have actually been significant changes in the make-up of Catholics in America during this period. In 1976, almost 30% of white, emerging adults identified themselves with the Roman Catholic Church. By 2008, this number had dropped to less than 20% of white, emerging adults. So, how did the percentage of young Catholics remain constant? The percentage of Hispanics in our emerging adult culture grew significantly during that period and well over 60% of them identified themselves as Roman Catholic.

Another interesting fact shown in the chart is the decline of Mainline Protestant affiliations (or more precisely Protestants who do not indicate being born-again). This group has dropped from over 25% of the population to less than 15% over this period of time. The number of emerging adults indicating they are born-again has remained near 25% of the emerging adult population; yet the percentage still dropped by 17% from 1976 to 2010 (i.e. from 27.5% of the population in 1976 down to 23% of the population in 2010).

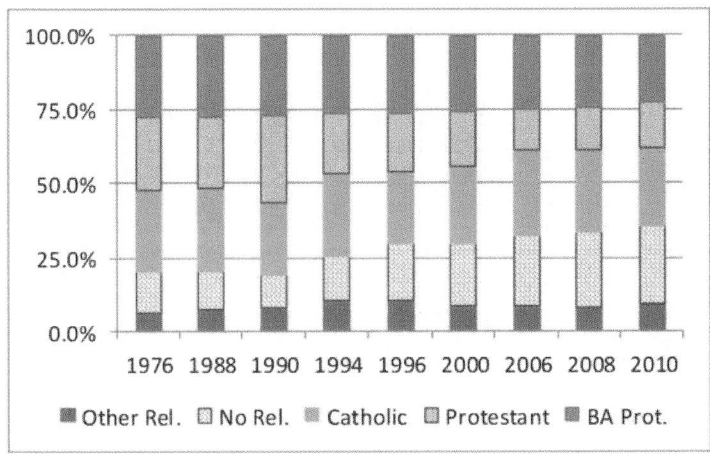

Figure 1-2 GSS Survey: Religious Affiliation of American Ages 18-29

Overall, this chart raises a critical question as we consider the role of Christianity in the future of America. Clearly, the percentage of non-Christians is growing and the percentage of Protestants is decreasing. To turn this trend around, born-again, Evangelical Christians must become more adept at sharing the reasons for their belief in order to win more to Christ. If not, it appears we will have a country with a consistent minority of 25% born-again believers. But perhaps, even that perception is gilding the lily. What do these self-identified, born-agains believe? Do they really have a message and life style that could draw others to faith in Christ? In the remainder of this book, we will look at just this question. Warning: the answer is not encouraging. We need to undertake a new course of action if we want born-again, Evangelical Christians to be a growing group influencing our culture for Christ.

Taking Stock of Emerging Adults

Let us continue this examination of the trajectory of Christianity in America by looking at what researchers are learning about "the religious and spiritual lives of emerging adults". This last phrase is the subtitle of a recent book by Christian Smith summarizing the results of a groundbreaking study based on the National Study of Youth and Religion (NSYR)[1]. In 2002/3, Smith and his team surveyed over 3,000 teenagers and conducted detailed interviews with over 250 of the survey respondents. These same people were surveyed again in 2005 and again in 2007/8. The 2007/8 survey also included over 230 in depth interviews. Through this effort, we can gain insight not only into the current beliefs and practices of these new adults but also how those beliefs and practices have changed over the five-year transition from teenager to new adult.

In general, the other surveys used in this analysis give a similar view of the state of new adult beliefs, but the results reported by the NSYR delve into these issues somewhat deeper drawing upon face to face interviews as well as survey data. So, in this introductory paragraph, we will rely heavily upon the works of Smith to help us paint a picture of emerging adult religious views in this decade.

Emerging Adults: A New Life Stage

These 18 to 23 year olds represent the future leaders of our nation and our churches and will be the parents of the children who will lead America into the second half of the 21st century. Barring a major state change in our culture, their attitudes toward Christianity are a preview of the role of Christianity in America in the near future. Those of us committed to Jesus' Great Commission should recognize the importance of understanding these cultural trends so that we effectively communicate the truth of the gospel to an increasingly confused culture.

Let's begin by highlighting a few aspects of the culture which shape the thinking and actions of these emerging adults (note: drawing upon the survey of new adults and other relevant data, Smith extends his analysis to consider all emerging adults ages 18 to 30). The first point Smith makes is that a new life phase has developed in American culture. The experience of young Americans as they age from 18 to 30 is much different today than during most of the 20th century. Full adulthood "is culturally defined as the end of schooling, a stable career job, financial independence, and new family formation."[2] Four factors have contributed to making today's transition to full adulthood an extended complex process:

1. the dramatic growth in higher education
2. the delay of marriage
3. the expectation of an unstable career
4. the willingness of parents to extend support well into their twenties

Because of these factors, most emerging adults assume that they will go through an extended period of transition trying different life experiences, living arrangements, careers, relationships and viewpoints until they finally are able to stand on their own and settle down. Many of those surveyed are smarting from poor life choices and harmful lifestyles, yet they profess to have "no regrets" and are generally optimistic about their personal future when they finally get to the point they are able to stand on their own. Some researchers refer to this recently created life phase as "emerging adulthood" covering the period from 18 to 30.

These emerging adults face a period of significant changes in their lives and in the culture around them. We will see that for many professing Christians, they have already established a set of beliefs and attitudes that have them on a trajectory moving away from a vital Christian walk with Jesus Christ. To put it in the words of Paul, they have already been "taken captive"[3] by their culture.

The General Social Survey (GSS) data shows us that the number of emerging adults who identify themselves either as not religious or as practicing a non-Christian religion (e.g. Islam, Buddhism, Mormonism) has grown from one in five emerging adults from 1976 through 1990 to almost two out of five emerging adults in 2010. This doubling reflects a change in the dominant culture from supporting Christian beliefs to now being basically counter to them. If this erosion continues at this pace for the next twenty years, we could see well over 50% of emerging adults who do not profess Christianity. As Smith reports, today's emerging adults are immersed in a postmodern culture that "stressed difference over unity, relativity over universals, subjective experience over rational authorities, feeling over reason."[4] In the postmodern mindset, one cannot ascribe to a universal truth applicable to all. Instead, one can only hold to local truths which may be useful to you but cannot be assumed or shown to be universal in their application.

This culture has produced a set of young Americans who may still claim to be associated with Protestant or Catholic beliefs, but in reality have accepted the view that God and Christ are potentially helpful upon death, but are of little value until then. As these young people moved from teenagers into emerging adults, Smith found that over four out of ten of them became less religious over a five-year span. However, he did find that about one in three would identify themselves as Evangelical and probably continue to identify themselves that way for the foreseeable future.

Themes Defining this New Life Stage

Through their interviews and the results of other studies, Smith and his team identified over 40 cultural themes that impact the overall religious perspective of emerging adults. A sampling of four of those themes gives a feel for the general cultural milieu shaping the lives of today's emerging adults.

Theme #1: Reality and morality are personal and subjective not objective – Most emerging adults cannot even conceive of, much less believe in, the existence of a common shared reality that applies to all people. According to Smith, "They cannot, for whatever reason, believe in – or sometimes even conceive of – a given, objective truth, fact, reality, or nature of the world that is independent of their subjective self-experience and that in relation to which they and others might learn or be persuaded to change. . . People are thus trying to communicate with each other in order to simply be able to get along and enjoy life as they see fit. Beyond that, anything truly objectively shared or common or real seems impossible to access." [5] It appears that the perceived inability to know objective truth causes emerging adults to settle for getting along and enjoying life as the highest good they can aspire to for their life. This cultural theme is driving them into a life of vanity. Solomon warned of this danger in Ecclesiastes when he wrote

> *Vanity of vanities! All is vanity. . . So I hated life, for the work which had been done under the sun was grievous to me; because everything is futility and striving after wind.*
> Eccl 1:2, 2:17

rather than the life of higher calling Paul knew when he wrote,

> *"one thing I do: forgetting what lies behind and reaching forward to what lies ahead, I press on toward the goal for the prize of the upward call of God in Christ Jesus."*
> Phil 3:13-14

For Solomon in Ecclesiastes, the best one could hope for was to enjoy ones work as an end in itself rather than as part of a greater good, a bigger truth. On the other hand, Paul saw his efforts as a part of the greater plan of God to redeem mankind bringing it back into an eternal relationship with their Creator. It appears the majority of emerging adults empathize more with Solomon's view than with Paul's.

This subjective view of reality is clearly reflected in the conversations of emerging adults. Based on interviews with emerging adults, Smith reports, "The phrase "I feel that" has nearly ubiquitously replaced the phrases "I think that", "I believe that," and "I would argue that" – a shift in language use that express an essentially subjectivistic and emotivistic approach to moral reasoning and rational argument. . . which leads to speech in which claims are not staked, rational arguments are not developed, differences are not engaged, nature is not referenced, and universals are not recognized. Rather, differences in viewpoints and ways of life are mostly acknowledged, respected, and then set aside as incommensurate and off limits for evaluation."[6] Our young people are growing up into a culture where there is no context for real dialogue about truth and truth's impact on our life choices.

The inability to believe in or search for objective truth stands in contrast to the central claim of Christianity to provide the Truth that we cannot obtain from other sources. When Jesus came to earth, John told us

> *For the Law was given through Moses; grace and* ***truth*** *were realized through Jesus Christ.* John 1:17

and Jesus told those following Him,

> *If you continue in My word, then you are truly disciples of Mine; and you will know* ***the truth,*** *and* ***the truth*** *will make you free.*" John 8:31-32

and Jesus told Pilate that He came "*to testify to* ***the Truth***" (John 18:37) and told His disciples that He is "*the way,* ***the Truth*** *and the life*" (John 14:6). As followers of Christ, we should have the same commitment to share the truth of Christ with a confused and hurting world as Paul wrote in his instruction to Christians to "*speak* ***the truth*** *in love.*" (Eph 4:15)

Without any concept of an objective standard, morality is determined by one's individual feelings. If you feel good about an action, it is right for you. If you feel bad about an action, it is wrong for you. Most emerging adults would say, "if something would hurt another person, it is probably bad; if it does not and is not illegal, it's probably fine."[7] The truth Jesus calls us to is a much higher, objective standard for living that calls us to consider the needs of others as more important than my own.

Theme #2: It's up to the individual, but don't expect to change the world – Most emerging adults have no concept of a common good that would motivate us to put another's interests ahead of our own or to attempt to influence another's behavior for the common good. "The most one should ever do toward influencing another person is to ask him or her to consider what one thinks. Nobody is bound to any course of action by virtue of belonging to a group or because of a common good."[8] They have essentially adopted the concept that asking someone to change or adopt a new behavior is in itself unacceptable behavior. You are telling that other person that they could be better, do better, think better than they currently do which is just rude. How would you feel if they turned around and tried to change you? "Again, any notion of the responsibilities of a common humanity, a transcendent call to protect the life and dignity of one's neighbor, or a moral responsibility to seek the common good was almost entirely absent among the respondents."[9]

Once again, this prevalent theme among our emerging adults runs counter to a biblical perspective of our responsibility in the world around us. What are some attitudes a Christian should employ in engaging the world:

- Be involved in making disciples of all Mt 28:19-20
- Go the extra mile in helping my neighbors Mt 5:42, Phil 2:3-4
- Seek to do good to those in need Gal 6:9-10
- Show love for my brothers in ways that can be observed by others John 13:34-35
- Pray for those who need to come to Christ Col 4:2-4

The attitude behind these instructions is that irrespective of the response we receive, we need to do our part in helping to minister to God's creation and specifically those created in His image. Our responsibility is to do what is right and trust God to accomplish His purpose through our obedience. However, most emerging adults take a very pragmatic view of good works. "Most emerging adults in America have extremely modest to no expectations for ways society or the world can be changed for the better. . . Many are totally disconnected from politics, and countless others are only marginally aware of what today's pressing political issues might be. . ."[10] Their attitude is often based on the idea that if you cannot make everything right all by yourself, then do not waste your time trying. Just go along with the flow and do your own thing.

Theme #3: Uncertain purpose, but consumerism is good stuff – Most emerging adults are still unsure as to what their purpose in life might be. Is there something greater that they should devote themselves to? Lacking any concept of a common good takes the teeth out of God's command to "*love your neighbor as yourself*" (Matt 22:39) and to "*regard others as more important than yourself, do not merely look out for your own personal interests, but also for the interests of others.*" (Phil 2:3-4) Self-sacrifice for others was clearly not a part of their life purpose.

In contrast, almost all of them are sure that being able to buy the things they want and to live a comfortable affluent lifestyle are key aspects of their purpose. There does not appear to be any tension in their thinking between loving God and loving material things as well. "Not only was there no danger of leading emerging adults into expressing false opposition to materialistic consumerism; interviewers could not, no matter how hard they pushed, get emerging adults to express any serious concerns about any aspect of mass-consumer materialism."[11] In this cultural environment, Jesus admonition in Luke 12 is desperately needed,

> "*Beware, and be on your guard against every form of greed; for not even when one has an abundance does his life consist of his possessions.*" Luke 12:15

To be on our guard against every form of greed requires continual vigilance in a country like America where greed takes on many forms which appear on the surface to be good. We need to regularly check our possessions and our desires to counter any tendencies towards greedy behavior. We can enjoy the bounty of life but not at the expense of turning our back on those with true needs. However, this is not the message communicated by television, advertising or YouTube videos, where constant consumption of goods with no regrets or concerns is advocated.

Theme #4: Sex is not a moral issue - Partying, hooking up, having sex and cohabitating are generally viewed as an essential aspect of the transition from teen years to adulthood. Whether one is personally engaged in casual sexual relationships at the moment or not, almost everyone reports having friends who are. For most emerging adults, hooking up with (i.e. having casual sex with) someone you hardly know is much less serious a relationship than seriously dating someone. The media and popular culture have succeeded in recasting sexual involvement as a passing recreational activity rather than as a part of a lifelong, partnership commitment.

This cultural theme creates a dissonance with their attitude toward serious practice of religion since they recognize that most religions are not favorable towards drunken partying and sex outside of marriage. Choosing to ignore any religious moral teaching from their teen years, "the vast majority of emerging adults nonetheless believe that cohabiting is a smart if not absolutely necessary experience and phase for moving toward an eventual successful and happy marriage. . . none of the emerging adults who are enthusiastic about cohabiting as a means to prevent unsuccessful marriages seem aware that nearly all studies consistently show that couples who live together before they marry are more, not less, likely to later divorce than couples who did not live together before their weddings."[12] Thus the popular wisdom of the time outweighs the hard fact that living together does not produce the knowledge or experience necessary to ensure a long, happy married life.

These four themes present a representative sample of the major themes on attitude and behavior identified by Smith and his team. To restate what we have seen, many emerging adults would resonate with the following:

1. There is no real truth or morality in this world; only what my friends and I establish for ourselves.
2. Consequently, there is no reason for me to get involved in helping create a society with high moral standards, as I can't even say what those standards should be.
3. But, there are a lot of good reasons to make sure that I am in a position to consume as much as possible during my stay on this earth; this is my primary objective in life.
4. This can certainly be seen in my attitude towards sexuality; where my emerging adulthood is a time of experiencing as much as possible before settling down to have a family (until I decide that I would enjoy another spouse better than my current one).

If these four themes represent the dominant attitudes of emerging adults, we have produced a generation that will introduce an essentially non-Christian worldview to succeeding generations.

Dispelling Some Common Myths Concerning Emerging Adults

As important as it is to understand the key themes driving the beliefs of a generation, it is equally important to unmask myths about that generation which are not supported by the data. A careful examination of well-designed cultural research identifies weaknesses in popularly held perceptions of reality; that is, facts often expose myths. Now consider three popular myths that must be modified or discarded in the light of the NYSR results.

Myth 1: Emerging adults are very spiritual but are not into religion

A popular perception is that although most young adults are not that interested in the external practice of organized religion, they are strongly committed to a personal faith and development of their spirituality. Although their outward involvement has declined, their inward commitment remains strong and their public involvement can be expected to return as they settle down into marriage and children. However, the data does not support this perception. As Smith states, "little evidence supports the idea that emerging adults who decline in regular external religious practice nonetheless retain over time high levels of subjectively important, privately committed, internal religious faith. Quite the contrary is indicated by our analysis."[13]

Smith and his team used the survey responses to categorize the respondents into six different religious types. Four of these types (Selective Adherents, Religiously Indifferent, Religiously Disconnected, and Irreligious) are generally indifferent to both traditional religions and spiritual topics. These four types of emerging adults make up about 70% of the population. Of the remaining 30%, half of those are what Smith labels Committed Traditionalists who are actively involved with organized religion. Another half of the remaining (i.e. 15% of the total) are labeled Spiritually Open. It is important to understand that Spiritually Open is not the same as Spiritually Interested. Smith reports, "Most are in fact nothing more than simply open. They are not actively seeking, not taking a lot of initiative in pursuit of the spiritual."[14] So, when the data is analyzed less than 15% (most likely much less than) of emerging adults could be considered as spiritual but not religious in the sense that spiritual concerns are a significant part of their lives.

It is interesting to note that Smith found approximately 35% of the respondents indicated an association with an evangelical church (including Pentecostal denominations) but only found that 15% were Committed Traditionalists. Thus, well over 60% of those identifying with evangelical churches are not actively involved with organized religion.

Consequently, it appears that the challenge for the church is not redirecting a pent up spiritual interest into orthodox Christianity, but, instead, demonstrating that spiritual issues are worthy of any real attention at all. Our challenge is to raise their interest in the spiritual dimension of life to a level at least consistent with their current focus on consumerism as the purpose for life.

Myth 2: Emerging adults are hostile toward the church

Several recent books have suggested that the dominant attitude of unchurched emerging adults is one of critical indifference if not hostility toward the church. As Kinnaman reports, "younger adults have little trust in the Christian faith, and esteem for the lifestyle of Christ followers is quickly fading among outsiders".[15] Their research suggests that emerging adults view the church as hypocritical, hateful and irrelevant. Although he acknowledges that some of these feelings exist, Smith believes that the data demonstrates that these attitudes are not as prevalent as others suggest. In fact, eight out of ten emerging adults state that they have "a lot of respect for organized religion in this country" and seven out of ten disagree that "organized religion is usually a big turnoff for me." Going a step further, a strong majority of emerging adults would disagree with the statement that "most mainstream religion is irrelevant to the needs and concerns of most people my age."[16] However, a large majority believe too many religious people are negative, angry, and judgmental. So there appears to be a larger disconnect with individuals than with religion as an institution.

Given these results, why are we presented with strong cases to the contrary? First, there are a significant minority who view the church as an irrelevant turnoff and a majority who believe that too many religious people are negative angry and judgmental. Second, Smith surmises that some of this perception comes from conducting "interviews with non-representative samples of emerging adults . . . by authors who are themselves alienated from mainstream religion . . . (or) by pastoral and ecclesial reformers within mainstream religion who want to make the case that traditional churches are failing to reach young people today and so need to be dramatically transformed in a postmodern or some other allegedly promising way."[17]

Once again this is a good news / bad news story. The good news is that most emerging adults do not have strong emotional barriers built up against organized religion. However, the vast majority of them are indifferent to religion and confused about its role in their life. According to Smith, "Most emerging adults are okay with talking about religion as a topic, although they are *largely indifferent to it* – religion is just not that important to most of them. . . To whatever extent they do talk about it, most of them think that most religions share the same core principles, which they generally believe are good."[18]

Myth 3: Religious practice does not impact personal behavior

Another common perception is that religiously devoted emerging adults are not appreciably different from other emerging adults in their actual life practices when it comes to sexuality, generosity, community service, drug use and integrity. We are often told that out of wedlock pregnancy, cheating and drug use are the same for Evangelical emerging adults as for the rest of society. It is certainly true that affiliation with an Evangelical denomination makes only a small difference in those behaviors. But, does a deep personal commitment to a relationship with Jesus Christ make a difference? The survey data allowed Smith and his team to differentiate between simple affiliation and devotion. What he discovered is that those emerging adults who are devoted to their faith exhibit significantly different lifestyles than the norm. In particular, these devoted emerging adults are

- more than twice as likely to give and volunteer their time,
- more than four times less likely to engage in binge drinking or drugs,
- 25% more likely to have attended college,
- almost two times less likely to think that buying more things would make them happier,
- twice as likely to abstain from pornography, and
- more than twice as likely to have abstained from sexual intercourse outside of marriage.

The results clearly show that a deep commitment to a Christian religious faith has a significant impact on one's lifestyle. As Smith concludes, "emerging adult religion – whatever its depth, character, and substance – correlates significantly with, and we think actually often acts as a causal influence producing, what most consider to be more positive outcomes in life for emerging adults."[19]

Exposing these myths helps us focus on the key challenge for the future. It is not redirecting a pent up spiritual interest into orthodox Christianity or overcoming an emotional aversion to organized religion. Instead, the key challenge is demonstrating to these young adults that spiritual issues are worthy of any real attention at all;challenging them to adopt new attitudes and behaviors consistent with an eternal, biblical worldview.

This first chapter presents a feel for the fundamental changes in beliefs which will drive the future direction of Christianity in our country. In the remainder of this first section, we will examine in some depth the religious and cultural beliefs behind the themes and myths discussed above.

Chapter 2 A Clear Warning Against Cultural Captivity

Before examining the spiritual and cultural beliefs of America's young adults in more detail, let us consider the biblical context for such a discussion. Cultural captivity is one concept introduced in the Bible that helps us understand our current situation. In the New Testament, we are warned to reject the different types of cultural captivity promoted by the Pharisees, the Sadducees, and the Greco-Roman culture.

Cultural captivity is a voluntary limiting of the work of Christ in our lives. It is a captivity caused by

1. putting our trust in something other than the person and promises of Christ, *or*
2. misunderstanding the truths by which Christ has called us to live, *or*
3. a combination of these two deceptions.

- Cultural captivity as used herein refers to Christians whose thinking about some (or all) aspects of life is aligned with the attitudes of the popular culture (or some subset of the culture) rather than the pure truth of Christ. In this context, non-Christians are dwelling in the domain of darkness as prisoners of the forces of darkness. They cannot choose to adopt a biblical worldview prior to being "*rescued from the domain of darkness and transferred to the kingdom of Jesus Christ by faith*" (Col 1:13) So, in this book, the term cultural captivity is a malady only infecting born-again believers. However, cultural captivity assumes there exists a dominant (or at least influential) cultural milieu of non-Christian views in order to have an opportunity to flourish.

Is our cultural captivity a new phenomenon or was it prevalent in New Testament times as well? An unbiblical cultural milieu was certainly prevalent in the Roman world of the first century. Paul's letter to the Colossians (along with several other New Testament books) deals specifically with the types of cultural captivity encountered by first century Christians. In Colossians 2:8, Paul warns the local Christians, "*See to it that no one takes you captive through philosophy and empty deception . . .*" which would be a foolish thing to allow since they are "complete in (Christ)". (Col 2:10)

"What does this danger look like that can capture someone who is complete in Christ? How can I avoid it or free myself from it in the power of Christ?" Surely, the Christians in Colossae were asking these types of questions. Paul thought as much for he goes on to point out four different views that may take genuine Christians captive and keep them from siding with Christ in the war of ideas. Let us review the first two chapters of Paul's letter to the Colossians to understand these issues.

The Context of the Problem

In the first chapter of Colossians, Paul wants to make sure that these new believers in Colossae fully understand the completeness of their salvation in Christ. He reminds them of

- the gospel which saved them (v. 3-8),
- the knowledge of God's will which allows them to walk in a manner worthy of the Lord (v. 8-14),
- the incomparable value of Christ Jesus who through Him and for Him and By Him created all things in heaven and on earth (v. 15-20), and
- the mystery hidden prior to Christ's resurrection of God's salvation for the Gentiles, "Christ in you, the hope of glory." (v. 21-29)

In Colossians 2:1-4, Paul sums up his review of the fullness of Christ's provision and reiterates our critical need for a true knowledge of "Christ, in whom are hidden all the treasures of wisdom and knowledge." Paul knows that if we don't completely understand the fullness of Christ and His work of redemption, we are setting ourselves up for those who would "*delude you with persuasive arguments.* " (Col 2:4) We must fully grasp that Christ alone is necessary and sufficient for our salvation. We must believe it in the day to day living of our lives; being "*rooted and grounded in Him*". (Col 2:7)

Cultural Captivity – Paul's Admonition

"... a true knowledge of ... Christ Himself, in whom are hidden all the treasures of wisdom and knowledge."

TRUTH

DELUSION

"... so that no one will delude you with persuasive argument."

"... as you have received Christ Jesus the Lord, so walk in Him, having been firmly rooted ..."

ROOTED IN HIM

CAPTIVITY

"See to it that no one takes you captive ..."

In the remainder of the second chapter, Paul lists four specific ways that our thinking can be taken captive by the philosophy of men through persuasive arguments. It is important to remember that these arguments are called 'persuasive' meaning that they appear to make good sense and have the power to sway our thinking. It is only by examining these arguments in the light of Christ's truth that their falsehood comes to light. Let's examine each of the four considering how they would appear to the Colossian Christians of that day and how they might play out in this decade.

The examples of cultural captivity exposed by Paul are still relevant to our lives today. Paul's examples can generally be characterized as naturalism, legalism, mysticism and asceticism. Let's examine each in turn.

Naturalism – Captive to Scientific Deception

The first type of cultural captivity highlighted in Colossians is found in chapter 2 verse 8.

> *See to it that no one takes you captive through philosophy and empty deception, according to the tradition of men, according to the elementary principles of the world, rather than according to Christ.*

This verse includes the only occurrence of the word 'philosophy' in the bible. This Greek word means "the investigation of truth and nature"[1] as emphasized by the remainder of this verse. Thinking in accordance with the tradition of men and the elementary principles of the world can captivate us. The ways in which man explains how the world works and how we fit into it can be a deceptive trap.

In Galatians 4:3, Paul tells us that apart from Christ, we are held in bondage by the elementary principles of the world.

> "*So also we, while we were children, were held in bondage under the elemental things of the world.*" Gal 4:3

When we try to limit the forces at work in our universe to simply those elementary forces operating in our daily lives, we are missing out on the powerful work of Christ in our world far above and beyond the everyday forces of nature. In the first century, thinking men were swayed by the philosophies of Socrates, Plato, Aristotle and other thinkers, philosophies that recognized some of the truth about humanity, but totally missed the role of the creator God and his Son Jesus Christ.

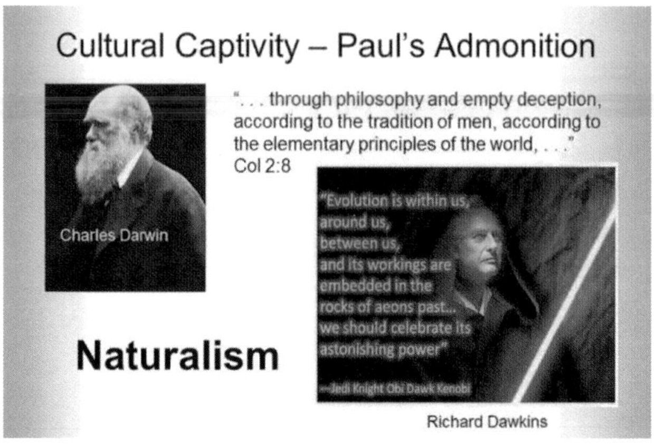

So what are the elementary principles that lure us into captivity today. Certainly, one of the most influential is Neo-Darwinism. Neo-Darwinists, such as Richard Dawkins, say the world is the result of the strictly natural processes of random mutation and natural selection. This theory, attempting to describe the current diversity and complexity of life on this earth, is the dominant view in our society. It is seen by many as the culmination of understanding our existence in this world. In fact, it is full of problems having no plausible explanation for 1) the existence of a planet supporting carbon-based life forms, 2) the first occurrence of life on this planet or, 3) the irreducible complexity of life forms on this planet. To learn more about the gaping holes in the Darwinian description of our existence, please check out our many related articles and books at www.probe.org.[2]

I would suggest that those Christians who put Christ's role in our creation at a level below that of these elementary principles are allowing themselves to be taken captive. If one believes these principles are lord over Christ instead of the other way around, that person is living practically as a citizen of this earth rather than as a citizen of heaven. Paul makes this clear in Colossians when he states,

> *For by Him all things were created,both in the heavens and on earth, visible and invisible, whether thrones or dominions or rulers or authorities — all things have been created through Him and for Him. He is before all things, and in Him all things hold together.* (Col 1:16-18)

Regardless of the period of time over which this creation occurred, Jesus Christ was the active agent in every aspect and still is holding it all together. Apart from the purposes and power of Jesus, there would be no humans and no universe. Far from being a purposeless result of random events, our world is the direct of result of an intelligent, powerful creator.

Legalism – Captive to Self-Made Godliness

The second form of cultural captivity identified by Paul in his letter to the Colossians can be called legalism. In the context of the first century church, Paul discusses it as follows:

> *Therefore no one is to act as your judge in regard to food or drink or in respect to a festival or a new moon or a Sabbath day — things which are a mere shadow of what is to come; but the substance belongs to Christ.*(Col 2:16-17)

Paul warned against those attempting to take Christians captive through the subtle lies of legalism. These false teachers were telling the new, Gentile followers that believing in Christ was a good start, BUT you also need to follow some (or all) of the laws of Moses if you are to be righteous before God.

Notice the items listed in this verse are not instructions on purity and righteous behavior. Rather they are specific practices given to Israel as precursors of the coming Messiah. For example, the festival of Passover is a marvelous foreshadowing of Christ's sacrifice of Himself as the Lamb of God to deliver us from slavery to the world of sin and separation from God. Why celebrate the Passover, when one can celebrate the real event? These behaviors designed to prepare us for the coming of Christ are no longer necessary now that we have the presence of Christ in our lives.

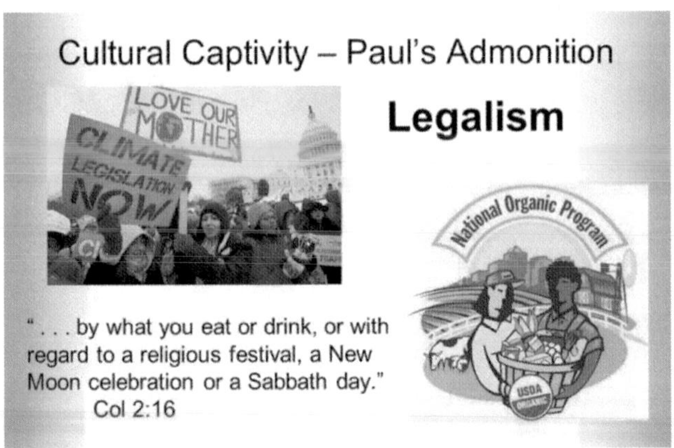

In our American culture, legalism appears to have been more prevalent in the 19th and 20th century, than it is today. But, there are certainly forms of legalism which take people captive today. If you are more interested in passing laws to make some form of Christian behavior the law of the land, than you are in changing the hearts of men through the gospel of Jesus Christ, you may be captive to legalistic thinking.

Another form of legalism is the practice of picking only parts of the truth as applicable to you. Jesus noted in Matthew 15:3-6, this type of legalism was present in the Pharisaical view of committing their resources to God so that they would not have to help their mother and father. Today, I can customize my religious beliefs to conform to what I expect from my religion rather than what my religion sets as a standard for my life. The National Survey of Youth and Religion tells us that over half of 18- to 23-year-olds in American say "it is okay to pick and choose their religious beliefs without having to accept the teachings of their religious faith as a whole."[3] A postmodern view rejecting any overarching truth standard is one form of this restructured legalism. It is discussed more at the end of this chapter.

Mysticism – Captive to Man's Composite View of God

The third form of cultural captivity listed by Paul after naturalism and legalism can be broadly defined as mysticism. In Colossians 2:18-19, Paul writes:

> *Let no one keep defrauding you of your prize by delighting in self-abasement and the worship of the angels, taking his stand on visions he has seen, inflated without cause by his fleshly mind, and not holding fast to the head, from whom the entire body, being supplied and held together by the joints and ligaments, grows with a growth which is from God.* (Col 2:18-19)

Here Paul is describing someone who drifts away by delighting in self-derived sources of truth, that is "visions he has seen", and other religious practices not taught by Christ. This person delights in mixing together teachings from different religions to come up with one's own personalized religious experience. However, Christ calls us to worship the Father and the Son not angels or our own self-sacrifice.

Your first reaction may be that this is not a major area of captivity for today's Christians. However, when we begin to consider examples of this type of thinking, we realize that it is very prevalent in our society. For example, consider the millions of people joining Oprah Winfrey in extolling and following the teachings of Eckhart Tolle, author of "A New Earth, Awakening to Your Life's Purpose"[4]. Tolle teaches a version of Eastern mysticism which he claims to have discovered in a vision. "*Taking his stand on visions*", he teaches we are all part of the universal life force to which we should desire to return. He selectively misquotes Jesus throughout the book, identifying Him as one of the early proponents of this mystic religion. Most of Tolle's followers claim to be professing Christians trying to find a way to integrate his teaching with the teachings of Jesus. However, since these teachings are directly counter to the truth taught by Jesus, they are going to continue to struggle with this integration.[5]

One feature of Tolle's teaching is the view that Jesus was one of many who are bringing a form of truth to us. He believes Buddha, Krishna, Mohammed are all trying to communicate the same truth in different ways. This viewpoint is seen in the National Study of Youth and Religion where over 70% of American 18- to 23-year-olds disagreed with the idea that only one religion was true. In our own study of American born-agains between 18 and 40, we found that less than half of these born-agains believe that Jesus is the only way to heaven, not Mohammed or Buddha. Even as born-agains, they believe Jesus is *a way* to heaven, just not the *only way*.

Asceticism – Focused on the Flesh

Asceticism captures the idea behind the fourth form of cultural captivity identified by Paul in his letter to the Colossians. The American Heritage Dictionary defines asceticism as "the doctrine that a life of extreme self-denial and austerity releases the soul from bondage with the body and permits union with the divine." Versions of asceticism were promoted in Jesus time by the Essenes of the Jewish culture and the Stoics of the Greek culture. The Essenes removed themselves from the mixed up culture of 1st century Palestine in order to practice their brand of asceticism in their own enclaves such as Masada. The Stoics practiced a different type of asceticism where denial of emotions (rather than things) characterized a person who had obtained moral and intellectual perfection.

Since our hope is rooted in an imperishable life in heaven, one could adopt the view that this earthly body needs to be denied in light of our heavenly home. However, Paul warns us:

> *If you have died with Christ to the elementary principles of the world, why, as if you were living in the world, do you submit yourself to decrees, such as, "Do not handle, do not taste, do not touch!" (which all refer to things destined to perish with use) — in accordance with the commandments and teachings of men? These are matters which have, to be sure, the appearance of wisdom in self-made religion and self-abasement and severe treatment of the body, but are of no value against fleshly indulgence.* (Col 2:20-23)

Paul warns the Christians at Colossae not to fall for the idea that we must remove our body from all pleasures of the world to partake of the divine. He points out that obsession with self-abasement and severe treatment of the body actually focuses our attention on the flesh. Thus, our focus is on eliminating fleshly indulgence rather than on living lives that please Jesus.

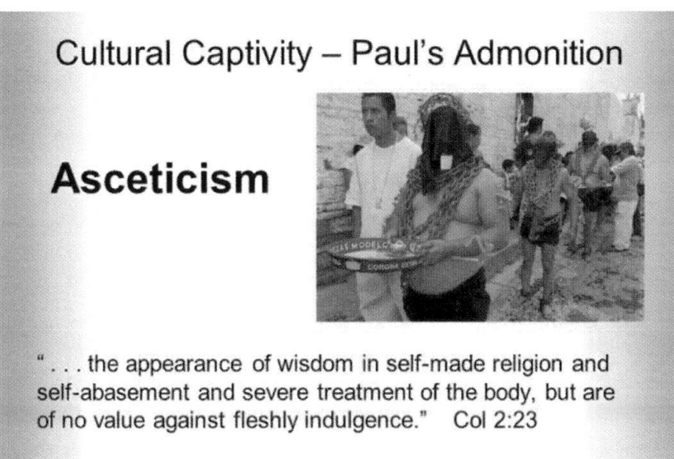

In our post-modern American culture, severe treatment of the body does not appear to be attractive to most young adults. Perhaps, it is evidenced by some forms of the "buy green" movement. What we do see is the opposite extreme where an emphasis on bodily enhancement for the here and now takes our focus off the work of Christ. Of course, in other parts of the world, e.g. South America, extreme asceticism is practiced among some Christian groups.

Today's Emerging Adults – Pop Postmodernism

Paul points out four types of false thinking that could take Christians captive in Colossae of the first century and can do the same in America today. If we recognize these forms of captivity, as Christians, we can be free of them. We must ask ourselves, "Does this way of thinking add anything to the fullness of Christ?" If I am already "complete in Him"[6], how can these add-ons make me more complete? Obviously, they cannot. So leave them behind and "*as you have received Christ Jesus as Lord so walk in Him.*" (Col 2:6)

These examples presented by Paul represent a broad range of ways Christian thinking can be taken captive. However, they are representative not comprehensive. The thought systems of the world that captivate us are unique, yet similar, across generations. How does the captive thinking of today's emerging adults relate to the four areas identified by Paul?

As we will see in greater detail in subsequent chapters, the thinking of many emerging adults in America is immersed in popular postmodernism. This popular thinking is characterized by several key elements including:

- There is no objective moral standard. What is moral is what my friends and I choose to believe is moral.
- Jesus may be a way to heaven, but He is not the only way. Other people's beliefs will work just as well.
- The worst thing I can do is to criticize other's beliefs. Tolerance is the most important virtue.
- Consumerism is the primary, practical objective in life. If I am able to consume as much as I want, I have lived a successful life.
- Enhancing my body through exercise, diet, cosmetics and surgery takes precedence over developing godliness (in contrast to 1st Timothy 4:7-8)
- I cannot really help less fortunate people and have no obligation to do so.

How do these views relate to the four basic types of false thinking listed by Paul?

First, these views appear to be an outright *rejection of legalism.* Legalism was probably the most prevalent form of cultural captivity in America from its founding through most of the 20th century. Postmodernism in its essence is counter to the concept of having a large meta-narrative into which every person is expected to conform.

Instead, these contemporary views appear to be primarily a strange *mixture of mysticism and naturalism.* Mysticism is the dominant factor in their perception of the spiritual. They accept that there are many ways to heaven and we really cannot discern which is best. I can chose an existing one or make up my own version with a few friends and that will accomplish my spiritual objectives. Naturalism comes into play in giving science a role in defining how this world operates. In our normal daily life, naturalism is how we look at what is going on and how we should respond. To a lesser degree, these views are *a perverted form of asceticism* in that what you consume on this earth is of utmost concern. However, for most, it is focused on how much can one consume rather than how little. My selfish consumerism now is not relevant to what may happen when I am no longer on this earth. Therefore my views about heaven are consistent with my temporal emphasis on comfort and material wealth.

Looking at both Paul's admonition and our current situation clearly shows that the current sets of false beliefs assailing our culture are not new. They are perhaps retooled and given new paint jobs, but they are certainly variations of the captivating views Paul warned the early church to avoid. The following chapters delve into how today's beliefs relate to a biblical worldview across religious and cultural topics.

Chapter 3 The Confusing Clamor of Statistical Studies

How is the Evangelical church doing in America as we begin to make our way through the second decade of this century? Are we growing in numbers and in the clarity of our message *or* are we fighting to hold our own against a tide of secularism *or* are we on the verge of a major collapse partially obscured by relatively stable attendance within some denominations? The people who should have the best handle on this question are the sociologists and pollsters who map and track many different aspects of our society. What are they saying about the Evangelical church?

In reviewing the published data, we found three different views promoted as the current state of evangelicalism in America. These views ranged from those who bring out data suggesting Evangelicals are doing well and perhaps better than in the past to those who point to data appearing to identify serious cracks in the beliefs of Evangelicals. None of these views are based on non-representative surveys or anecdotal data, but rather on statistically rigorous surveys. Let's explore this range of views further.

Case 1: Other Religious Groups May be Struggling, but Evangelicals Are Doing Great!

First, consider Bradley Wright, professor of Sociology at the University of Connecticut. In his 2010 book, *Christians Are Hate-filled Hypocrites . . . and Other Lies You've Been Told*, he finds "there seems to be no compelling evidence – based on the data we have about our young people – that the church in America is on the verge of collapse."[1] Wright takes it upon himself to correct the impression spread by others that there is a looming problem of unbelief among American Evangelicals.

Looking at the data from the Pew U. S. Religious Landscape Survey, 2008, and the General Social Survey (from 1972 through 2008), he concludes "On the negative side, the number of young people who do not affiliate with any religion has increased in recent decades just as it has for the whole population. . . . On the positive side, the percentage of young people who attend church or who think that religion is important has remained mostly stable. . . . What I don't see in the data are evidence of a cataclysmic loss of young people."[2]

Wright notes that the percentage of Evangelicals has remained fairly constant in recent years, while Mainline Protestantism has declined. He suggests that one reason Mainline Protestantism has decreased as a percentage of the population is that most Mainline churches have not emphasized church planting. Therefore, "the number of Americans has grown every year but the number of seats in Mainline churches has not."[3] This interpretation of the data seems a strange inversion of cause and effect, but one cannot know if it is true without crafting a new set of survey questions aimed at determining which is the cause and which is the effect. That is: Did the lack of growth cause Mainline churches not to build new and bigger churches OR did the lack of buildings contribute to the lack of growth OR some of both?

Another set of sociologists looking at this question are Byron Johnson and Rodney Stark, professors of Social Sciences at Baylor University. Baylor undertook extensive surveys in 2005 and 2007. These surveys were intended to restart an effort originally begun back in the 1960's to truly understand what was happening around religious thought and behavior in America. This effort is important given that those in academia had often mischaracterized the dominant beliefs of Americans to line up with their own experience rather than taking the effort to ask Americans what they actually believe.

Considering data from the 2005 survey,[4] Johnson concludes, "Leading religious observers claim that evangelicalism is shrinking and the next generation of Evangelicals is becoming less religious and more secular, but these are empirical questions, and the evidence shows that neither of these claims is true. . . . Those who argue that a new American landscape is emerging – one in which the conservative evangelicalism of the past few decades is losing numbers and influence – are simply ignoring the data."[5]

As Johnson points out, "For starters, evangelicals have not lost members . . . Fully one-third of Americans (approximately 100 million) affiliate with an evangelical Protestant congregation."[6]

In his book examining the same survey data, *What Americans Really Believe*, Stark states, ". . . the younger they are, the less likely Americans are to attend church. But, the concern generated by this finding is a false alarm. This same effect can be found in *every* national survey of church attendance ever done."[7] Of course, the behavior of past generations can be a valuable indicator of what will happen in the current generation, but there have been times and issues where significant changes occur that move away from the historical behavior of the past. In the case of church attendance, only time will tell with certainty. However, the GSS survey data, used extensively by Wright, shows that from 1972 to 2006 the number of Mainline Protestant and Catholic emerging adults attending religious services weekly has dropped in half.

Reading what these two sources have to say about the survey data on Evangelicals, one would conclude that Evangelicals have never been better positioned within society. With the weakening position of Mainline Protestant and Catholic denominations, perhaps Evangelical churches will be the only strong, growing Christian voice in America. Or, perhaps the Evangelical church attenders will become more like Mainline Protestants in their set of beliefs as suggested by our next case.

Case 2: Evangelicals Are Okay but There Are Some Very Disturbing Trends

Another eminent sociologist, Christian Smith of the University of Notre Dame, led an extensive study of young Americans over the five years from 2003 to 2008 which is summarized in the book *Souls in Transition, The Religious and Spiritual Lives of Emerging Adults*.[8] As discussed in Chapter 1 herein, he begins by identifying the distinctly different culture of today's twenty-somethings in contrast with those of prior generations. The major source of distinction is the view that they don't really need to start living as married adults until they reach their thirties. The twenties are for exploring different jobs, lifestyles, and relationships before getting married and settling down. But when it comes to religion, he states, "the preponderance of evidence here shows emerging adults ages 18 to 25 actually remaining the same or growing more religious between 1972 and 2006 – with the notable exceptions of *significantly declining* regular church attendance among Catholics and Mainline Protestants, a near *doubling in the percent of nonreligious emerging adults*, and *significant growth* in the percent of emerging adults identifying as *religiously liberal*."[9] (emphasis added, not in the original) Clearly, these "notable exceptions" are extremely significant in their implications for the future as can be seen in his in-depth analysis.

However, looking at the more detailed data from his surveys, he concludes, "Most emerging adults are okay with talking about religion as a topic, although they are largely indifferent to it – religion is just not that important to most of them. . . . Most of them think that most religions share the same core principles, which they generally believe are good."[10] In other words, the dominant views of emerging adults today include some form of pluralism saying all religions are equally effective. This pluralistic view essentially would make Evangelicals practicing non-Evangelicals since there is no need to evangelize people of other faiths.

He goes on to say, "Furthermore, among emerging adults, religious beliefs do not seem to be important, action-driving commitments, but rather mental assents to ideas that have few obvious consequences."[11] The very essence of the Christian faith is that our understanding of Jesus teaching and example forms the basis for how we live our daily lives. Mental assents are like the son in the parable who told his father that he would obey and then proceeded to ignore his father's request. These verbal assents may sound good but they are essentially counter to a true faith in Jesus Christ. He also concludes that among these emerging adults the tenets of liberal Protestantism have won the day, influencing many Evangelicals, Catholics and Jews as well as Mainline Protestants. One surprising outcome of this trend is the demise of Mainline Protestant churches since their teaching is "redundant to the taken-for-granted mainstream" that they helped create. [12]

Smith was very concerned about some of the findings of his survey prompting him to write a second book on the data, *Lost in Transition – The Dark Side of Emerging Adulthood.* In this book, he focused on data from the verbal interviews done during their survey work which showed common trends across this age group. After reviewing their extensive data, he states "emerging adult life in the United States today is beset with real problems, in some cases troubling and even heartbreaking problems."[13] He identified five disturbing trends. He labeled these trends:

1. morality adrift
2. captive to consumerism
3. intoxication's "fake feeling of happiness"
4. the shadow side of sexual liberation
5. civic and political disengagement.

One of his conclusions is that "the farthest boundary of sight that youth today can envision as real and being worth pursuit is entirely imminent, purely material, and completely mundane" and this limited view of life is one they received from their parents.

Case 3: Evangelicals Have Traded the Core Teachings of Christ for Captivity to the World

Standing in contrast to the findings of these eminent sociologists are the findings of George Barna, David Kinnaman and the Barna Group. Their surveys between 1995 and 2009[14] indicate that among all Americans who self-identify as being born-again about 18% of them agree with six basic historic Christian beliefs,[15] which Barna associates with a biblical worldview. These beliefs comprising a Barna biblical worldview are:

1. Absolute moral truth exists.
2. The Bible is totally accurate in all of the principles it teaches.
3. Satan is considered to be a real being or force, not merely symbolic.
4. A person cannot earn their way into Heaven by trying to be good or doing good works.
5. Jesus Christ lived a sinless life on earth.
6. God is the all-knowing, all-powerful creator of the world who still rules the universe today.

Barna defines born-agains as those people who said they have made a personal commitment to Jesus Christ that is still important in their life today and who also indicated they believe that when they die they will go to Heaven because they had confessed their sins and had accepted Jesus Christ as their savior. Since only about 45% of Americans profess to being born-again and only 18% of those born-agains hold to a biblical worldview, we can calculate that only about 9% (i.e. 45% times 18%) of American adults hold a biblical worldview. Among those between 18 and 29, this number drops even lower. Young people may be affiliating with Evangelical churches at similar rates over the last fifty years, but that affiliation does not mean that they have beliefs similar to prior generations. More importantly, it does not mean that they have beliefs that are reasonably consistent with biblical teaching on how Christians should live as citizens of heaven temporarily residing on this earth.

David Kinnaman in The Buster Report[16] found that 78% of young Americans (under the age of 30) did not strongly disagree with the statement "the Bible, the Koran and the Book of Mormon are different expressions of the same spiritual truths". This pluralistic belief shows both an ignorance of the vastly differing messages of these three books and a total disregard for the heavy cost God undertook in dying for our sins. God would not have undergone the excruciating pain of the cross if there were other less painful ways to provide for our redemption.

In his book, ***unChristian***, Kinnaman examined what young Americans outside the Christian community thought about Christians and Christianity. He states, "Our research shows that many of those outside of Christianity, especially younger adults, have little trust in the Christian faith, and esteem for the lifestyle of Christ followers is quickly fading

among outsiders. They admit their emotional and intellectual barriers go up when they are around Christians, and they reject Jesus because they feel rejected by Christians."[17] As Evangelicals, our very name states that our primary purpose is to share the message of Christ with the world around us. Yet, if we are interacting with the world in ways that erode trust and raise barriers, we are living in ways that are counter to our purpose as God's ambassadors in this world.

In his companion book, *You Lost Me: Why Young Christians Are Leaving Church . . . and Rethinking Faith*, Kinnaman examines the thoughts of young Christians who are turning away from the church. In a survey conducted in 2011, he found that 59 percent of young people with a Christian background report that they had or have "dropped out of attending church, after going regularly." He goes on to say "The next generation is caught between two possible destinies – one moored by the power and depth of the Jesus-centered gospel and one anchored to a cheap, Americanized version of the historic faith that will snap at the slightest puff of wind. Without a clear path to pursue the true gospel, millions of young Christians will look back on their twenty-something years as a series of lost opportunities for Christ."[18] These emerging adults represent an age group that is disconnected from the church life of their youth and in most cases not overly interested in reconnecting to the shallow life of American Christianity.

How Can We Determine Who is Right?

So what is right? Is it true that there is no compelling evidence that the church in America is on the verge of collapse? Or, do we have more religious young people who are heavily influenced by the 'social gospel' beliefs of Mainline Protestantism? Or, is the dearth of a biblical worldview an early warning sign of a significant collapse?

How can we have such a divergent set of beliefs on the status of Christian belief in America? Are different surveys getting disparate groups of respondents? Or, are some of the surveys flawed in the questions they ask? Or, are the surveys very similar and it is the techniques used to analyze the data and the biases of the evaluators that cause such different conclusions?

As you can imagine, these are questions that we at Probe just had to get to the bottom of. So, we dove in to analyze the data behind the statements above, using their own data to validate or question their conclusions. We also commissioned our own survey of 18- to 40-year-old, born-again Americans to probe deeper into this question. Unfortunately, what we found convinced us that things are not only worse than what Wright, Johnson, and Smith concluded, but they appear to be worse in some ways than our prior assumptions from the existing Barna surveys.

Chapter 4 Sorting Out the Confusion

Looking at the underlying survey data used by Wright, Johnson & Stark, Smith, *and* Barna & Kinnaman, we discover a somewhat surprising result: on similar questions they get similar results. In their analysis, they come to starkly different conclusions and, yet, their underlying data is essentially the same. In this chapter, we are going to look at survey results for all young adults, for young adults who are born-again and for those who are not born-again. Looking across the relevant surveys, we want to find where they are consistent and where they tell a divergent story.

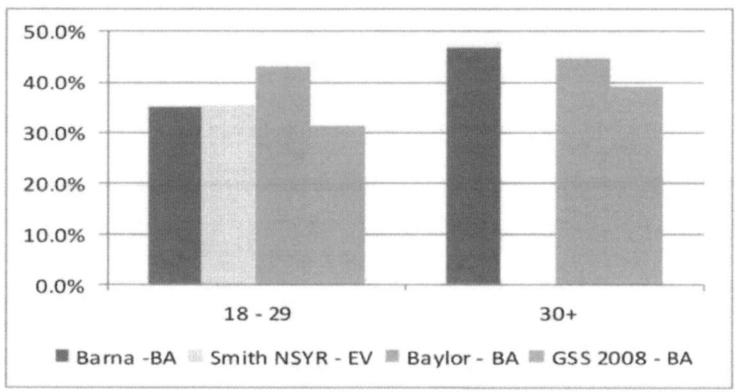

Figure 4-1 Multiple Surveys: Born-Agains

Figure 4-1 shows what these four surveys discovered about the number of people who profess being born-again (or in the case of the NSYR survey, the number of people who affiliate with an evangelical church). Among those over 30, approximately 45% claim to be born-again. For those under 30, about 35% profess to being born-again. As you can see, all four surveys have similar results. However, apart from this high level question, one would expect to encounter very different results from these surveys to account for the very different conclusions drawn from them as discussed in the previous chapter.

Now, let us look at four basic questions important in understanding the status of today's religious beliefs. The questions are variants of what do you believe about God, Jesus, the Bible and salvation. Of course, each survey poses the question somewhat differently from the others. Table 4-1 below shows how these questions were worded in each survey.

Table 4-1 Questions on Basic Religious Beliefs

Topic	Barna & Kinnaman[1]	Smith (NSYR)[2]	Johnson & Stark (Baylor)[3]	Wright (GSS)[4]
God	The all-knowing, all-powerful creator who rules the universe today.	A personal being involved in the lives of people today.	I have no doubt that God exists.	I know God really exists and I have no doubts about it.
Hea-ven	A person cannot earn their way into Heaven by trying to be good or do good works.	Only people whose sins are forgiven through faith in Jesus Christ go to heaven.	My religion is the one true faith that leads to salvation and only a few or no non-Christians will go to heaven[5]	*I definitely believe in life after death, and* *I definitely believe in heaven.*
Jesus	*Jesus lived a sinless life on earth.*	Jesus was the Son of God who was raised from the dead.	Jesus is the Son of God.	**No question on Jesus.**
Bible	Is totally accurate in all of the principles it teaches. **Strongly Agree or Agree**	**No question on the Bible.**	Means exactly what it says & should be taken literally and/or it is perfectly true but should not be taken literally.	The actual word of God and to be taken literally, word for word OR the inspired word of God but not everything should be taken literally, word for word.

Note that the item in bold following a question (e.g. Strongly Agree, Disagree, etc.) indicates the answer(s) to the question which we are tracking in the graphs.

The questions in italics are sufficiently different from other questions in that category to result in different answers. On the topic of heaven, the GSS survey only asks about the existence of heaven and life after death without asking how one enters heaven. On the topic of Jesus, the Barna survey asks about the type of life Jesus lived while the others state He was the Son of God. In aggregate, these four surveys should provide a consistent look at how young Americans relate to the basic tenets of Christianity. We can compare the results of these surveys on these questions to see if they obtain similar results. First, look at the data for all 18- to 30-year-olds in each survey (18- to 23-year-olds for the NSYR).

As you can see in Figure 4-2, all sources have reasonably similar results given the variations in their questions. The Barna Group's question on Jesus is significantly different from the other surveys resulting in a lower percentage of belief in that statement. Since the differences in results can be attributed to differences in the content of the questions and the way in which they were asked, it appears these surveys should portray similar conclusions about American religious beliefs.

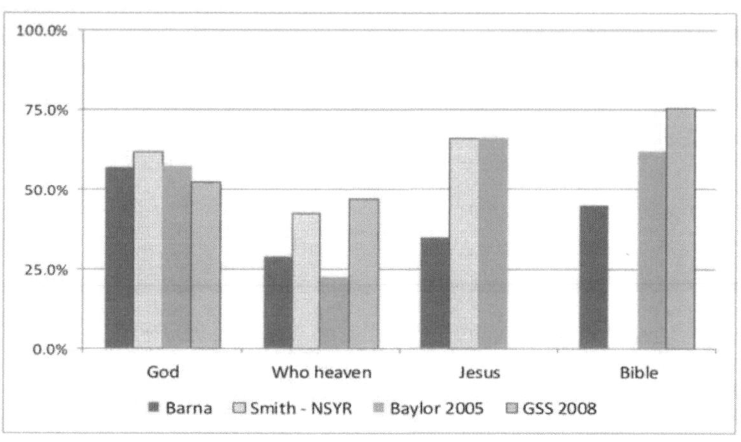

Figure 4-2 Multiple Surveys: Basic Religion

Look at the same questions when we only consider those who affiliate with an evangelical church (NSYR and Baylor) or profess to being born-again (GSS, Barna and Probe). In this comparison, we have also added the results of Probe's survey of born-again Americans from age 18 to 40. Probe's survey used the same four questions as the Barna surveys.

As shown, the beliefs of these Christians are very consistent on God and the Bible. On the questions about Jesus and who goes to heaven, we have a greater variation primarily caused by the more restrictive question used in the Barna and Probe surveys. A greater percentage of people state they believe Jesus is the son of God than state they believe Jesus lived a sinless life on earth. This result may strike some as odd since it implies some think that living a sinless life is more unlikely than being God in the flesh. On the question of who goes to heaven, the NSYR and GSS responses leave more room for a pluralistic view as compared to the Baylor, Barna and Probe questions. Even with those differences, the responses are sufficiently close to elicit similar interpretations of their meaning.

So, how did these sociologists come to such different conclusions about similar sets of data? Looking at these relatively high percentages of basic Christian beliefs, how could Smith say there is something different about this emerging generation, or how could Barna say that "Jesus would be disappointed by the answers He received from today's Americans?" The answer comes from two sources. First, you need to ask more questions about their beliefs and practices than just "Do you believe in a God and in Jesus as His Son?" A person can mean many different things when answering yes to those questions. Second (and it turns out to be extremely important), you must look at the combined answers to a set of related questions. In his book, Smith took the first step by asking a lot of probing questions, both in the survey and in face-to-face interviews. By doing this, it became clear that their answers to a few questions about God and Jesus did not mean that they were biblically literate Christians.

Barna took the second step of looking at the answers to a combined set of questions. He discovered that the beliefs of Americans were disjointed and inconsistent particularly among the younger generations. So, even though between 82% to 93% of 18- to 30-year-olds who professed to be born-again believed that God is all powerful and involved in the world today, only a small subset of them believed all six biblical worldview questions evaluated in the Barna research.[6]

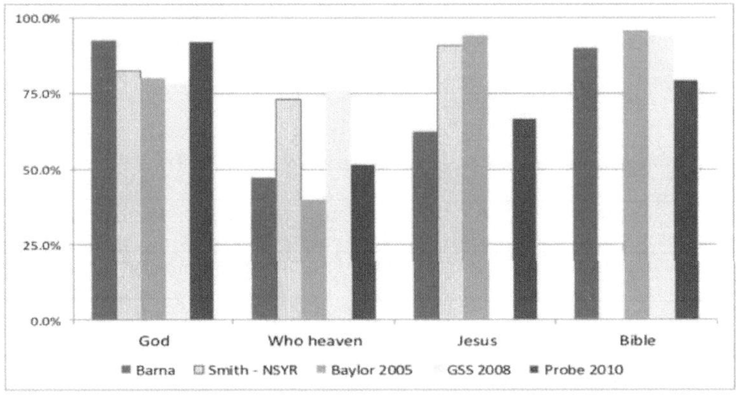

Figure 4-3 Multiple Surveys: Religious Beliefs of Born-agains

What happens if we look at the results of the surveys used by Wright, Johnson, and Smith in the same way the Barna group looked at their results? Will we see a distinctly different set of results? Or, will the data sets continue to line up? Fortunately, we were able to access the raw questionnaire results using the Association of Religious Data Archives online database. As noted previously, these surveys did not ask exactly the same questions, but we were able to find a set of roughly equivalent questions within each survey. In addition to the four questions listed for Barna in Table 4-1 above, the two questions on Satan and morality listed in Table 4-2 below make up the six questions the Barna Group considers in ascribing a biblical worldview.

Table 4-2 Biblical Worldview Questions

Topic	Barna & Kinnaman and Probe	Smith (NSYR)	Johnson & Stark (Baylor)	Wright (GSS)
Satan / Demons	Is not a living being but is a symbol of evil. **Disagree Strongly**	Do you believe in the existence of demons or evil spirits?	Satan does exist.	I definitely believe in hell.
Morality	Do you believe that there are moral absolutes that are unchanging, or that it always depends upon circumstances? **Unchanging**	Morals are relative; there are no definite rights and wrongs for everybody. **Disagree / Strongly Disagree**	No similar question.	A personal matter and society should not force everyone to follow one standard. **Disagree Somewhat / Strongly**
Life Change	No similar question.	How important is religious faith in shaping how you live daily? **Extremely Or Very**	No similar question.	Have you had a religious/spiritual experience that changed your life? **Yes**
Personal God	No similar question.	No similar question.	Is concerned with the well-being of the world.	God concerns Himself with every human being personally.
One True Religion	No similar question.	Only one religion is true.	How many non-Christians will get into heaven? **None/A Few**[7]	There is truth in one religion.

The remaining three questions in the table 4-2 (on Life Change, a Personal God, and One True Religion) were selected from some of the other surveys to make up for those surveys not covering all six of the topics in the Barna Group's definition of a biblical worldview.

The results are shown in Figure 4-4 for all 18- to 30-year-olds. Across the four surveys, approximately 30% believe in a biblical idea of God, Jesus and salvation. Adding in the other questions identified for each survey as establishing a biblical worldview, we have an average of 12% of these young Americans who profess a biblical worldview. The results from the Barna survey are lower because of the more specific questions about Jesus (i.e. He lived a sinless life), Satan (not a concept but a living being) and morality (ultimate moral truths). In every survey, a very small percentage of young Americans apply a biblical worldview to their life decisions.

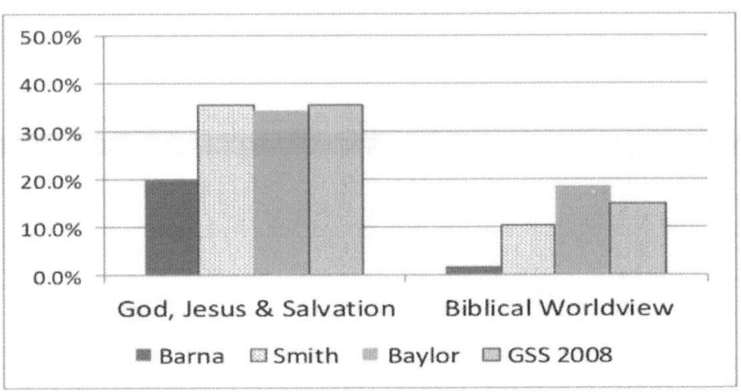

Figure 4-4 Multiple Surveys: Religious Beliefs of American 18 – 30 years olds

What happens when we divide the results between those who are Evangelical (or born-again) and those who are not? Looking at the results for those who are Evangelical or have professed to being born-again in Figure 4-5, we, naturally, see an increase in biblical beliefs. On the average, about 2 out of 3 profess a basic set of beliefs in God, Jesus and salvation while the number with a full biblical worldview drops to about 1 in 3. Of course, at the same time, we see those who are not Evangelical have only one in five who believe in God, Jesus and salvation by faith. Almost none of them have a full biblical worldview.

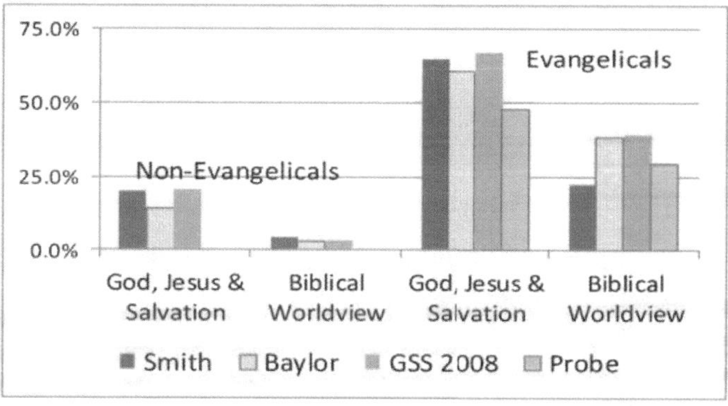

Figure 4-5 Multiple Surveys: Non-evangelicals vs. Evangelicals on Biblical Worldview

Clearly, considering oneself to be born-again or affiliating with an Evangelical church does not mean one is going to apply a biblical worldview to the issues they face and the decisions they make in life. This decay in belief is clearly seen later in this chapter when we look at areas of cultural belief on which the Bible takes a clear stand.

Table 4-3 below shows the questions we considered from the various surveys to determine this result. Note, we did not have access to this type of question from Barna other than for the Probe survey (administered for us by the Barna Group).

Table 4-3 Questions Related to Religious Practice

Topic	Smith (NSYR)	Johnson & Stark (Baylor)	Wright (GSS)	Probe Survey
Prayer	Pray daily and experienced a specific answer to prayer in the last two years.	Pray at least daily outside of worship services.	About how often do you pray? **At Least Daily**	Pray regularly in a typical month.
Read the Bible	I read from the Bible at least once a week.	Outside of attending religious services, about how often do you read it? **At Least Weekly**	No question on this topic	Read Bible at least Weekly.

Topic	**Smith (NSYR)**	**Johnson & Stark (Baylor)**	**Wright (GSS)**	**Probe Survey**
Attend church services	Attend at least 2-3 times per month.	Attend religious services 2-3 times per month or more.	Attend religious services 2 to 3 times a month or more.	Attend church in a typical month.
Involved in church activities	Attend Sunday School or other religious group during the week.	Participate in religious education programs, such as Bible study or Sunday school. **At Least Monthly**	Take part in the activities of a church or place of worship other than attending services. **At Least Monthly**	Attend Small Group at least monthly.
Share their faith with others	In the last year, I have shared my faith with someone else not of my faith.	Witness/share your faith with your friends **At Least Once During The Last Month**	No question on this topic	Believe I should share my religious experience with others.
Giving	No question on this topic	During the last year, contributed more than $500 to your current place of worship.	I try hard to carry my religious beliefs over into all my other dealings in life. **Strongly Agree**	No question on this topic

This second set of questions deals with basic practices of a Christian disciple: prayer, reading the Bible, attending church, giving money and sharing their faith. How many people practice these basic disciplines of the Christian life across our four different surveys? Figure 4-6 shows that around 5% of non-Evangelicals and close to 20% (or 1 in 5) of Evangelicals regularly practice the basic disciplines of their faith.

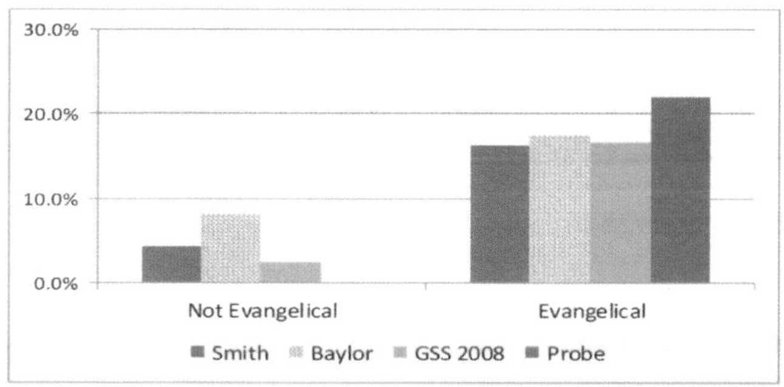

Figure 4-6 Multiple Surveys: Minimal Religious Practice

Finally, does this consistency across the surveys continue when looking at their cultural beliefs in areas where the Bible provides clear guidance? Specifically, what do emerging adults believe about abortion, sex before marriage, adultery, homosexual behavior, pornography, suicide, and materialism? Once again the relevant surveys do not all cover the same questions. The questions considered for each survey are listed in Table 4-4 below. The Probe survey questions differ in that rather than asking what the respondent thinks about a particular behavior, it asks do they personally face difficulties in dealing with the item in question.

Table 4-4 Questions on Cultural Behavior

Topic	Smith (NSYR)	Johnson & Stark (Baylor)	GSS (Wright)	Probe Survey
Divorce	A couple without children should stick with it even if they are not happy.	Divorce is almost always wrong.	No related question	No related question
Abortion	No related question	Abortion because the woman does not want the child is wrong	It should be possible to get an abortion if married and doesn't want more children or not married and does not want to marry.	No related question

Topic	Smith (NSYR)	Johnson & Stark (Baylor)	GSS (Wright)	Probe Survey
Sex before marriage	1) Should wait until they are married. 2) Unmarried people who are not in love should not. 3) It is NOT IMPORTANT to live with the person you are thinking of marrying before getting married?	Sex before marriage and living together before marriage is always wrong.	If a man and woman have sex relations before marriage, I think it is always wrong.	1) I do not face difficulties or challenges in: having sex prior to marriage. 2) I do not face difficulties or challenges in: living with someone who I'm not married to.
Adultery	No related question	No related question	A married person should not have sexual relations with someone other than the marriage partner.	I do not face difficulties or challenges in: having sex with someone other than my spouse.
Gay sex	No related question	Sex between two adults of the same sex is always wrong.	Between two adults of the same sex is always wrong.	No difficulties or challenges in: homosexual thoughts or actions.
Gay marriage	No related question	Gay marriage is always wrong.	Homosexuals should have the right to marry one another. **Wrong**	No related question
Lying / Cheating	No related question	No related question	No related question	I do not face difficulties in: lying or being dishonest or in cheating.
Porno-graphy	About how many X-rated movies, videos, or cable programs have you watched in the last year? **Zero**	Viewing of porn is always wrong.	I have not seen an X-rated movie in the last year and there should be laws against distribution, for any age.	I do not face difficulties or challenges in: watching pornography

Topic	Smith (NSYR)	Johnson & Stark (Baylor)	GSS (Wright)	Probe Survey
Suicide	No related question	Physician assisted suicide always wrong.	No related question	No related question
Material-ism	I would be happier if I could afford to buy more things. **Disagree**	No related question	No related question	I do not face difficulties in: not being generous or giving to those in need and/or not having everything I want in terms of possessions

Before looking at the survey results in these areas of cultural behavior, consider what the results should be by comparing how these activities are addressed by the media (television and movies), by popular opinion and by the Bible.

Table 4-5 Comparing Positions on Topics of Cultural Behavior

Topic	Television and Movies	Popular Opinion	Biblical Teaching
Abortion	Woman's right to choose. Only extremists oppose it.	Many support woman's right to choose.	Always Wrong (some exceptions considered)
Sex before marriage	Encouraged and expected. Only nerds are not doing it.	Expected, if not encouraged.	Always Wrong
Adultery	Depends on situation. Is normal state for most people.	Depends on situation. Common activity	Always Wrong
Divorce	Standard condition and the right thing to do in most cases.	Not good but a common out to an unsatisfying marriage.	Wrong except in the case of adultery and abusive behavior.
Gay Sex	Promoted as being right Well-adjusted gays are everywhere.	Uncomfortable acceptance Around 5% or less	Always Wrong
Gay Marriage	An absolute right	Support civil unions but oppose gay marriage.	Always Wrong

Topic	Television and Movies	Popular Opinion	Biblical Teaching
Pornography	Soft is great; hard core is not generally acceptable.	Soft is fine and hard core is tolerated and readily available.	Always Wrong
Suicide	Depends on situation; generally not favorable.	Depends on situation; generally not favorable.	Always Wrong
Materialism	Differing messages	The New American Dream	Generally Wrong
Lying / Cheating	Depends on the situation but generally the end justifies the means.	Standard practice for most in some areas of life.	Always Wrong

Based on Table 4-5 above, we would expect to see very different responses from Evangelical/born-again emerging adults compared with the rest of the emerging adults. As you can see in Figure 4-7 below, the results are significantly different but not encouraging. Almost no emerging adult who is not an Evangelical believes that all of these cultural issues are wrong. However, the vast majority of young Evangelicals also do not adhere to what the Bible clearly teaches on these subjects. In fact only about 10% of them (when averaged across the four surveys) adhere to a consistent set of biblical beliefs concerning these cultural topics. In a later chapter, we will look at their response to the individual questions. For now, we are interested in their views regarding a set of culturally relevant questions.

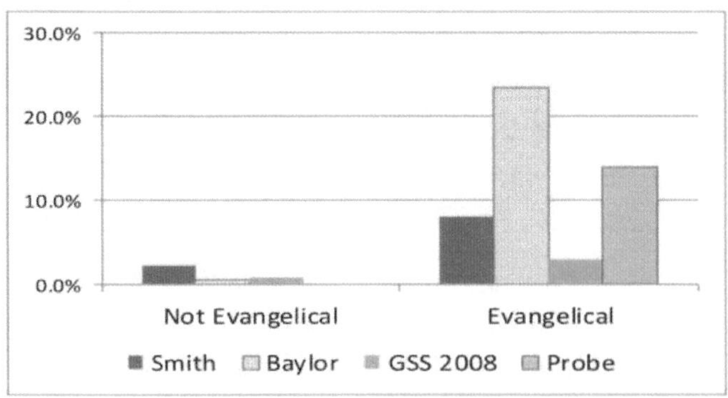

Figure 4-7 Multiple Surveys: Biblical View on Cultural Topics

If we look at the cumulative set of questions: religious beliefs, religious practice, and cultural beliefs, what do we find? As shown in Figure 4-8 below, we see a common problem declared by all four surveys. No non-Evangelicals and virtually no Evangelicals hold a consistent set of beliefs and practices clearly called out in the Bible.

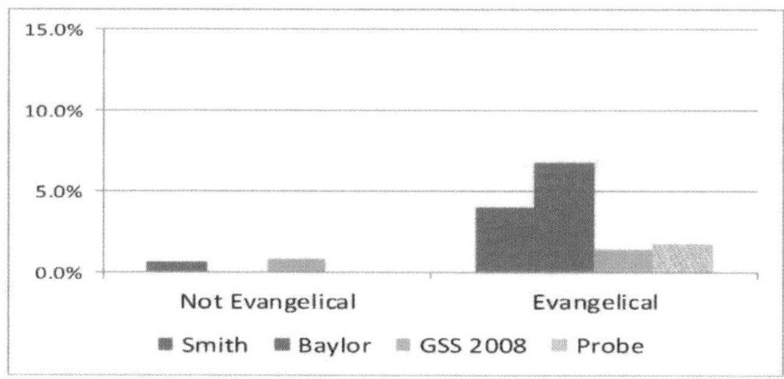

Figure 4-8 Multiple Surveys: Biblical Worldview Beliefs, Practice and Cultural Beliefs

So each of the surveys used by the four different sociologists basically shows the same result:

- less than one third of born-agains (or Evangelicals) had a set of beliefs consistent with the biblical worldview taught by Jesus and
- less than 8% had a biblical worldview and a set of cultural beliefs (e.g. beliefs about sex outside of marriage, abortion, materialism, caring for the poor, etc.) taught by Jesus in the New Testament.

Therefore, it appears that if they had done more in-depth analysis of their own survey data, Wright, Johnson and Smith may have been espousing the same message as the Barna survey.

This surprising result (at least to Wright and Johnson) that their data actually is consistent with Barna's data allows us to quit worrying about the differences and concentrate on the common message of these surveys. Among several, three major messages from the survey results are important for us to consider here.

1. As the culture has adopted unbiblical views regarding pluralism, sexuality, honesty, etc., the majority of Evangelical church members have adapted to accept the new cultural positions rather than stand

firm in the truth taught by Christ and his apostles. In other words, they have been taken "*captive by the empty deception and philosophy according to the traditions of men, according to the elementary principles of the world, rather than according to Christ*"(Col. 2:8).

2. 18- to 29-year-olds are leaving a classical evangelical faith in large numbers. A third of them directly leave any involvement with an Evangelical church with half of that number going into the more liberal Mainline Protestant denominations and the other half leaving behind all church affiliation. Of those who remain associated with an Evangelical church, one-third of them attend church but do not hold to a biblical worldview and another third do not go to church or hold to a biblical worldview. Thus, far fewer than 10% of American teenagers move into emerging adulthood with a strong, evangelical worldview.

3. The percentage of Americans belonging to Evangelical churches has remained fairly consistent, but that does not mean that the beliefs of the members have remained constant. The sacred / secular split, described by Nancy Pearcey in her book *Total Truth,*[8] allows them to ascribe to at least a limited set of evangelical beliefs in their sacred side while keeping the "real truths" of the secular side isolated and unaffected by any evangelical beliefs.

Chapter 5 Disconnected Religious Beliefs and Behaviors

The prior chapters have clearly shown:

1. The various surveys on religious belief and practice are reasonably consistent with one another; not vastly different as one might be led to believe by the articles and books written about them.
2. There appears to be an overwhelming trend toward self-defined mixtures of religious beliefs rather than a few consistent belief systems established by the primary Christian traditions in the United States, e.g. Evangelical, Mainline Protestant, and Roman Catholic.
3. Many more young adults than in prior generations are unwilling to identify with any Christian faith.

In the previous chapter, we saw that all the surveys demonstrated a considerable lack of consistency in the religious beliefs and practices of emerging adults. In this chapter, we will take a deeper look at young adults' core religious beliefs: what those religious beliefs are and in what ways, if any, they influence their lives.

Changing Affiliations

Let us begin by considering the changes in religious affiliation that occur over the five years from the teen years to new adulthood. The only data available on this topic from the surveys we have evaluated is from the NSYR survey. The NSYR initiative surveyed the same set of almost 3,000 people in 2003 when they were ages 13 to 18 and again in 2008 when they were ages 18 to 23. By questioning the same people at different stages of their lives, we gather some sense of changes occurring across this critical period of life. Figure 5-1 shows the changes that occurred over this five-year period. Relative to the original size of each group, the number of Evangelical Protestants went down by 15% and Roman Catholics went down by 27%, while those espousing another religion or no religion grew by 64%. So for 18- to 23-year-olds, there are as many non-Christians as there are Evangelicals: about 35% of the population.

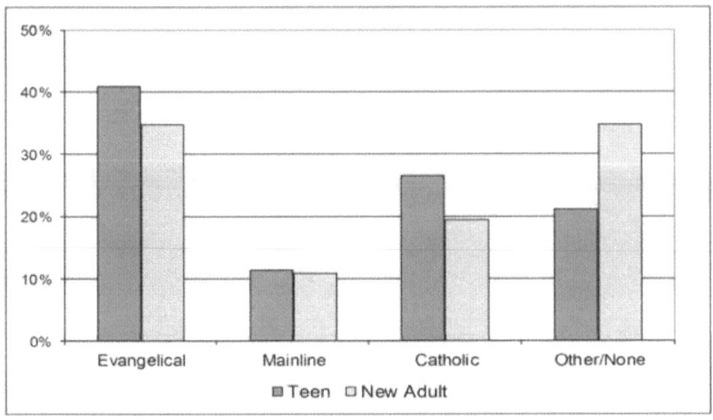

Figure 5-1 NSYR: Change in Faith Affiliation with Age

Note how this data from the NSYR tracks with the GSS data presented in Figure 1-2 for 18- to 29-year-old Americans. As shown, the GSS data for 2008 showed 25% identified as born-again Protestant, 14% as Protestants not identifying as born-again, 28% as Catholic and 33% as other/no religion. Both of them show a large percentage of emerging adults who do not see themselves as affiliated with any Christian religion.

However, there was much more change going on than revealed by the chart above. Why? The chart above shows the overall difference in affiliations over the five-year period, but it does not show who makes up each column shown for the young adults. For example, what if all those who were Mainline Protestants as teenagers became something else as young adults AND about 40% of those who were Catholic as teenagers became Mainline Protestants as young adults? In that case, you would have two columns for Mainline Protestants (one for teenagers and one for young adults) that looked identical (much like what we actually show in the graph), but each column would represent a totally different group of people. So one can see, it is important to look at what actually happened over the five years and who now makes up the columns representing each religious group.

First, the emerging adults who identify as Evangelical were not all Evangelicals as teenagers. In Figure 5-1, the bar for teenage Evangelicals represents 1064 of the respondents in 2003 while the bar for new adult Evangelicals represents 881 of the respondents in 2008. However, only

728 of the 881 new adult Evangelicals came from the group of teenage Evangelicals. The other 153 new adult Evangelicals were affiliated with one of the other groups as teenagers. So, we really had 336 new adults (i.e. 1064 – 728) who identified as Evangelicals in high school, but now identify with another group as new adults. The 153 young adult, new Evangelicals were about equal parts from Mainline Protestant, Catholic and from not religious or non-Christian religions. Of the 336 who left evangelical Christianity about half went to other Christian religions and the other half went to nonreligious or indeterminate religious beliefs. Undoubtedly, if we were to include these original Evangelicals in our Evangelical statistics, we would see even less commitment to basic evangelical beliefs.

This information is shown graphically in Figure 5-2. Those who were evangelical as teenagers are represented by the solid color bar. As shown, we can see that some of them became Mainline Protestants, a few became Catholic, and a large number became Other/None, but the majority remained Evangelical just as they had been as a teenager. These four solid bars represent the 1,064 teenage Evangelicals from 2003. Similarly, the bars above "Evangl" in the chart include some Mainline Protestant teenagers, Catholic teenagers and Other/None teenagers, who now affiliate with an Evangelical congregation as a new adult.

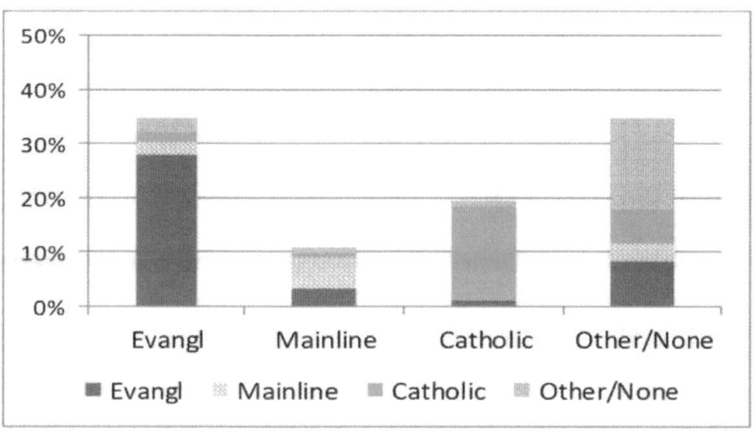

Figure 5-2 NSYR: Where Current New Adult Faith Affiliations Came From as Youth

What about other religious backgrounds? Almost 50% of teenage Mainline Protestants no longer affiliate with a Mainline Protestant church. About half of those are now Evangelicals and about half are not religious or non-Christian, i.e. Mainline youth leaving their home church broke half and half either to Evangelical churches or chucking any affiliation with a church. Interestingly enough, the 50% who left were replaced by former Evangelicals and Roman Catholics, keeping Mainline Protestants at about 10% of the population. The Roman Catholics lost about 30% of their members between teenage and emerging adult years and picked up very few from other faiths. The not religious or non-Christian category nearly doubled in size, picking up 20% of teenage Evangelicals, 27% of teenage Mainline Protestants and 24% of teenage Roman Catholics.

Overall, about 32% of emerging adults changed their religious affiliation from their teenage years. Well over half of those changing their affiliation migrated away from faith institutions altogether.

Feelings Towards Religion

The general feelings of emerging adults toward religion appear to be driven by their years of diversity training in public schools and encouragement to adopt religious pluralism. Religion does not seem to be viewed as a controversial topic by emerging adults. They are not averse to talking about religion, but they are not very likely to bring it up for discussion. As Smith and his team discovered, "there are many more important things to think and talk about. In any case, for most it's just not a big issue, not a problem, nothing to get worked up over. . . For very many emerging adults, religion is mostly a matter of indifference. Once one has gotten belief in God figured out . . . and . . . feels confident about going to heaven . . . there is really not much more to think about or pay attention to. In this way, religion has a status on the relevance structures or priority lists of most emerging adults that is similar to, say, the oil refinery industry."[1] Once you are reasonably confident that you have selected a set of beliefs to call your own that fall within the list of approved religions, you are as assured as one can be of getting into heaven. With that taken care of, put it aside and get on with living your life on this earth.

Even though they realize that religions claim to be different and to have the truth, most emerging adults' belief that all religions share the same basic principles. Basically, religion is about belief in God and learning to be a good person. One respondent put it this way: "The line of thought that I follow is that it doesn't matter what you practice. Faith is important to everybody, and it does the same thing for everybody, no matter what your religion is." Another said, "I find it really hard to believe that one religion is exactly true, I would say that if anything's right, it would be probably something common in most religions."[2] Of course, that statement does not hold up to a study of different religions. Their claims about the nature of the universe and God are so disparate that it is obvious that they cannot all be true. They all may be entirely false. But, if one of them is true, the others must be false.

Let's look at some relevant questions from our surveys to see how they match up with Smith's interviews. A few questions in each survey deal with pluralism as summarized in Table 5-1 below.

Table 5-1 Questions Related to Pluralism

Topic	Smith (NSYR)	Johnson & Stark (Baylor)	Wright (GSS)	Probe
One True Religion	Only one religion is true.	How many non-Christians in heaven? NONE or A FEW[3]	There is truth in one religion.	Mohammed, Buddha and Jesus are not all valid ways to God.
One way to heaven	Only people whose sins are forgiven through faith in Jesus go to heaven. **Agree**	No similar question.	No similar question.	Jesus Christ is the only path to God.
My Religion is All True	It is okay to pick and choose religious beliefs without having to accept the teachings of their faith as a whole. **Disagree**	My religion is the one true faith that leads to salvation	No similar question.	If a person is good/does enough good for others during their life, they will earn a place in heaven. **Disagree strongly**

So, how many young adults believe that Jesus is the only way to eternal life with God? As you can see in Figure 5-3, only about 10% of non-Evangelicals and about 30% of Evangelicals profess to a consistent view that only through faith in Jesus Christ can one receive eternal life. So, more than 2 out of 3 Evangelicals do not believe that Christianity is the only valid way to heaven. Consequently, if you affiliate with one religious tradition, it is fine to only select those aspects that feel right to you and mix in aspects from other faiths to find what works for you. It is perfectly acceptable to call myself a follower of one religion while actually ascribing to a set of mutually inconsistent beliefs from multiple religions.

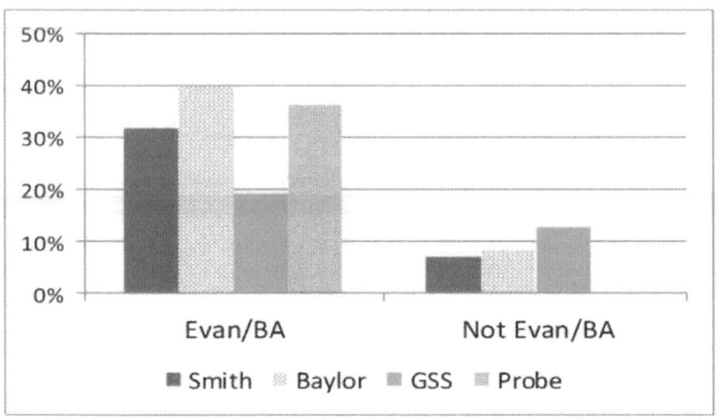

Figure 5-3 Multiple Surveys: Do Not Support Religious Pluralism

Purpose of Religion. All major world religions attempt to answer the major questions of life: Where did I come from? Why am I here? What happens when I die? Is there anything I can do during this life which will impact what happens to me after I die? Consequently, religions provide a perspective on how to be in a right relationship with our creator during this life and how to maximize our benefits in the afterlife (or repeating lives for some religions). However, most emerging adults take a more pragmatic view. According to the interviews, "The real point of religion, ultimately, in the eyes of most emerging adults, is to help people be good, to live good lives."[4] If this is the case, then adopting one's own personalized religious viewpoint works well as long as it encourages you to live a good life (with the definition of "good" left up to your own personalized set of beliefs). It is a "no fail" approach to religion.

In fact, it is not really important if they have true answers to these key questions. As one of the interviewees stated, "What do you mean by religious truth? Because all religions pretty much have a good message that people can follow. I would say that basic premise of the religions, like where they get their message from, is false, but the message itself is good, so."[5] What an interesting proposition:

- The world religions all have been misled or have intentionally lied about where their message came from.
- They have devised significantly different explanations on how to achieve eternal life and live life on this earth.
- But, they all have a good message to live your life by even though it is false.
- So, pick one, a combination, or none of them and live what you think is good and you will be fine.
- *However*, if one of them is actually telling the truth about God and eternal life, you have missed the truth and will live with the results of believing a lie forever.

One important purpose that many emerging adults see for religion is to set our kids on a good path in life. Kids learn right and wrong from church activities. As Smith notes, ". . . by the time a kid becomes a teenager or young adult, that person has pretty much learned his or her morals and so can effectively "graduate" and stop attending services at the congregation. What is the point, after all, of staying in school after you have been taught everything it has to teach?"[6] Therefore, for many emerging adults, the benefit of being involved in religion has already occurred and there is no good reason to continue your involvement, with the one exception of looking into it again when your children need training on what is good behavior in life.

Most emerging adults have religious beliefs, but "they do not particularly drive the majority's priorities, commitments, values, or goals." One observed, "I don't think it's the basis of how I live, it's just, I guess I'm just learning about my religion and my beliefs. But I still kinda retain my own decision or at least a lot of it on situations I've had and experiences."[7]

Perhaps the most chilling quote from Smith is his conclusion on this theme. "It was clear in many interviews that emerging adults felt entirely comfortable describing various religious beliefs that they affirmed but that appeared to have no connection whatsoever to the living of their lives."[8]

The results of this research confirm that the "cultural captivity" or "sacred/secular split" (identified by Nancy Pearcy as a major challenge for American Christianity) is a dominant factor among emerging adults. Nancy Pearcy defines this sacred/secular split as follows: "Many believers have absorbed the fact/value, public/private dichotomy, restricting their faith to the religious sphere while adopting whatever views are current in their professional and social circles."[9] The split means that their religious beliefs deal with at best a future hope and have no impact on the living of their lives. Their daily lives are driven by the secular view of life. Today, those two split parts of life are becoming most like the chart below.

POSTMODERN "MYSTICISM"
Moral and humane ideals have no basis in truth,
******<u>*BUT WE AFFIRM THEM ANYWAY*</u> ******

SCIENTIFIC NATURALISM
Humans are machines[10]

The spiritual half of the sacred/secular split is an interesting combination of postmodern thought and classic mysticism. Basically saying that, although we know that our spiritual ideas cannot possibly be true, we are going to affirm them anyway as being good ideas for our spiritual lives. This idea is not as big a stretch as it seems, when we remember that the sacred side of the split is a private kind of long-term hope. The real living of my life occurs in the secular side of the split that takes scientific naturalism as an undisputed fact.

These insights make it very clear that it is not enough to equip teenagers with a set of basic Christian doctrines defining a good Christian. They must also understand that these truths relate to ***the real, everyday world*** and can be trusted to inform and enlighten our daily choices, attitudes and activities.

Related Religious Attitudes

In Smith's research, he identified a number of other themes characterizing the dominate beliefs of new adults (which he felt would apply to most emerging adults as well). A few of them are listed below.

- My family's faith is associated with dependence. – As an independent person I need to distance myself in some way from my parent's faith
- A church or religious group is not a place of real belonging. - You attend or affiliate with it but it is not where one really hangs ones hat
- Friends hardly talk about religion. – "Many, if not most, emerging adults do not even know the religious backgrounds or basic beliefs and commitments of their friends."[11] Talking about it is a good way to not have many friends since they really do not want to talk about it.
- Moral Therapeutic Deism (MTD) is still alive and well. – MTD was identified in Smith's earlier work on the survey results for 13 to 18 year olds. MTD says there is a God who wants people to be good to one another and be happy, but God does not need to be involved in your life unless you need Him to resolve a problem. This view was a dominant theme among the teenagers he interviewed and it was still the primary view when they were re-interviewed five years later.
- "What seems right to me" is authority. - It is not what my religion teaches, but rather what I feel or believe takes precedence.
- Take or leave what you want. – Since parts of all religions are not up to date with our post-modern understanding, emerging adults are the ultimate authority on what parts of religious teachings are relevant in their lives. In other words, their own personal views take precedence over the teachings of Jesus, Buddha, Mohammed or any religious teacher from the past.
- Evidence and proof trump "blind faith." – As one emerging adult put it, "I mean there is proven fact and then there is what's written in the Bible – and they don't match up."[12] So don't believe any part that seems to go against your concept of the real world.
- Mainstream religion is fine, probably. – They don't feel alienated from mainstream religion but it is not the source one goes to for real life answers. Mainstream religion is not a primary source of the problems we face today, but it does not offer any answers either.

- Personal (not social or institutional) Religion is totally a personal choice. - It is not a group activity.
- There is no way to finally know what is true. – Since one cannot know what is really true, the only option is to fall back on what works for you and not really worry about whether it could be universally true.

As you can see from the list above, these beliefs are generally different versions of the same theme. That theme could be expressed as, "No religious teaching can be considered to be really true, so I will make up a religious view that I think works for me and not really think about it very much." It is important not to spend much time thinking about it because most of these self-made religions do not stand up to logical examination.

Inconsistent Religious Beliefs Lacking a Biblical Worldview

Let us take a deeper look at data on religious beliefs as shown in Figure 5-4 through Figure 5-7. Before considering the data, a brief explanation of the chart formats is in order. Figure 5-4 presents the percent of non-evangelicals who affirm a belief in the items stated in the x-axis, e.g. God & Jesus, Heaven thru Faith, etc. For each item stated in the x-axis, there are three percentages shown, one for each survey consulted (e.g. Smith NSYR, Baylor 2005, GSS 2008). Figure 5-5 presents the same items and surveys as Figure 5-4. However, Figure 5-5 provides the *cumulative* percentages starting from left to right. Thus, the leftmost bar in Figure 5-5 is the percentage of respondents in the Smith NSYR survey that indicated a belief in God & Jesus. That same bar in the second group, Heaven thru Faith, is the percentage of respondents in the Smith NSYR survey who

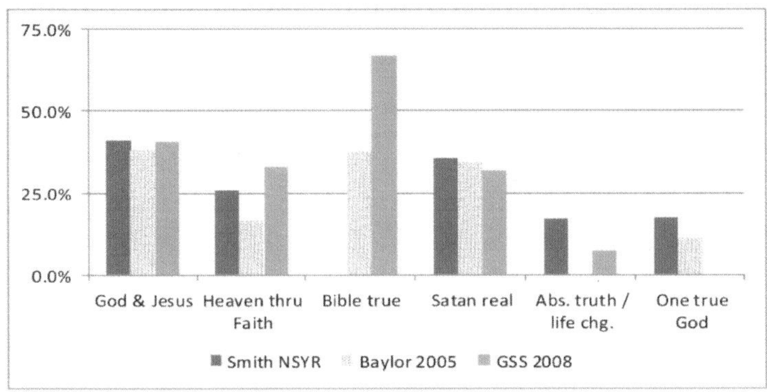

Figure 5-4 Religious Beliefs of Non-Evangelicals Age 18 – 30

indicated a belief in God & Jesus *and* a belief in Heaven thru Faith. The same bar in the sixth group of Figure 5-5, One True God, is the percentage of respondents in the Smith NSYR survey who indicated a belief in *all six* items listed on the chart. A few charts later on in the book include independent and cumulative bars in the same figure and are labeled accordingly. The cumulative bars have the same meaning in those charts as described here.

By itself, this data on religious beliefs is very interesting. First, we find that 60% of non-Evangelicals (including one third of Mainline Protestants and nearly half of Catholics) do not believe in God as a personal being and Jesus as His Son who was raised from the dead. In stark contrast, roughly three out of four of those associated with an Evangelical church believe in these basic Christian doctrines. Unfortunately, it also means we are starting with one fourth of those still associated with an Evangelical church who either don't believe in God or Jesus as His Son (or both). However, the number of Evangelicals who believe in God or Christ is still a significant number close to 30% of the total population of 18- to 29-year-olds in America. When we add in the Mainline Protestant and

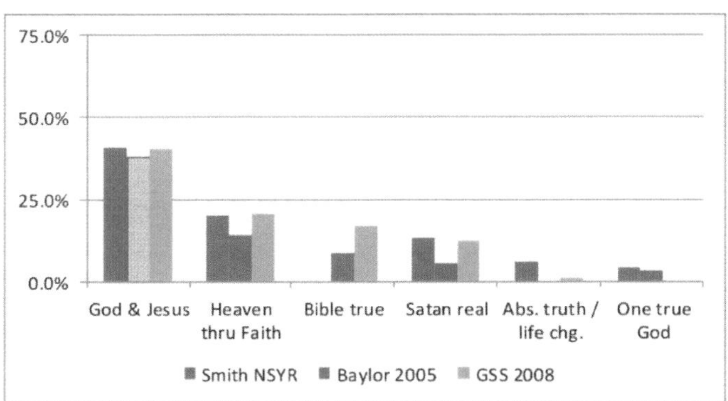

Figure 5-5 Multiple Surveys: Cumulative Religious Beliefs of Non-Evangelicals Ages 18 - 30

Catholic believers, we find approximately half of all emerging adults have a Christian view of God and Jesus at this very basic level. Although half is not what we would like, it is probably more than one would expect to find as active Christians in today's culture.

Let us begin to add in some other basic concepts typically associated with Christian faith as seen in the figures above. When the concept that only people whose sins are forgiven through faith in Jesus Christ go to heaven is considered, we find only one in four non-Evangelicals ascribe to this pivotal Christian belief. Looking at Figure 5-6 below, we see about seven out of ten emerging adult Evangelicals believe this concept, but when we look at those who believe in this concept and in God and Jesus Christ it drops down to about six out of ten as shown in Figure 5-7. This means that 4 out of 10 young Evangelicals do not appear to hold to the basic tenets of evangelical Christianity.

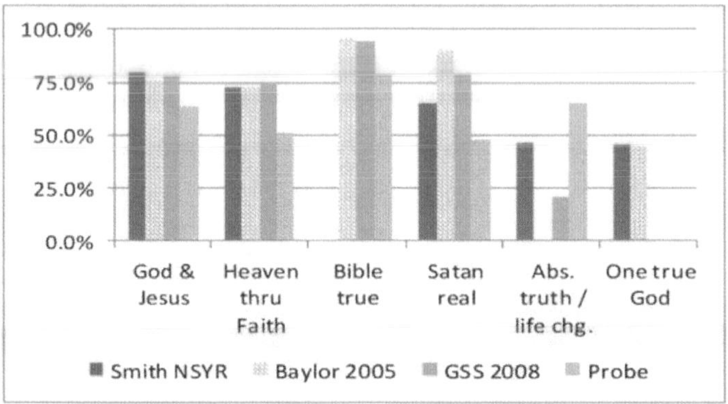

Figure 5-6 Multiple Sources: Evangelical Religious Beliefs Ages 18 – 30

When we add in the concept that the Bible is true (although not necessarily inerrant), we observe a further degradation in Christian beliefs. On the average, about 12% of non-Evangelicals and about 55% of Evangelical emerging adults ascribe to these four basic tenets of evangelical Christianity. When one adds in the concepts that Satan or demons are real beings, that there are some actions that are always right or wrong and there is one true faith, we find very few emerging adults ascribe to all of these beliefs. Among non-Evangelical emerging adults, we discover less that 5% adhere to these beliefs. More disturbing is that only 1 out of 4 Evangelical emerging adults hold to these basic Christian worldview beliefs. Looking across independent data from four different surveys, we can conclude that our Evangelical churches are losing the battle of ideas with the popular culture.

Clearly, we have a major disconnect of belief for this age group even among those who are associated with an Evangelical church. As we probe beyond God and Jesus, we find that most of them do not have a set of beliefs consistent with the basic truths of the Bible. Although 50% hold to biblical beliefs on God, Jesus, salvation by faith, Satan and the Bible, it drops to only 25% when we add in absolute moral truth and the existence of one true God.

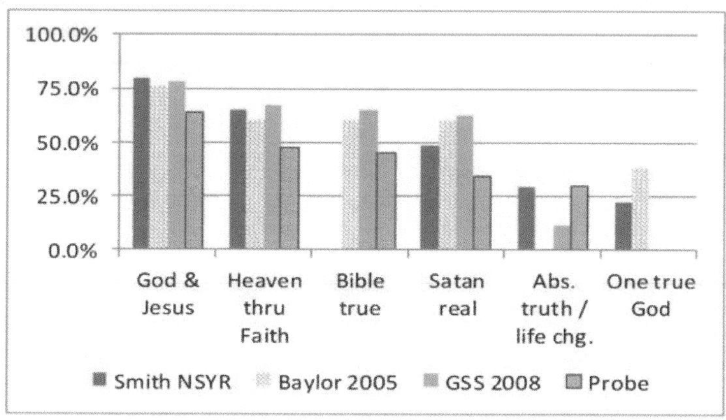

Figure 5-7 Multiple Sources: Cumulative Evangelical Beliefs Ages 18 - 30

In his book, Smith points out that for emerging adults "evidence and proof trump blind faith".[13] By this statement, he means that most emerging adults view scientific pronouncements as based on evidence and truth while religious beliefs are simply blind faith. As one young person put it, "I mean there is proven fact and then there is what's written in the Bible – and they don't match up."[14] Or as another young person put it, "You have to take the Bible as symbolic sometimes. If you take it as literal there's definitely a problem. There is scientific proof [that contradicts it]. So you have to take it piece by piece and choose what you want to believe."[15]

The interesting result of this belief is that it does not primarily apply to the extremely small segment of the Bible which some might consider at odds with scientific theories (e.g., creation of the universe). Rather, they apply it to things like teachings on sexuality, the uniqueness of Jesus, and the beginning of life. Therefore, they use the excuse of science to modify any beliefs taught by the Bible that are inconsistent with current cultural beliefs.

Perhaps we have now found the truly religious 18-to 23-year-olds in the one out of four Evangelicals that express a set of core religious beliefs. Looking at the NSYR data, we can consider six similar questions on religious belief. These questions are similar but not identical. These questions are as follows:

1. Do you believe in the possibility of divine miracles from God?
2. Do you believe that there will come a judgment day when God will reward some and punish others?
3. Do you believe that there is life after death?
4. Do you believe in heaven as a place where some people go after death?
5. People believe that it is sometimes okay to break moral rules if it works to your advantage and you can get away with it. Disagree
6. Some people think that it is okay to pick and choose their religious beliefs without having to accept the teachings of their religious faith as a whole. Disagree

The responses of 18- to 23-year-olds are shown in Figure 5-8 below. Note that for non-Evangelicals, the cumulative percentage concurring with these basic Christian beliefs quickly drops from 50% down to 11% of the population. Then when combined with the prior questions defined as constituting a biblical worldview, the cumulative probability drops to less than 4%. For Evangelicals, those agreeing with these five questions (which do not include any questions about Jesus) individually range from 60% to 90%.

However, when considered in combination, the probability of Evangelicals concurring with all five statements drops to under 40%. Then when combined with the biblical worldview set, the cumulative probability bottoms out at 19% of Evangelical new adults. This result shows a further reduction from the 25% of Evangelical new adults who hold a biblical worldview. However, since it only drops from 25% down to 19%, it appears to show some leveling off in the amount of reduction introduced by these additional questions. Perhaps, we can expect about 20% of Evangelical emerging adults who hold a consistent biblical worldview and reflect it in their religious practice and cultural decisions.

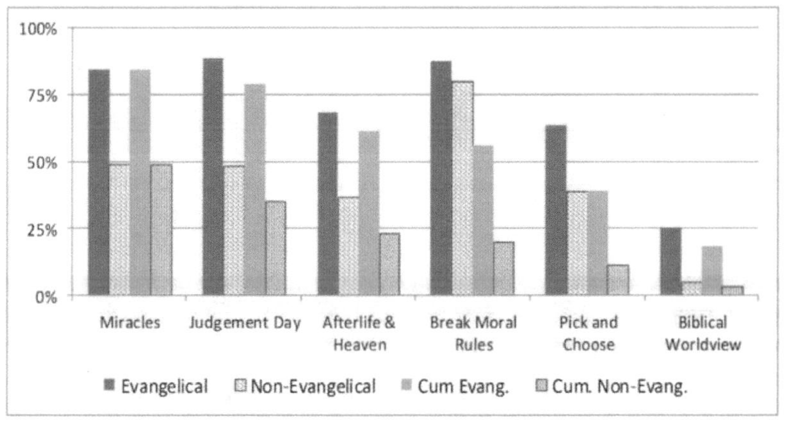

Figure 5-8 NSYR Survey: Additional Religious Beliefs for New Adults

Basic Religious Practice If this group of emerging adults is the core group, we would expect them to be engaged in the basic religious practices of their Christian faith:

- prayer on a daily basis
- attend church several times a month
- read the Bible at least once per week
- involvement with a Sunday school class or small group

How involved are they in the basic activities of their faith? Results from the four surveys are shown below in Figure 5-9 through Figure 5-12.

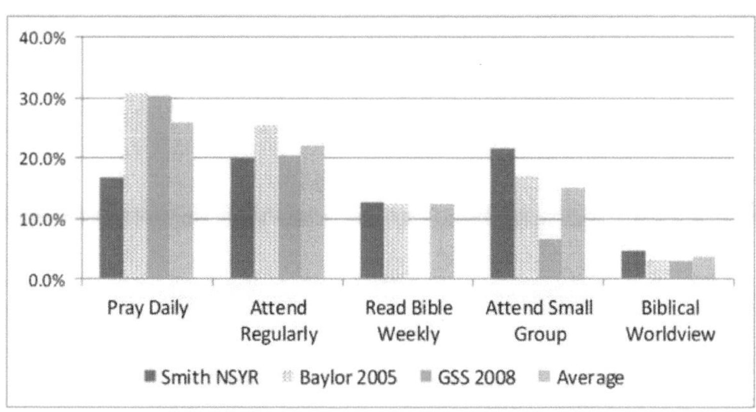

Figure 5-9 Multiple Surveys: Religious Practices of Non-Evangelical Emerging Adults

First, note that about one in four non-Evangelical, emerging adults pray on a daily basis and about one in five attend church more than twice a month. However, only about one out of ten read the Bible at least weekly and attend a small group to study the Bible with others. When we consider the cumulative results, they drop quickly down to about 5% for those practicing all four Christian disciplines. When we add a biblical worldview to the cumulative measure, it **drops to about 2%.** So, we can say that about 98 out of 100 non-Evangelical, emerging adults do not combine a biblical worldview and basic religious practices in their lives.

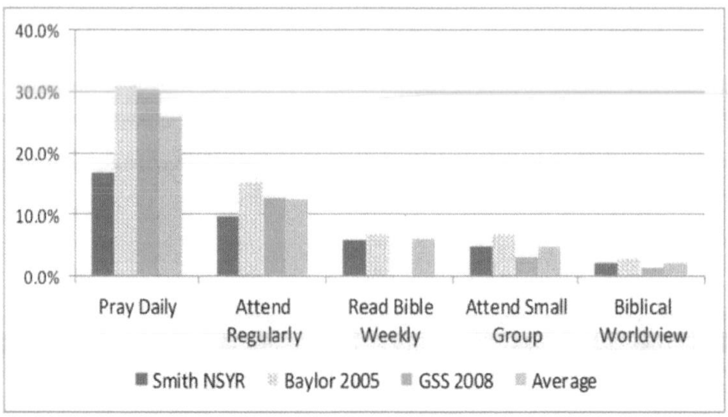

Figure 5-10 Multiple Surveys: Cumulative Religious Practices of Non-Evangelical Emerging Adults

Looking at Figure 5-11 and Figure 5-12 mapping common Evangelical religious practices, we see that two out of three pray at least daily and one out of two attend church fairly regularly. However, only 40% of them read the Bible on a weekly basis and only 40% attend a small group to discuss the lessons from the Bible with other believers. Looking at the cumulative results, we see that they also drop down quickly to about one in four who practice all four disciplines. Adding in a biblical worldview with these practices drops the number down to 14%. So, even *among Evangelicals, 86 out of 100 of them do not have a biblical worldview and a set of basic religious practices* to help them live out their faith as ambassadors for Christ.

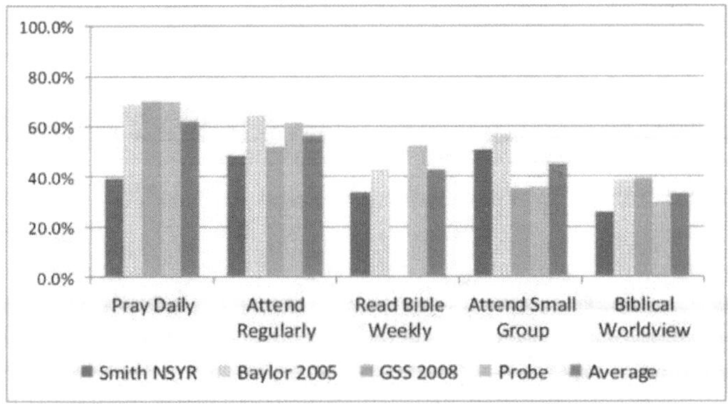

Figure 5-11 Multiple Surveys: Religious Practices of Evangelical Emerging Adults

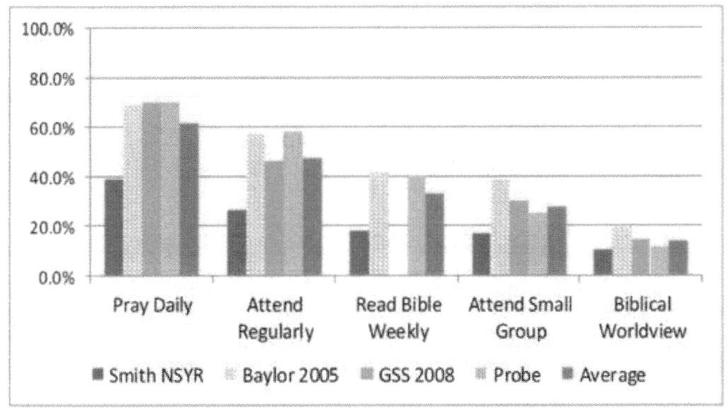

Figure 5-12 Multiple Surveys: Cumulative Religious Practices of Evangelical Emerging Adults

It is interesting to note that about 35% of Evangelical, emerging adults have a biblical worldview and almost 30% of them are regularly engaged in the four practices list above. Yet, only 14% do both. Many with a biblical worldview do not fully participate in the disciplines of a disciple of Christ. At the same time, many of those who participate in the disciplines do not hold to a complete biblical worldview.

This data clearly shows for Evangelical, emerging adults that beyond a belief in God and Jesus there is no common set of beliefs and practices. Virtually every Evangelical young adult will depart from the faith on one or more basic core beliefs and practices. It appears that there is essentially *no common core group* of dedicated faithful believers among this age group.

As Christian Smith points out, emerging adults view religious ideas as a cafeteria line where you take the ones you like and leave the rest behind. As he says, "People should take and use what is helpful in it, . . . and they can leave the rest. . . At least some parts of religions are 'outdated.' Emerging adults are the authorities for themselves on what in religion is good or useful or relevant for them."[16] As one of the emerging adults put it, "Instead of fighting various religions, I just kinda combined religious ideas that were similar or sounded good . . ."[17] So, since the emerging adult is the authority on what religious beliefs to accept rather than the Scriptures, their culture determines their religious beliefs rather than the other way around.

Changes in Affiliation and Practice

What impact does this postmodern cultural milieu have on the religious lives of emerging adults? The survey results provide insight into that question as well. We find that these emerging adults are much less involved in organized religion and personal religious practice than are older adults. For example, the percentage of emerging adults praying daily is only about 2/3 of the percentage of baby boomers who currently are daily prayers. Similarly, the percentage of emerging adults who regularly attend worship services is only about half of the percentage of baby boomers who currently are regular worship service attendees. It is important to note that when these metrics are compared against the behavior of baby boomers when they were in their twenties, the baby boomers had numbers that were almost as low as todays' emerging adults. This comparison gives some reason to hope that today's emerging adults will exhibit increased levels of religious involvement as they mature.

However, before banking on that historical trend, we need to remember that these emerging adults will be entering their thirties in a culture very different from the culture of the late '70s and early '80s. During this period, as Smith points out, "the larger popular culture of that era was still oriented around the outlook of ideological modernity." This outlook supported the ideal that if we applied ourselves diligently we could uncover absolute truths on which to base a successful life. Today's emerging adults are immersed in a postmodern culture that "stressed difference over unity, relativity over universals, subjective experience over rational authorities, feeling over reason". In this cultural environment, there is little reason to be hostile toward organized religion, but there is also little reason to pursue it.

The effects can be seen in two major differences between the religious practices of baby boomers during their early twenties and those of today's emerging adults. First, the survey results show that the number of Mainline Protestants and Catholic emerging adults regularly attending church has dropped by almost 50% from the 1970s to today. Today, less than 15% of Catholic emerging adults and less than 10% of Mainline Protestants attend religious services on a weekly basis. In contrast, the attendance percentages for evangelical Protestants have actually grown slightly over the same time period. *Second, as noted earlier, the number of emerging adults who identify themselves as not religious or as another non-Christian religion has grown by 80% from 1990 to 2010 increasing from 20% to 36%.*

The NSYR not only gives us insight into the differences between generations and age groups, it also lets us examine the changes in the practices and thinking of these young people as they moved from teenage high school students into their early twenties. For our purposes, we will look at two primary areas of change: religious affiliation and religious beliefs. At the top level, these surveys show that there is a high degree of continuity in these two areas. That is, the majority of the emerging adults surveyed have retained the same affiliation and basic beliefs through this five year period. At the same time, a large minority has experienced changes in these areas.

Over 1/3 of the emerging adults surveyed are now affiliated with a different religious group than they were five years ago. On the positive side, 25% of those who originally identified themselves as Not Religious are now affiliated with a Christian religion (mostly Evangelical denominations). However, over the same period, 17% of those who originally identified themselves as Christian now identify themselves as Not Religious. The greatest changes were seen among Mainline

Protestant denominations where fully one-half of the emerging adults changed their affiliations with half of those identifying as Not Religious and most of the rest now affiliated with Evangelical Protestant denominations.

Lest we mistake these changes for a positive trend, keep in mind that the absolute number of emerging adults converting to Not Religious is five times the number of those converting from Not Religious to a Christian affiliation. When we analyze the change in religious beliefs and activities as those surveyed moved from teenagers to emerging adults, *we find that over 41% of them became less religious over the five-year span while only 3.6% of them became more religious during that period.*

Cultural Captivity

If we define cultural captivity as looking to the culture rather than to Christ and the Bible as truth and our primary guide for living, then the following seven beliefs from Table 5-2 would give a good indication of someone who is not culturally captive.

Table 5-2 Those Who Ascribed to a Particular Religious Belief

Belief	U.S.	Evangelical		MP
	2008	2003	2008	2008
My religious faith is very or extremely important in shaping my daily life.	44%	70%	57%	33%
Jesus was the Son of God who was raised from the dead.	68%	NA	83%	59%
Only people whose sins are forgiven through faith in Jesus go to heaven.	43%	NA	64%	33%
Only one religion is true.	29%	49%	45%	22%
Morals are not relative; there is a standard	51%	NA	65%	50%
God is a personal being involved in the lives of people today	63%	79%	74%	57%
Demons or evil spirits exist	47%	66%	63%	32%
Ascribe to 7 biblical beliefs above (based on 2008 affiliation)	10%	NA	22%	10%

MP – Mainline Protestant Source: NSYR Survey

As seen in the last row of the table, nine out of ten new adults do not hold to a consistent set of basic biblical teachings. For those affiliated with an Evangelical Protestant church, the number drops slightly to about eight out of ten, an alarming figure for denominations stressing the authority and accuracy of the Bible. For those affiliated with a Mainline Protestant church, the number remains at nine out of ten consistent with the average for all new adults.

Christian Smith and other researchers suggest that one interpretation of this data is that it is a result of the success of liberal Protestantism capturing the culture. The views taken by the majority of emerging adults are more consistent with those espoused by liberal Protestant theologians than by those espoused by conservative theologians. However, this success has the effect of making Mainline Protestant churches irrelevant to the younger generations since the church offers the same relativism as the culture.

Factors Influencing Beliefs

One topic of interest to Evangelicals is what aspects of a teenager's life will most impact their religious beliefs and behaviors as an emerging adult. In his study, Smith analyzed the religious trajectories from the teenage years into emerging adulthood. As these teenagers left home for college and careers, moving out from under the more or less watchful eyes of their parents, how did their religious beliefs and behaviors change? Overall, they found a significant decline in religious fervor with the percent of the group that was highly religious dropping from 34% in 2003 down to 22% in 2008. Basically, one in three highly religious teenagers are no longer highly religious as emerging adults.

Smith and his team used statistical analysis techniques, comparing the original teenage survey results with the emerging adult survey results taken five years later, to identify the factors in teenage lives that were associated with significantly higher levels of religious fervor during emerging adulthood. The teenage period factors they found consistently very important in producing emerging adults with higher involvement in their religion were:

- frequent personal prayer and Scripture reading

- parents who were strongly religious
- a high importance placed on their own religious faith
- having few religious doubts
- having religious experiences (e.g. making a commitment to God, answered prayers, experiencing a miracle)

Some teenage practices had a surprisingly weak correlation with emerging adult religious involvement. These weaker factors included

- level of education
- frequency of religious service attendance
- frequency of Sunday School attendance
- participating in mission trips
- attending a religious high school

Let's explore these influencing factors to see what lessons we can glean.

Religiously Strong Parents. First, teenagers who view their parents as strongly committed to their religion are more likely to be highly religious as emerging adults. Even though the teenage years begin the process of developing independence from one's parents, it does not mean that what parents think, do and say is not important. As Smith points out, "the best empirical evidence shows that . . . when it comes to religion, parents are in fact hugely important . . . by contrast it is well worth noting, the direct religious influence of peers during the teenage years . . . proved to have a significantly weaker and more qualified influence on emerging adult religious outcomes than parents. **Parental influences, in short, trump peer influences.**"[18] Note this result is true regardless of whether the emerging adult felt close to their parents during their teen years.

These results led Smith to chastise American adults for swallowing the myth that "parents of teenagers are irrelevant."[19] He encourages us not to back away from discussing and promoting our religious beliefs with our children during their teenage years when they are first able to begin asking some of life's most important questions.

Personal Religious Disciplines. Second, the analysis showed that it was not participation in religious events, trips or peer groups, but rather commitment to individual religious disciplines that was a strong factor in predicting high religious involvement as an emerging adult. In other words, putting teenagers into a religious setting is not sufficient. However, if they come to the point where they realize the value of personal interaction with God through prayer and Scripture, they are much more likely to continue in that path. One reason for that correlation is that the practice of personal devotion, not directly observed by peers, parents or youth leaders, indicates a teenager that has placed a high value on the role of God and His Truth in his or her life.

Another reason may be that a consistent intake of God's Truth helps to confirm the power and validity of the Scripture as our guide for living. As Jesus told his followers, "If you abide in My Word, you are truly disciples of mine and you will know the truth and the truth will set you free" (John 8:32). Perhaps we should judge the success of our youth groups less on the number of teenagers attending events, trips and classes and more on the number who are committed to personal spiritual disciplines because they recognize the value they bring. Perhaps it is worth risking the "attendance hit" of having fewer fun times, in order teach them the importance of "longing for the pure milk of the Word" (1 Peter 2:2).

College vs. Culture. One somewhat surprising result dealt with the impact of college attendance on religious faith and practice. Prior research on baby boomers had shown that higher education had an undermining effect on the religious and spiritual lives of young adults in these preceding generations. Many of us baby boomers discovered that the social network of our high school years, which was generally supportive of religious belief and involvement, was in stark contrast to our college campus. In college, those beliefs were often viewed as backward and inappropriate for an educated person. This environment contributed to a higher decline in religious participation among college attendees compared to those who did not attend college. Today, however, several studies, including the NYSR, have shown that "in fact those who do not attend college are the most likely to experience declines in religious service attendance, self-reported importance of religion and religious affiliation."[20] For most measures, the differences are not large, but they are certainly counter to the results from the '70s and '80s.

Smith and other researchers have suggested several reasons for this major change. These possible causes include:

- the growing influence of campus based religious groups
- colleges changing attitudes to be more supportive of religious interests
- a growing number of committed Christian faculty
- the growth of religious colleges and universities
- the major long term decline in American college students' interest in answering questions about the meaning of life
- the influence of postmodern relativism which undercuts the authority of the professors as a source of truth
- adolescents who are less rebellious and more conventional than earlier generations

However, I would suggest that if all of these factors were significant we should see less decline in religiousness from the teen to emerging adult years than for the baby boomer generation. As we saw earlier, this is not the case. The decline in religious involvement and belief is greater for today's emerging adults as a whole than for the baby boomers. The transition period is just as corrosive if not more so. A reasonable conclusion is ***the culture itself has become just as corrosive as the college.*** Movies, television, music and public schools are promoting the same counter-religious message once found primarily in academia.

Other studies have found that many teenagers have already conformed to the culture in their "real lives" before leaving high school and are maintaining the appearance of religiousness to please their parents and authority figures. Once they leave that environment to attend college or pursue a career, they are relieved to be able to set aside their faux religion and focus on their real life pursuits.

Certainly, this data appears to show that the types of training and perspective that Probe offers to prepare students for the college environment are equally important for those students who are not headed for college. All teenagers need to be shown why they should value the perspectives taught in the Bible over the perspectives of their popular culture because the Biblical perspectives are rooted in verifiable reality rather than the subjective postmodern morass of our popular culture.

Chapter 6 Combined with Inconsistent Practices

As seen in the prior chapter, there is a significant disconnect between what the Bible teaches and the common religious beliefs and practices of Evangelical emerging adults. Less than 15% of Evangelical emerging adults combined basic, evangelical religious beliefs with a reasonably limited set of religious practices. At this point, one might expect to find a small but significant subset that shared an evangelical belief and practice *and* applied those beliefs consistently in their response to the prevailing culture. Let's see how that expectation lines up with the survey data.

To do this, we will look at different areas of our cultural lives that significantly define who we are and are directly dealt with by the truth of Scripture. In other words, we will look into areas where the Bible clearly states how we are to think about real events in our lives. We will look at several areas, including sexual ideas and behavior, cultural hot points (e.g. homosexual behavior, abortion), and the relationship between science and religion. As Christians our faith should play a significant role in informing our response to these issues.

Sexual Practices

First, let us look at how emerging adults view issues related to heterosexuality. These issues include divorce, pornography, sex outside of marriage, and cohabitation prior to marriage. Once again, let's use Table 6-1 to reiterate the major chasm between the positions espoused by most television and movie offerings, the popular opinion expressed by most emerging adults, and the teaching of the Bible.

Table 6-1 Three Standards of Culturally Relevant Behavior

Topic	Television and Movies	Popular Opinion	Biblical Teaching
Divorce	Standard condition and the right thing to do most of the time.	Not good but a common out to an unsatisfying marriage.	Wrong except for adultery and abusive behavior. Mt 19:3-9

Topic	Television and Movies	Popular Opinion	Biblical Teaching
Pornography	Soft is great; hard core is not generally acceptable.	Soft is fine and hard core is tolerated and readily available.	Always wrong Eph. 5:3-5, Col 3:5
Sex before marriage	Encouraged and expected Only nerds are not doing it and only because they can't attract someone of the opposite sex.	Expected, if not encouraged.	Always wrong Acts 15:29, Rom 13:13-14
Living together	Smart way to keep from making a mistake.	Expected, and often encouraged.	Always wrong John 4:17-18; Mt 14:3-4
Adultery	Depends on situation. Is normal state for most people.	Depends on situation. Common activity	Always wrong Mt 5:27-30, 2 Pet 2:12-14

The table highlights the stark difference in this area between what our emerging adults are being bombarded with from every side and the clear truth presented in the Bible. Jesus made it clear that divorce was only to be considered in the event of adultery or continuing abusive behavior. Marriage was created by God with the intent that it be a vow for life. Of course, our media outlets and our popular culture take a different view. Divorce is a ready escape from dealing with any problems. After all, marriage is entered into on a trial basis and divorce is the way to end it. For more information on a biblical view of divorce, check out www.probe.org.[1]

From a biblical perspective, we are clearly not to take into our minds pornographic material encouraging sexual fantasies with multiple, nameless partners. As Paul wrote to the Ephesians,

> *But immorality or any impurity or greed must not even be named among you, as is proper among saints; and there must be no*

> *filthiness and silly talk, or coarse jesting, which are not fitting, but rather giving of thanks. For this you know with certainty, that no immoral or impure person or covetous man, who is an idolater, has an inheritance in the kingdom of Christ and God. (Eph 5:3-4)*

Of course, Paul was not aware of pornographic movies and xxx rated Internet sites but they are certainly covered by "filthiness and silly talk, or coarse jesting". In contrast, the popular culture is continually pumping out soft- and hard-core pornography over every type of media. In general, consumption of this material is tolerated in some quarters and encouraged in others. Once again, more information on a biblical view of pornography can be found on the Probe website.[2]

When it comes to sex outside of marriage (either fornication or adultery), the biblical truth is that it is a harmful activity. It is clearly and often stated that we are to avoid them not only in action but also in thought. As Paul wrote in Romans 13:13-14,

> *Let us behave properly as in the day, . . . not in sexual promiscuity and sensuality, . . . But put on the Lord Jesus Christ, and make no provision for the flesh in regard to its lusts.*

If we have put on Jesus Christ as Lord, we will avoid sexual promiscuity and sensuality. We will avoid activities and thoughts that promote those activities in our lives. As shown in the table above, this reaction to sexual activity outside of marriage runs counter to the prevalent views of our day. We are inundated with television and movies which assume that one time sexual encounters and living together as an unmarried couple are the natural, right way to go about our lives. For example, what could be a compelling television comedy about four intelligent male nerds and their normal intelligence, more socially adapted female neighbor is turned into a continuing saga of fornication with multiple partners and people living together outside of marriage.[3] Sadly, on this topic, our popular culture is right in line with the media. If you are socially capable of "hooking up" with multiple partners, feel free to do so. Before you think of getting married, be sure and live with that person in a sexual relationship to make sure you are compatible. For more information on this topic, check out the articles on our web site.[4]

What impact does this situation have on the beliefs of today's emerging adults? For these topics, we will look at survey results from three different sources. The results from the Probe survey of Evangelicals were not included here because the Probe survey looked at those who personally engaged in an activity and not just what they think about someone else engaging in it. In each area, we will look at a chart which looks at each topic by itself and a second chart looking at the cumulative probability as we add each topic to the chart. For example, in Figure 6-1 we show the percentage of people who take a biblical stance on divorce and the percentage of those who take a biblical stance on pornography and so on. Then, in Figure 6-2 we first show the percentage of people who take a biblical stance on divorce and then the percentage who take a biblical stance on both divorce *and* pornography, and so on; i.e. a cumulative probability.

Let's start by looking at non-Evangelical emerging adults. As shown in Figure 6-1 and Figure 6-2, only about 25% have any concerns about turning to divorce when things are not working out as they hoped. Excluding the NSYR data on pornography, less than 15% see any problem with pornography, casual sex outside of marriage, or sex before marriage (this last category refers to living together in a sexual relationship before marriage). Note that the 45% shown under NSYR data for pornography is in response to a question on whether they had watched a pornographic video during the last year. For the other surveys the statement was more along the lines of "I think viewing pornography is always wrong." So this tells us that while 45% have not viewed pornography in the last year, most of those do not believe that there is anything wrong with doing so. The specific questions used from each survey are listed in Appendix A.

When their views on these sexual issues are combined in Figure 6-2, we find that less than 4 out of 100 take a consistent biblical view on these sexual issues.

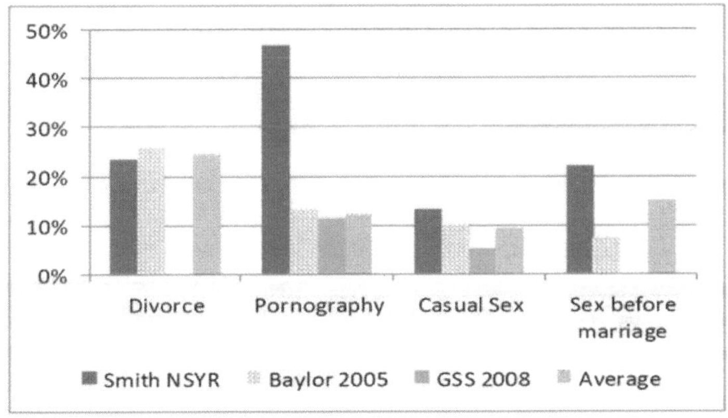

Figure 6-1 Multiple Surveys: Biblical View of Sexual Issues by Non-Evangelical Emerging Adults

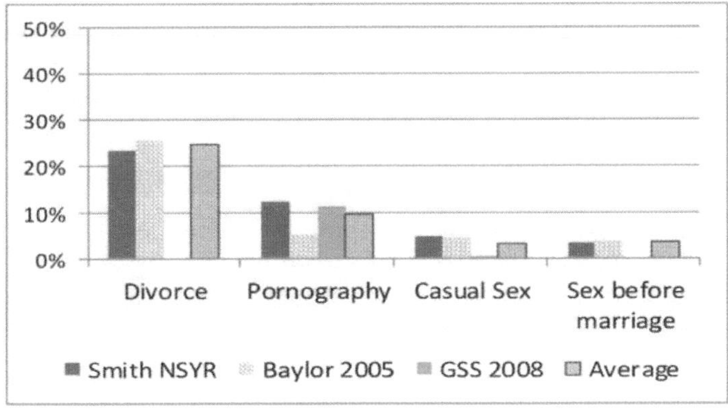

Figure 6-2 Multiple Surveys: Cumulative[5] Biblical View of Sexual Issues

Of course, these are non-Evangelicals who are not be expected to adopt a biblical view. However, most of them are Catholics or Mainline Protestants who should be applying biblical teaching to these topics. However as found in the Christian Smith study, only one out of six Mainline Protestants and less than one in ten Catholic young adults believe they should wait to have sex and don't need to try out sex with their partner before they get married. As Christian Smith points out, this belief is odd given the numerous studies showing that couples who do not live together before marriage have a significantly greater chance of success than those who do.

What about Evangelicals? How do they view these common sexual issues? Begin by looking at Figure 6-3 and Figure 6-4. Across the three surveys, we find that each of the four questions shows between 35% and 45% of these young Evangelicals taking a biblical worldview perspective. This means that roughly 6 out of 10 Evangelical, emerging adults do not take a biblical worldview on these sexual issues. Clearly, the culture is having a strong impact on the thinking of these young Evangelicals. Even worse, looking at the cumulative results, we find that only about 1 out of 7 Evangelical, emerging adults (i.e. about 14%) ascribe to a biblical stance on all four of these clear cut sexual issues.

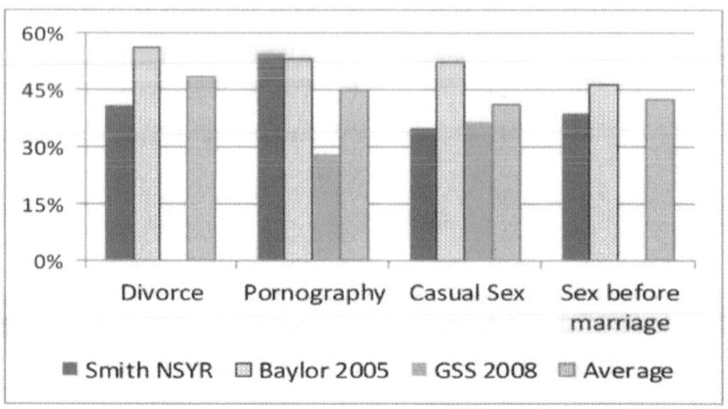

Figure 6-3 Multiple Surveys: View of Sexual Issues by Evangelical Emerging Adults

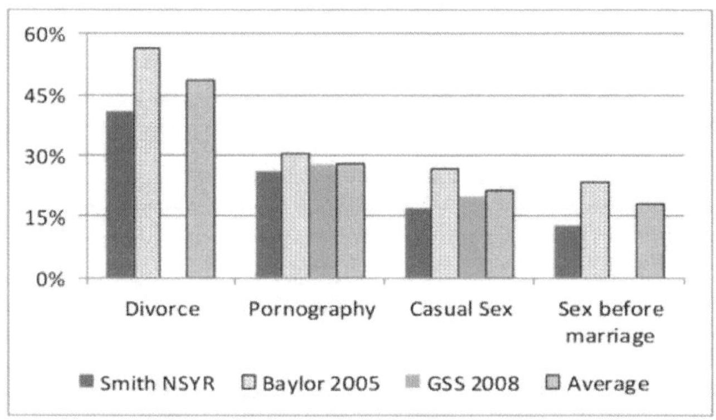

Figure 6-4 Multiple Surveys: Cumulative View of Sexual Issues by Evangelical Emerging Adults

Finally, when we look for young Evangelicals that

- hold these beliefs,
- have a basic biblical worldview, and
- engage in a minimal level of basic Christian practices,

we find that less than 8 out of 100 fall into that category. This result means that we have **8% of the most extreme Christians, i.e. Evangelicals, who stand up for these basic biblical teachings**. Therefore, approximately 2.5% of all American emerging adults (i.e.8%/3) apply a biblical worldview to their attitudes toward sexual behavior.

These beliefs are clearly counter to the teaching of Christianity, but they are dominant beliefs among Evangelical, emerging adults. As Christian Smith put it, "Most emerging adults reduce a certain cognitive dissonance they feel – arising from the conflict of religious teachings against partying and sex before marriage versus their wanting to engage in those behaviors – by mentally discounting the religious teachings and socially distancing themselves from the source of those teachings." In other words, they discount any religious teachings that would discourage them from doing what the culture promotes as acceptable. This thinking is in contrast to the Bible which says,

> "*Love not the world neither the things of the world. For all that is in the world, the lust of the flesh and the lust of the eyes and the boastful pride of life, are not of the Father but are of the world.*" (1 John 2:15-16)

Hot Behavioral Topics

Now let's investigate some related topics that are hot topics in America today. Those topics are abortion, homosexual acts, homosexual marriage, and suicide. These topics have all resulted in recent federal or state laws galvanizing our population on one side or the other. First, let's consider what the scripture teaches about these topics.

Abortion amounts to the killing of someone else to make your life easier. You think your life will be easier because you will not have to care for a new life *or* you will not have to put up with grief from your parents *or* you will not have your boyfriend upset with you. Whatever is pushing the person toward abortion, it is ultimately to make their life easier. This act is justified in the minds of some because this living soul is residing in its mother's womb at the time of its termination. However, the Bible makes it very clear that murder is a grievous sin (in fact even thinking about it is sinning according to Mt 5:21-22). And, it is clear that in God's eyes, we are people while in our mother's womb. This thought is clearly stated in Psalm 139:13-16, where we learn,

For You formed my inward parts; You wove me in my mother's womb.
I will give thanks to You, for I am fearfully and wonderfully made;
Wonderful are Your works, and my soul knows it very well.
My frame was not hidden from You, when I was made in secret,
And skillfully wrought in the depths of the earth;
Your eyes have seen my unformed substance;
and in Your book were all written
The days that were ordained for me,
when as yet there was not one of them.

Clearly, we are to honor the life that comes from God and not take it into our hands to end such a life for our convenience. You can find more information on this topic at www.probe.org.[6]

Homosexual activity is clearly identified as sin in the Bible in two regards. First, sexual activity was created to be shared in a marriage, not some other arrangement including civil unions. Second, it is to be shared with our spouse of the opposite sex. Homosexual behavior (along with other forms of sin) is clearly stated as being counter to God's will for us in numerous Scripture passages. One such passage is found in 1 Corinthians 6: 9-10:

> *Do you not know that the wicked will not inherit the kingdom of God? Do not be deceived: Neither the sexually immoral nor idolaters nor adulterers nor male prostitutes nor homosexual offenders nor thieves nor the greedy nor drunkards nor slanderers nor swindlers will inherit the kingdom of God.*

As Christians, we are to avoid homosexual activity just as we are to avoid heterosexual activity outside of a marriage relationship. For more insight in a biblical perspective on homosexuality check out our website at probe.org.[7]

Homosexual marriage is clearly incompatible with biblical teaching on the Christian life. Given God's instruction on sexual activity, the Bible clearly does not sanction homosexual marriages as discussed in Kerby Anderson's book entitled, *A Biblical Point of View on Homosexuality*, and other Probe resources.[8]

Whether self-administered or with outside help (i.e., euthanasia), suicide is clearly counter to God's will for us as expressed through the Bible. We are created in the image of God with an inherent dignity and value. The Bible is clear that God is the source of that life and that we are not to take it upon ourselves to end it, as stated in Deuteronomy 32:39,

> *See now that I myself am He!*
> *There is no god besides me. I put to death and I bring to life,*
> *I have wounded and I will heal,*
> *and no one can deliver out of my hand.*

For more information on a biblical view of suicide, check out these articles and more at probe.org.[9]

Now, look at what today's emerging adults feel about these four hot topics. For these topics, we will only look at results from the 2005 Baylor survey and the 2008 GSS survey as the other surveys do not ask about these issues. First, consider what non-Evangelicals think about these issues.

As you can see from Figure 6-5 and Figure 6-6, about 40% believe that abortion for convenience is wrong. About one in four believe that homosexual acts are wrong and that suicide should not be considered a valid option. Finally, only 16% believe that homosexual couples should not have the right to marry. Thus, the vast majority (ranging from 60% to 84%) of non-Evangelical, emerging adults hold to beliefs on these currently hot topics that are counter-biblical. The difference in the number opposed to homosexual liaisons between the 34% in the GSS survey and the 17% in the Baylor survey is interesting. It appears to reflect a fairly wide variation in sentiment rather than a significant difference in the question asked. Looking at the cumulative chart, we can see that once again inconsistencies in beliefs across these four questions result in a significant change when we consider all four questions at once. Less than 4% of non-Evangelical, emerging adults express a biblical worldview toward all four of these topics.

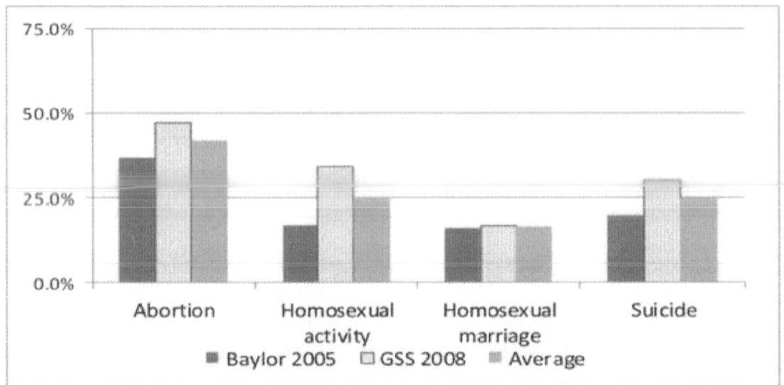

Figure 6-5 Multiple Surveys: Views of Non-Evangelical Emerging Adults on Current Hot Issues

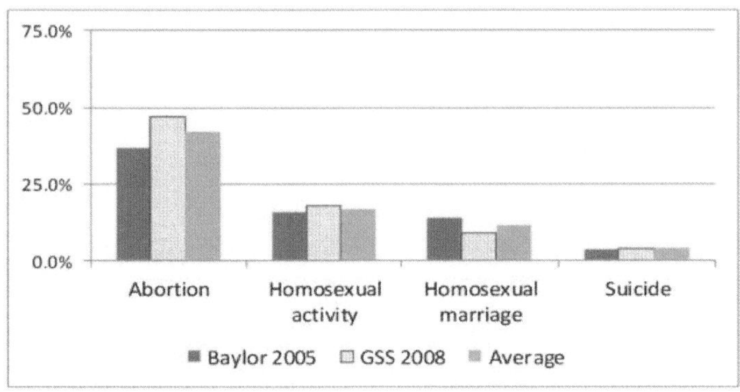

Figure 6-6 Multiple Surveys: Cumulative Views of Non-Evangelical Emerging Adults on Current Hot Issues

Comparing this data with that from the figures for Evangelicals (Figure 6-7 and Figure 6-8), these hot topics are areas where there is significant differences between the beliefs of emerging adults associated with Evangelical churches and their non-Evangelical brethren. On all four topics, about three times as many Evangelicals ascribe to a biblical belief.

They are not quite as strong on homosexual marriage and suicide, but still over 50% ascribe to a biblical view of these issues. Of course, that means between one-quarter and one-half of Evangelical, emerging adults hold beliefs that are counter to the Bible. When we consider the cumulative average, we find that over half do not hold views consistent with biblical teaching. Finally, when we look for young Evangelicals that hold these beliefs, have a basic biblical worldview, and engage at a minimal level in basic Christian practices, we find that less than 4 out of 100 fall into that category.

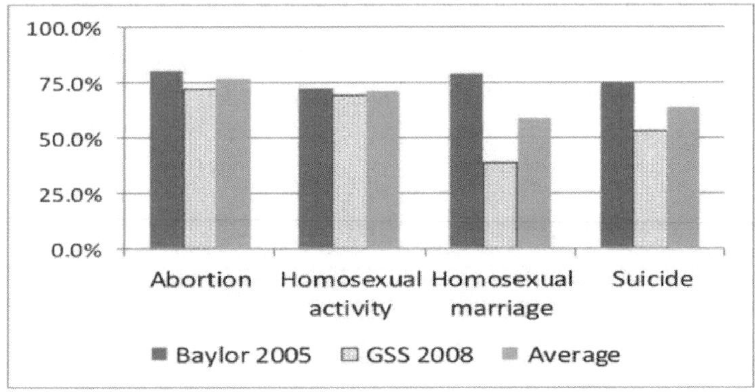

Figure 6-7 Multiple Surveys: Views of Evangelical Emerging Adults on Today's Hot Issues

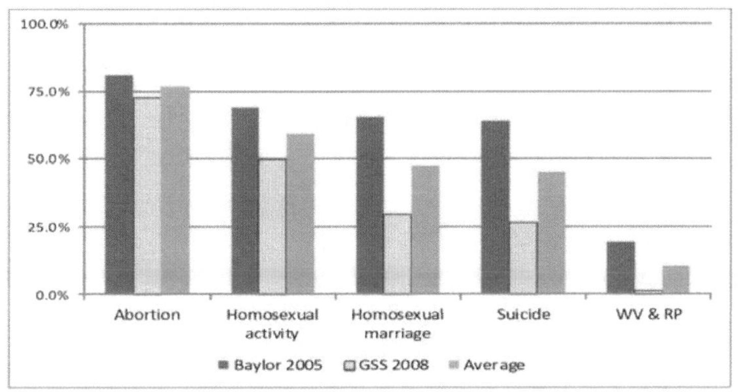

Figure 6-8 Multiple Surveys: Cumulative Views of Evangelical Emerging Adults on Today's Hot Issues

Questions of Science Another area where biblical principles encounter cultural beliefs is in the area of science. The surveys we are looking at do not give us a wide range of questions in this area. But they do allow us to look at the broad question of the relationship between religion and science. They also allow us to look at two specific areas: 1) evolution and 2) human cloning or embryonic stem cell research. Once again, let's begin by looking at the beliefs of non-Evangelical emerging adults (Figure 6-9) .

The first item on the chart is a belief that science and religion are compatible and do not ultimately conflict with one another. Someone who disagrees with this view basically believes that science and religion present two incompatible views of the world which cannot be reconciled. A biblical worldview looks at science as addressing repeatable processes in our natural world. Ultimately, science should be compatible with the Bible which addresses far more than the physical world and is not a science textbook. As revealed in Colossians, Jesus is responsible not only for creating all things, but also for holding them together.

He is the image of the invisible God, the firstborn of all creation. For by Him all things were created, both in the heavens and on earth, visible and invisible, whether thrones or dominions or rulers or authorities all things have been created through Him and for Him. He is before all things, and in Him all things hold together. (Col 1:15-17)

As shown below, only about one in three non-Evangelical emerging adults concur with a biblical worldview concept. The vast majority, roughly two out of three, concur with the idea that religion and science are set against one another, presenting distinctly different views of reality.

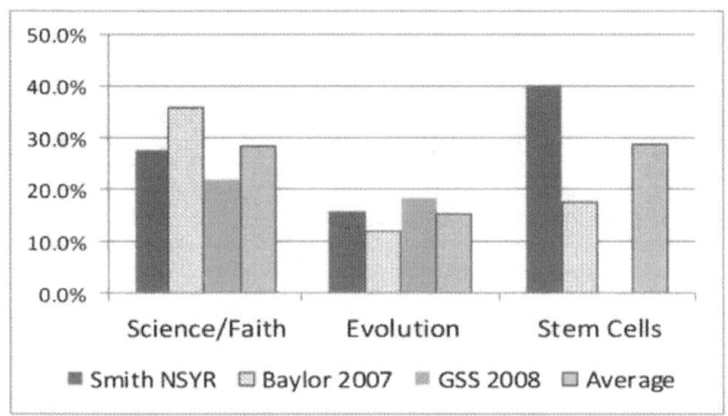

Figure 6-9 Multiple Surveys: View of Non-Evangelical Emerging Adults on Science Topics

Looking at evolution questions is a somewhat tricky proposition given the different views which could be considered consistent with the biblical record. A quick overview of those views is worthwhile to understand this question. There are four basic views of the history of life on this earth (and myriads of related views derived from the four basic views). One view is often called *young earth creationism.* This view states that the Bible claims the universe and all it contains was created in 6 literal days. The world is believed to be between 4,000 to 100,000 years old. The second view is referred to as *old earth creationism.* This view is that the earth is very old, approximately 4 billion years old. This view states that God intervened as described in Genesis chapter 1 to introduce the various forms of life on the earth. God was actively involved in creating the world and mankind, but over a much longer time span. The third view is called *theistic evolution.* Proponents of this view believe that God put all the elements which would result in our world of mankind into place at the beginning of the universe. He did not need to intervene to produce the world full of life we find today. The fourth view is *naturalistic evolution.* This view states that our world is purely the result of random events and natural selection processes. We are here by accident with no god involved or required. For more details, check out our website.[10]

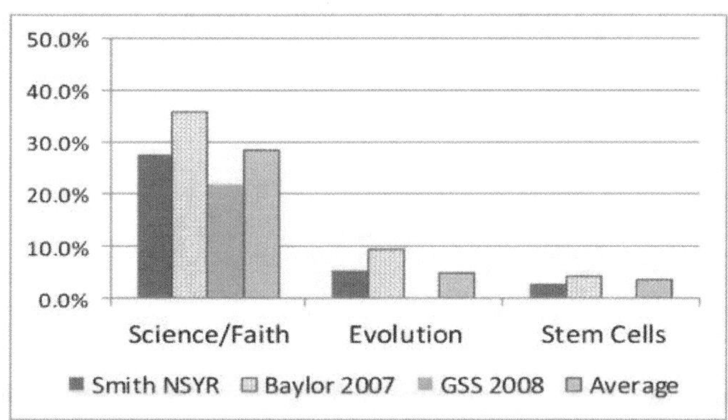

Figure 6-10 Multiple Surveys: Cumulative Views of Non-Evangelical Emerging Adults on Science Topics

However, the vast majority of emerging adults are only aware of the first option, young earth creationism, and the last option, naturalistic evolution. If they have a biblical worldview, they will believe that God had something to do with our existence. On the chart above, one who believes that human beings did not evolve from earlier species of animals or from other primates is assumed to hold a biblical worldview. As you can see, only about 15% of non-Evangelical emerging adults hold such a view.

The third area looks at placing limits on scientific research to protect the sanctity of life as the sole purview of God. In particular, one survey looks at human cloning and another looks at embryonic stem cell research. Human cloning is problematical at multiple levels. Most importantly, introducing humans as the direct creators of human –like creatures places them into the position of god for those clones. Embryonic stem cells are stem cells removed from potentially viable fetuses thereby rendering them unviable. Adult stem cells create no related ethical issue and are already used for a number of positive health treatments. Embryonic stem cell research has yet to produce anything worthwhile and requires the death of viable embryos. Most evangelical ethicists have taken a clear stand against embryonic stem cell research. But, as shown on the chart, more than 2 out of 3 non-Evangelical, emerging adults believe that embryonic stem cell research and/or human cloning are valid research areas. For more information on a biblical view of these topics, go to our web site.[11]

Looking at cumulative results of someone holding a biblical worldview on all three issues, we find that it shrinks to only about 4% of non-Evangelical, emerging adults. How do these views on science change for those who are affiliated with Evangelical churches? Consider the charts below (Figure 6-11 and Figure 6-12) for Evangelical, emerging adults.

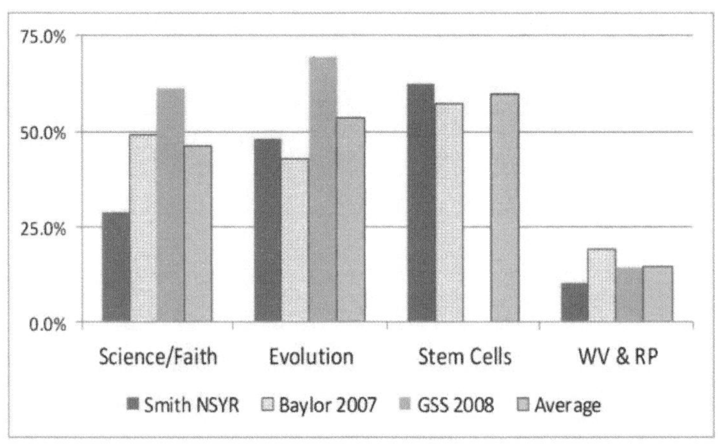

Figure 6-11 Multiple Surveys: Views of Evangelical Emerging Adults on Science Topics

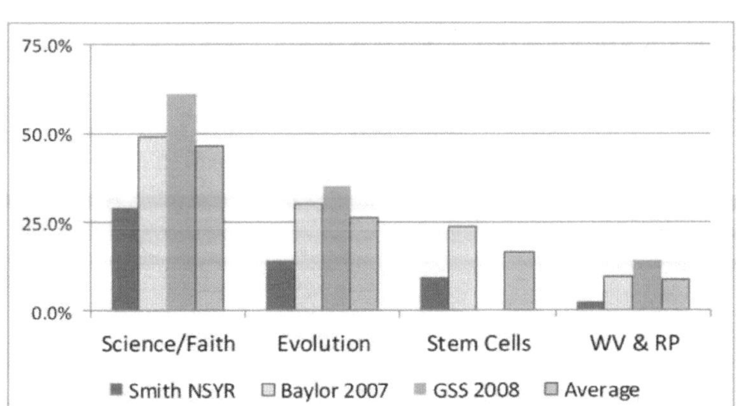

Figure 6-12 Multiple Surveys: Cumulative Views of Evangelical Emerging Adults on Science Topics

As shown, about half of Evangelical, emerging adults believe that science and religion are ultimately compatible versus only one-third of non-Evangelical, emerging adults. Similarly, we see that about half of them believe that some level of God's intervention is required to explain our existence as opposed to less than one-sixth of non-Evangelicals. About 60% of these Evangelicals oppose human cloning and/or embryonic stem cell research versus only 30% of non-Evangelicals. Although there is a significant difference between non-Evangelicals (~65% of population) and Evangelicals (~35% of population), this does not reflect a clear evangelical position on these topics. Roughly half of the Evangelicals take a position counter to the Bible. This dichotomy could be caused by a lack of understanding these issues or by a sacred/secular split in the thinking of these confused Evangelical, emerging adults.

Looking at the cumulative chart, we see an even more disturbing picture. Although approximately one-half hold a biblical view on each of the three questions, only about one-fifth hold a biblical worldview on all three questions. Once again, this result highlights the lack of a consistent application of biblical principles to current issues. When we add in the questions on a biblical worldview and a minimal level of religious engagement (WV & RP on the chart), we find *less than one in ten*

Evangelical, emerging adults applying a consistent biblical worldview across their actions and beliefs related to science and religion.

Other Cultural Topics and Practices

The topics we have looked at in this chapter are only a small subset of the cultural beliefs that should be impacted by our religious beliefs. Now, consider a few more found in the NSYR grouped into three rough categories: 1) their personal life, 2) attitudes toward material possessions and 3) sexual purity. Looking at their view of their personal life, let's consider those who have not felt guilty about things in their life over the last year, believe their life is meaningful and believe that they can change important things in their life as needed. We find that approximately one-third of non-Evangelicals and one-third of Evangelicals agree with these statements. Second, looking at how many don't need to buy more and care about the needs of the poor, we find about one in four of all new adults agree with these objectives. However, when we combine these two areas, we find that only about one in ten new adults agree. Now add in the idea that unmarried sex and divorce are not okay. We find that only 28% of Evangelicals and 14% of all new adults agree with this statement. Combining all three of these belief areas, we discover that only 2% of Evangelicals agree with all three areas. When combined with religious beliefs and practices, we find that less than one in two hundred Evangelicals has consistent beliefs across all these areas.

Perhaps the disturbing cultural beliefs are belied by the cultural practices. Let's look at some of the relevant cultural practices addressed in the National Study on Youth and Religion. Let's begin with the number of people who have not smoked pot or engaged in binge drinking in the two weeks before the survey. Amongst Evangelical, emerging adults over half (54%) have not engaged in these two activities. Of course this also means that almost half of them have engaged in one of both of these activities. Amongst Catholic emerging adults, two out of three have engaged in these behaviors.

Certainly Christians are called to "give thanks in all circumstances" and to "set their minds on heavenly things". So, let us consider those who are grateful for the present and sometimes think about the future. This includes almost half of all emerging adults. Thus, over half of emerging adults seldom give thanks and rarely think about the future.

Looking at the different sets of cultural topics examined in this chapter, we find for each set that the inconsistent views of American emerging adults result in almost no one maintaining a consistent biblical worldview.

Conclusion

When we consider all three primary areas considered together (sexuality, hot topics, and science), we obtain the results plotted in Figure 6-13. We find that no non-Evangelicals and only about 3% of Evangelicals have a consistent biblical worldview across these cultural topics. Looking at the combination of biblical worldview, some level of religious participation and these cultural views, we discover that only 1.5% of Evangelical, emerging adults express a consistent worldview derived from biblical teaching. For non-Evangelicals, the religious beliefs, religious practices and cultural beliefs are all much less than 10% of the group. For Evangelicals, close to one third of them have biblical beliefs and/or consistent religious practices which is a significantly greater percentage than for non-Evangelicals. But when we look at their cultural beliefs we find that they do not apply their biblical beliefs or religious practice in developing their beliefs on cultural issues.

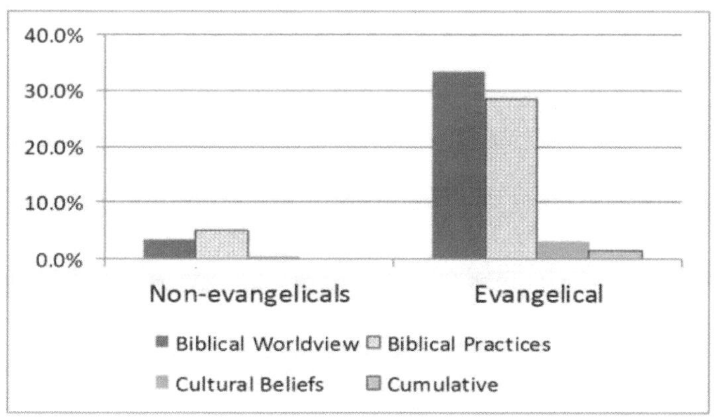

Figure 6-13 Multiple Surveys: Emerging Adults Holding a Biblical View on Worldview

As this chapter shows, the hodgepodge approach to picking a set of inconsistent beliefs and religious practices carries over into the application of religious convictions on current cultural issues. All the surveys carry a consistent message. Much less than 1% of emerging adults in America hold to a basic set of biblical truths *and* practice at least a light level of activities associated with their religion *and* carry the teachings of their religion into their views of cultural practices of today. *It appears they are influenced much more by pleasing their friends and not making anyone else uncomfortable than by the teaching found in the New Testament.* This statement is almost as true for those associated with an Evangelical church as for other emerging adults.

Chapter 7 Belief and Behavior Vary by Demographic

Up to this point, we have looked at American emerging adults as a homogeneous group. We have the means to consider some other factors in our analysis. Looking at race, education, location in the country, and gender, brings out other interesting truths about the religious beliefs and practices of young adults. In the consideration of religious beliefs and practices, data is drawn from the GSS 2008 Survey and the Probe Survey. In looking at cultural beliefs, the examination is limited to the GSS 2008 Survey data.[1] In this section, our consideration is extended to 18- to 44-year-olds (18 – 40 for Probe Survey) to give a greater sample size when we subdivide the respondents. Even so, for some groups, e.g. Asians, the small sample size means the uncertainty of the results will be significantly higher.

Racial Background and Religious Belief /Practice

In America today, there is still a significant level of self-imposed racial segregation among churches. Therefore, one may expect to find some differences in the worldviews being expressed in different ethnic congregations. Let's begin by looking at how many 18- to 44-year-old Americans are born-again before adding in a biblical worldview and religious practices. In the GSS 2008 survey, respondents were asked, "Would you say you have been "born-again" or have had a "born-again" experience? That is, a turning point in your life when you committed yourself to Christ?" How was this question answered by different races? The answer is shown along with the population break out in Table 7-1.

Table 7-1 Born-Agains by Race for 18 - 44 year olds

Racial Background	White	Black	Hispanic	Asian & Others
% of Population	60%	13%	20%	7%
% of Race Born-again	31%	51%	31%	23%
% of Total Population Born-again	19%	6%	6%	2%

Just over half of black, young adults claim to be born-again as compared to approximately one third of the other ethnic groups considered. Even though whites make up almost two-thirds of born-again Christians among young adults, on a percentage basis, blacks are much more likely to be born-again. It is also important to note, for 18 – 29 year old blacks, the percentage claiming to be born-again drops to 41%. This drop may indicate a generational change between the younger respondents and those over 30. But for the other races, there is very little difference between 18- to 29-year-olds and 30- to 44-year-olds. As noted earlier, 31% of all 18-to 29-year-olds are born-again while 33% of all 30- to 44-year-olds are born-again.

As a whole, 44% of born-again, 18- to 44-year-olds profess to a biblical worldview per the definition used with the GSS study (see Appendix A for the GSS worldview questions). Similarly, 18% of them participate in a minimal set of religious practices (i.e. pray daily, attend church at least twice a month, take part in a church related activity at least once a month, and try to carry their religious beliefs into other areas of their lives). How are those numbers distributed among the born-agains by race?

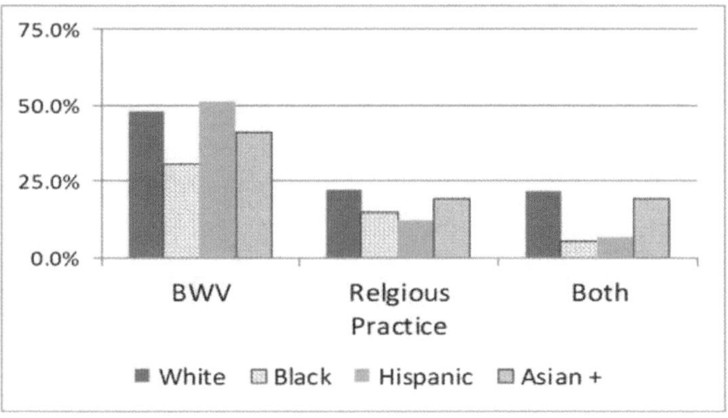

Figure 7-1 GSS Survey: Belief & Practice Across Ethnic Groups

As shown in Figure 7-1, almost half of born-again whites, Hispanics and Asians profess to a biblical worldview. However, blacks (who had over half professing to be born-again) have only just over one fourth of those born-agains professing to holding a biblical worldview. Is there one particular worldview question that causes this discrepancy? If that were the case, the percent of blacks holding to a biblical view of that question, should be only slightly higher than percent holding to all seven beliefs. Of the seven worldview questions, the lowest rated question[2] among born-again blacks is professed by almost twice the level holding a complete biblical worldview. So it wasn't one question, but rather the combination of questions that reduced their percentage.

Looking at religious practices, the Hispanics are significantly lower than the others. Looking at the combined probabilities for both biblical worldview and practice, we find that whites and Asians stayed at the level of religious practice. This means basically everyone who had a consistent set of religious practices also had a biblical worldview. However, among blacks and Hispanics, this was not the case. The result for those ethnic groups dropped to only 5% of born-agains having a biblical worldview and a minimally consistent set of religious practices.

The next chart, Figure 7-2 adds in the data from the Probe survey. Remember that the definition of a biblical worldview and a minimally consistent set of religious practices is somewhat different between these two studies (see Appendix A for the details). As shown, the percentage holding a biblical worldview are slightly lower and the percentage with a minimally consistent set of religious practices are higher, but the composite result from both surveys is essentially the same, around 20% of whites and Asians and around 7% for blacks and Hispanics.

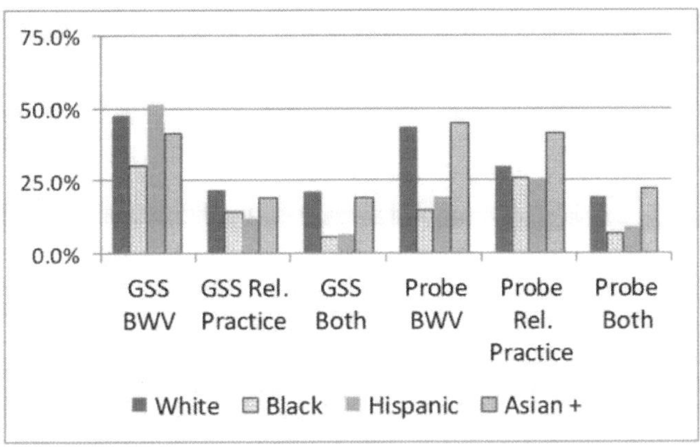

Figure 7-2 GSS/Probe Surveys: Belief & Practice Across Ethnic Groups

In summary is appears that black born-agains have on the average a somewhat different view of what constitutes a biblically sound worldview. Or possibly, the focus of the teaching in those churches does not focus on the areas addressed by these biblical worldview questions. Similarly, Hispanic born-agains have a lower commitment to religious practices and, in the case of the Probe study, also a different view of the worldview issues used in the Probe survey.

Geographic Location and Religious Belief and Practice

In some ways, the differences in language and perspective found in different areas of the country have diminished. But regarding some cultural aspects, significant differences still exist. Let's see if this is true for religious belief and practice considering the Northeast, the Midwest, the South and the West. Once again, we will begin by examining the GSS survey to find out how many people are born-again in each area of the country.

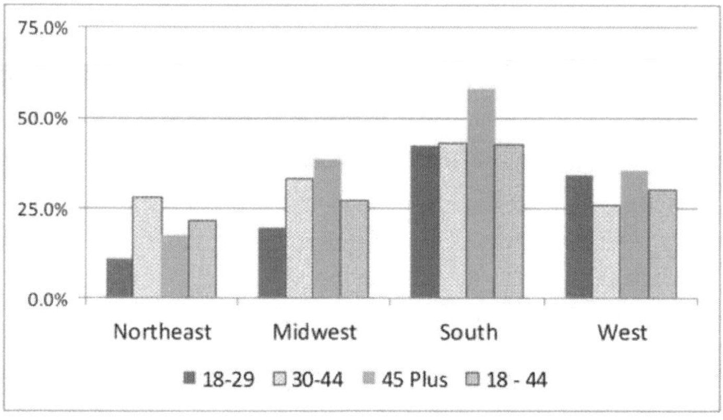

Figure 7-3 GSS Survey: Born-Agains by Age & Region of the Country

As shown in Figure 7-3, there is a significant difference in the percentage of born-agains across the regions. For 18 – 29 year olds, it ranges from 11% in the Northeast to 43% in the South, four times greater! For 18 – 44 year olds, it ranges from 22% in the Northeast to 43% in the South. Also of interest, is for 18 – 44 year olds the Midwest and the West are about the same level at about 30%, but for 18 -29 year olds, the Midwest lags the West by 75% (i.e. 20% vs. 35%).

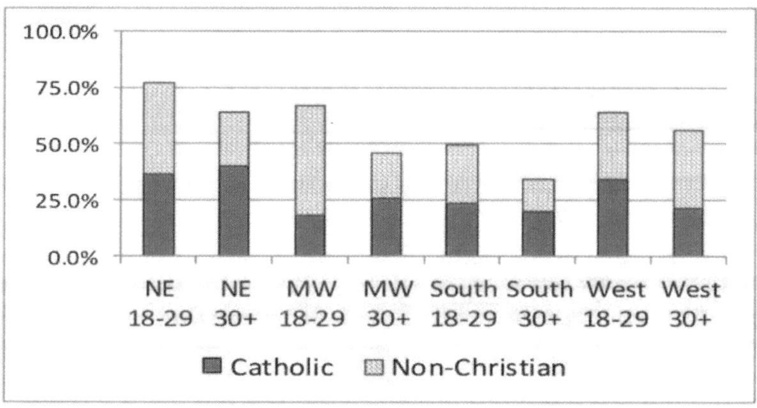

Figure 7-4 GSS Survey: Catholics and Non-Christians by Age and Region of the Country

Clearly, the probability of someone being an Evangelical is heavily dependent on the section of the country in which they were raised and the dominant religious views of that region. This can be clearly seen in Figure 7-4 on the distribution of Catholics and non-Christians across the regions. As shown, over 75% of emerging adults from the Northeast are identified as non-Protestants as compared to the South where 50% are non-Protestants. Equally interesting is the distinct difference between emerging adults under 30 and those 30 and over. In the Midwest and the South, emerging adults (i.e. 18- to 30-year-olds) are 40% more likely to state they are non-Protestant than are those 30-years-old and over. In all regions, we see a significant difference in the age groups. It is important to understand that this is not an issue of not going to church because you are busy with your friends or sleeping in which may all change when you have kids. This result indicates a significant increase in those who do not claim any affiliation with a Protestant church group.

Looking at the data from Figure 7-5 on biblical worldview and religious practice among born-agains across these four geographical segments, we find more interesting results. First, one sees that those in the West are significantly more likely to hold to a biblical worldview than those from other regions. However, all four regions are about the same with only 20% - 25% of the born-again respondents reporting at least a minimally active religious practice.

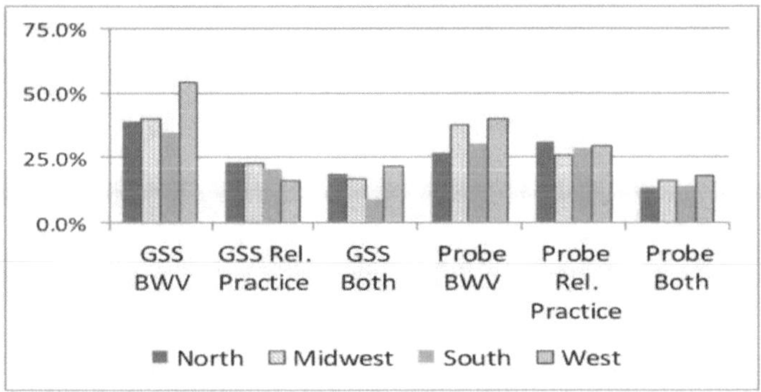

Figure 7-5 GSS/Probe: Belief & Practice By Region of the Country

When we combine a biblical worldview with an active religious practice, we see both surveys across all geographic regions reporting about 15% of the born-agains who combine both aspects in their lives. One exception is the GSS survey showing less than 10% of Southern born-agains with a biblical worldview and religious practice. In the GSS survey data, the anomaly of the Western region having a higher probability for both than for only religious practice is caused by looking at only of subset of respondents for the biblical worldview questions. Also, we need to keep in mind that this chart is only for born-agains in each region. When we look at the percentages of the entire group of 18- to 44-year-olds, we find from the GSS survey, 3.4% of Northeasterners, 3.9% of Southerners and Midwesterners and 7% of Westerners combine a biblical worldview and a minimally active religious practice.

In summary, a significant difference exists between regions regarding the percentage of born-again, young adults. However, among those born-again, young adults, there is a reasonable amount of uniformity in religious beliefs (i.e. biblical worldview) and religious practice. Unfortunately, it is uniformity around a disappointingly small percentage of those with a consistent biblical worldview and religious practice.

Education and Religious Belief and Practice

In the past, there has been a significant correlation between higher levels of education and lower levels of religious belief. However, Christian Smith has reported that this trend has changed in recent years with a slightly higher percentage of those graduating from college ascribing to a basic set of Christian beliefs than those who have not graduated from college.[3] Let us see what these surveys tell us about the relationship between education and Christian worldview belief and practice.

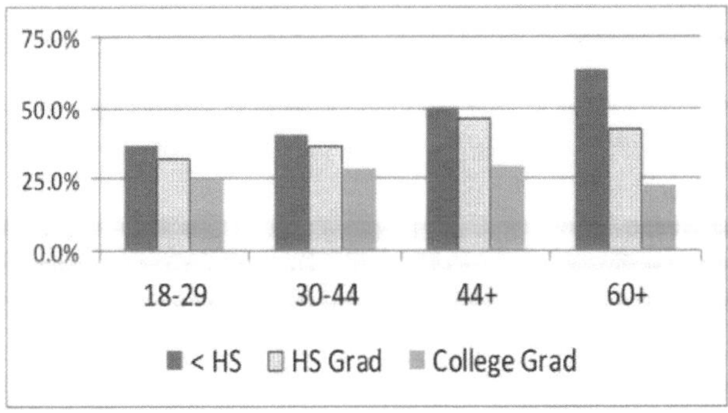

Figure 7-6 GSS Survey: Born-agains by Education Completed

Once again, we will begin by considering the GSS 2008 survey data on education and those who profess to being born-again as shown in Figure 7-6. First, we see a drop in the percentage of born-agains based on the level of education at each age level. Second, among those who did not graduate from college we see a decline in the percentage of born-again individuals as a function of age. However, for those who graduated from college, the percent is consistent (about 25%) regardless of age. It appears that for the last forty years about one fourth of American college students have been prepared to maintain their identify as born-again through their college experience. At the same, time, the percentages of born-again non-high school graduates and high school graduates have dropped by 36% and 28% respectively over the last twenty years.

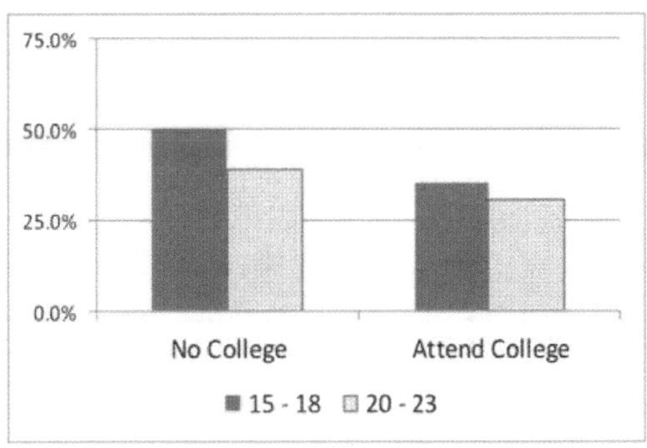

Figure 7-7 NSYR Survey: Evangelicals versus Age and Education

This graph raises the question: Were the beliefs of the college graduates created by their college experience or were they already predisposed as less likely to be born-again? We can explore this question by looking at data on Evangelicals in the first and third wave of the National Study on Youth and Religion as shown in Figure 7-7. Although this study does not ask whether the emerging adults are born-again, we can look at the number who are affiliated with an Evangelical denomination. What we find is a very interesting result. Both 'those who attend college' and 'those who do not' show a decrease in affiliation with Evangelical churches. Those who were not attending college began at 50% Evangelical and decreased to 39% (a decrease of 22%). Those who were attending college began at 35% Evangelical and decreased to 30% Evangelical (a decrease of almost 15%). It would appear from this result that it is not the college experience that degrades their faith as much as breaking free from parental influence and establishing their own pattern of beliefs.

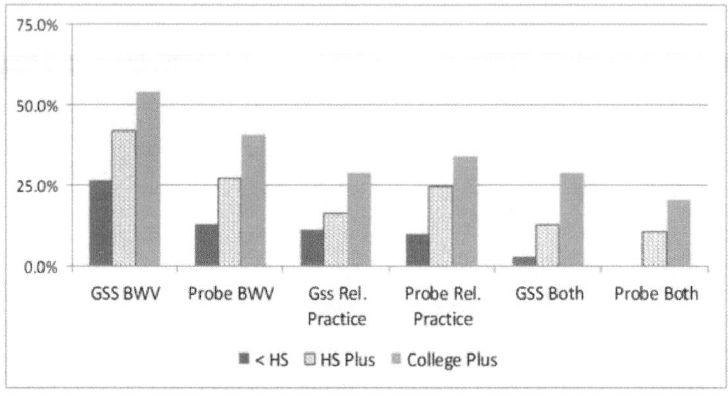

Figure 7-8 GSS/Probe Surveys: Belief & Practice versus Level of Education

When we consider biblical worldview and religious practice as a function of education, we discover a trend that is counter to that of who is born-again. In particular, we find that born-again, college graduates are much more likely to hold to a biblical worldview and a nominal set of religious practice than other emerging adults. As you can see in Figure 7-8, they are more than twice as likely as those without a high school degree to hold to a biblical worldview. They are more than three times as likely to engage in a consistent set of nominal religious practices. Interestingly, when we consider both worldview and religious practices, we find that virtually no young adults without a high school education have both those attributes. Between 20% to 28% of born-again, college graduates have both of these attributes. Of course, we should keep in mind that almost three out of four born-again college graduates do not ascribe to a biblical worldview and practice a nominal set of religious practices.

Gender and Religious Belief and Practice

Finally, let us look at the effect of gender on emerging and young adults religious beliefs and practice. As shown in Figure 7-9, females are somewhat more likely to identify themselves as being born-again and to ascribe to a biblical worldview than are males. This trend is true for all age groups.

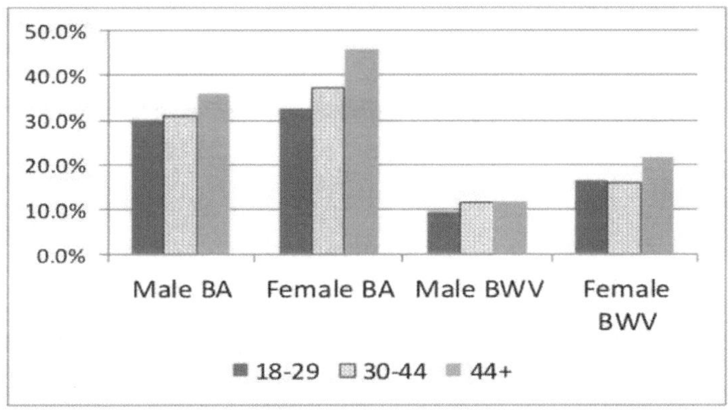

Figure 7-9 GSS Survey: Basic and Worldview Beliefs by Gender & Age

Looking at the second chart on this subject, we see slightly different results for the two surveys. The GSS survey with its definition of a biblical worldview shows a greater percentage of born-again women than born-again men ascribe to a biblical worldview. While the Probe survey, with a somewhat different definition, shows a greater percentage of born-again men than women with a biblical worldview.

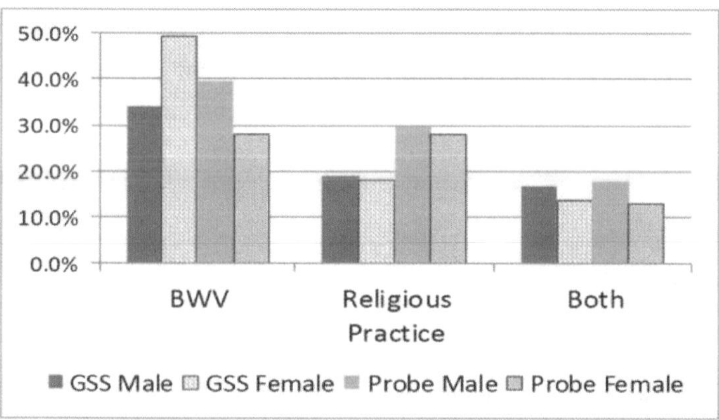

Figure 7-10 GSS/Probe Surveys: Worldview and Religious Practice by Gender

However, when we look at religious practices and the combination of worldview and practices in Figure 7-10, we find that the portion of men and women is virtually identical. Approximately 15% of men and women who are born-again ascribe to a biblical worldview and a nominal set of religious practices according to both surveys. When it comes to holding a biblical worldview and practicing its basic principles, neither men nor women stand out. In fact, they both fall far short in accepting biblical views with their born-again status.

Demographics and Cultural Belief

In the preceding chapter, we looked at three sets of cultural beliefs which should be driven by our worldview. The first set is Sexual Issues consisting of beliefs on divorce, pornography, fornication, and living together without marriage. The second set is labeled Hot Topics. These topics included abortion, homosexual activity, homosexual marriage, and suicide. The third set, Science Topics, includes views on evolution, the relationship between science and religion, and embryonic stem cell research. In this chapter, we will consider these three topics as we look at various demographic breakdowns of the young adult population. Because we will use only the GSS survey for these demographic topics, the Science Topics will not include stem cell research.

Racial Background and Cultural Belief

The first thing we should notice from Figure 7-11 for born-again, young adults is that the highest percentage is 40%, the lowest is 5%, and the average is around 20%. So regardless of race, most born-again, young adults do not appear to be applying a biblical worldview to these important cultural questions.

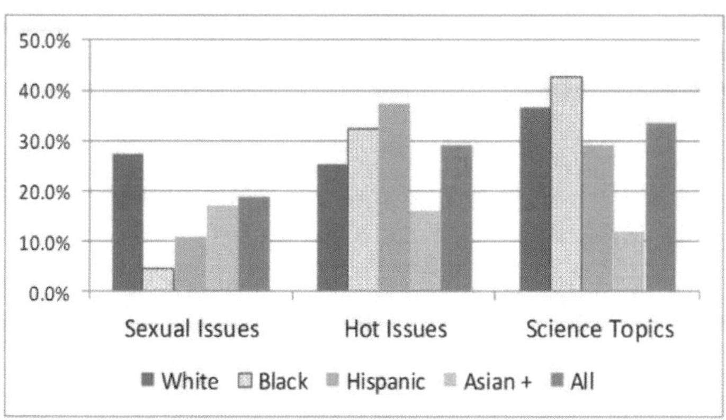

Figure 7-11 GSS Survey: Cultural Issues by Ethnic Background for Born-again Young Adults

There appears to be significant differences as a function of race on several of these topics. On sexual issues, white, born-agains, are almost twice as likely as any other race to hold a biblical position. Those from the black, born-again community were more than 5 times less likely than whites to hold a consistent biblical worldview on sexual issues. The area creating most of the difference was pornography, specifically 1) have you seen an X rated movie in the last year and 2) there should be laws against the distribution of pornography, whatever the age. Some of the difference may be more an opposition to government intervention than an opposition to limiting pornography.

On the Hot Issues, relating to suicide, abortion, homosexual acts, and homosexual marriage, the Asian community of born-agains are much less likely to subscribe to a biblical worldview. In this area, the Asian respondents were much less likely to hold a biblical worldview than other races on homosexual acts, homosexual marriage and suicide; with the lowest area being gay marriages at 19% for Asian respondents vs.

approximately 45% for the other races. It should be noted that the number of Asian respondents who were 18 – 44 year old born-agains was relatively small (~20) reducing the accuracy level of the responses. However, these differences were large enough to indicate a real difference in thinking on these issues may exist.

On the Science Topics, we find a large disparity between the white/black respondents and the Asian respondents. The white/black respondents were four times more likely to profess a biblical worldview than the Asians (i.e. 40% vs. 10%).

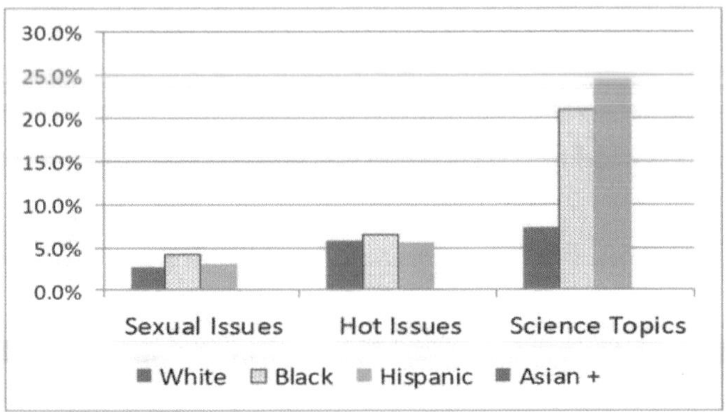

Figure 7-12 GSS: Cultural Issues by Ethnic Background for Not Born-agains Young Adults

Although the levels of biblical worldview thinking are low for born-again, young adults, they are significantly better than for those young adults who are not born-again. As shown in Figure 7-12 for those not born-again, most of the topics are less than 5% of the group; significantly less than the born-agains. The one area where there is a significant difference among races is on the science questions where a relatively large percentage of blacks and Hispanics espouse beliefs consistent with a biblical worldview.

For Asian young adults who are not born-again, there were no respondents (i.e. 0%) who espoused beliefs in any area consistent with a biblical worldview. Let's take a closer look in the area of Hot Issues breaking out each of the topics in Table 7-2. As shown, there are Asians in the survey who were not born-again and yet took a biblical position on each issue. But none of them took a biblical position on all four issues.

Table 7-2 Asian Cultural Beliefs of 18 - 44 year olds: Those Who Do Not Believe the Following Are Acceptable

Status	Abortion	Homosexual Acts	Gay Marriage	Suicide	Combined
Asian Born-again	84%	44%	19%	29%	16%
Asian Not Born-again	20%	34%	10%	17%	0%

For three of the topics above, the born-agains and the not born-agains track fairly well with about a 10% difference between them. On the topic of abortion there is a huge difference. Born-again, young Asian adults oppose abortion at a rate 4 times that found for those young, Asian adults who are not born-again. Clearly the Asian Evangelical churches take a strong stand on abortion. If they take a strong stand against homosexuality and suicide, it is not getting through to young adults.

Geographic Location and Cultural Belief

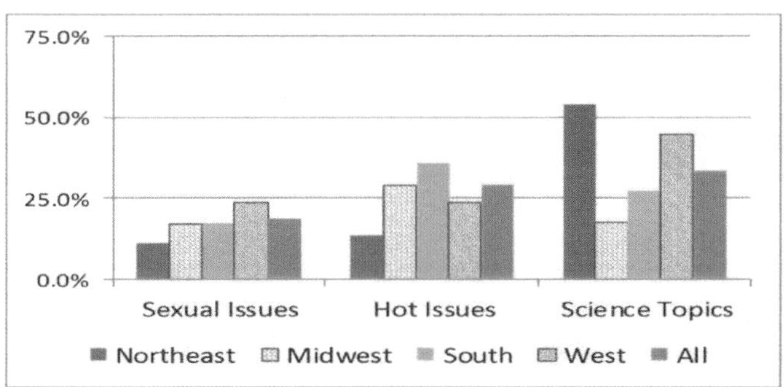

Figure 7-13 GSS Survey: Cultural Issues by Region for Born-again Young Adults

How do cultural beliefs vary by geographic location? As we can see in Figure 7-13 for born-again, young adults, the level of belief is fairly consistent across regions for most topics. The science topic shows a large discrepancy between the Northeast/West and the Midwest/South regions. What we may be seeing here is a situation where those in the less religious Northeast and West who choose to associate with Evangelical churches are less likely to buy into the materialistic view of science taking precedence over religion. This scenario is supported by the data shown in Figure 7-14 below for 18 to 44 year olds who do not profess being born-again. As shown, about 10 times as many born-again, young adults from the Northeast and the West ascribe to the views on science as the number of not born-again, young adults. In contrast, in the South where more conservative, evangelical views are prevalent, there is only a difference of 20% between these two groups (i.e. 25% of born-agains vs. 20% of non-born-agains).

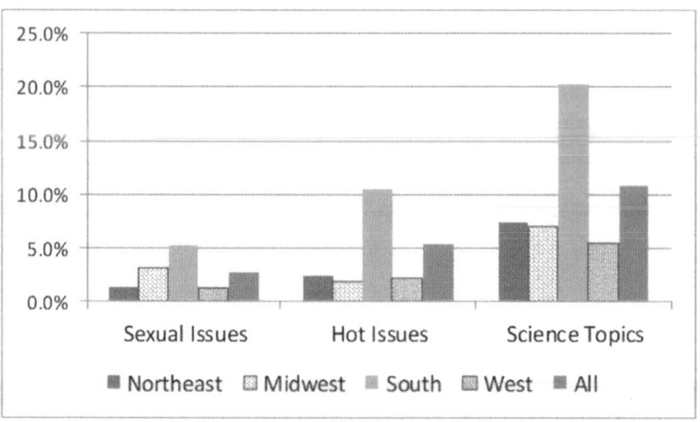

Figure 7-14 GSS Survey: Cultural Issues by Region for Not Born-again Young Adults

While young adults from the Northeast rank significantly higher than other regions on the science questions, they are much lower on the Sexual Issues and the Hot Issues at about only 12% of born-agains and 2% for those not born-again. In contrast, looking at the two charts, we can see that in the South these biblical worldviews leak over (at least to some extent) into the beliefs of those not born-again.

Education and Cultural Belief

How does their level of education play on the cultural beliefs of young adults? Looking at born-agains in Figure 7-15, we find two anomalies. Those with a college degree are almost twice as likely to take a biblical worldview on Sexual Issues as those with less education. This result probably is further evidence that those coming out of college professing to be born-again more consistently apply their Christian beliefs across all areas of their life. For those not born-again (Figure 7-16), only 2% of college graduates take a biblical worldview on these Sexual Issues (15 times less than the born-agains). The beliefs of born-again, college

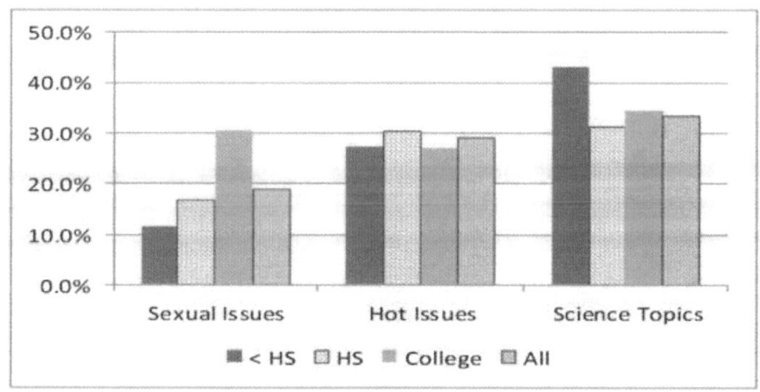

Figure 7-15 GSS Survey: Cultural Issues by Education Achieved for Born-again Young Adults

graduates are distinctly different from the population at large. And yet, only 30% of them hold to a biblical view regarding Sexual Issues.

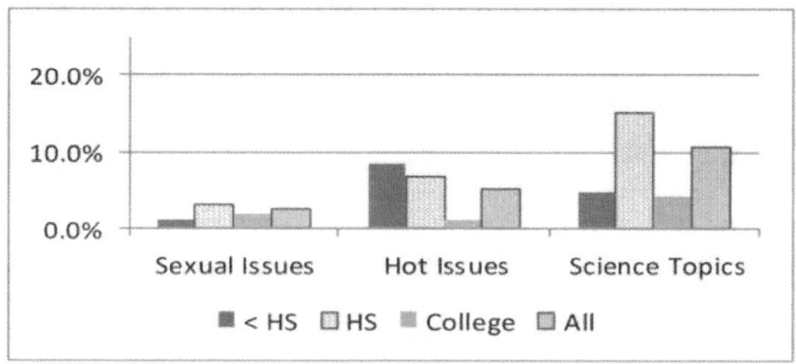

Figure 7-16 GSS Survey: Cultural Issues by Education Achieved for Not Born-again Young Adults

Secondly, those born-agains without a high school diploma are 33% more likely to have a biblical worldview on the Science Topics (i.e. 42% vs. 31%). This outcome may be the result of those without a high school diploma avoiding the dominant teaching in high school science classes that Neo-Darwinism is an accepted fact. Looking at the results for not born-again, young adults, we find that only 5% of those without a high school diploma have a biblical view of the Science Topics. This large discrepancy may be caused by the born-agains being influenced by their peers in church and by those not born-again being influenced by their secular peers.

Gender and Cultural Belief

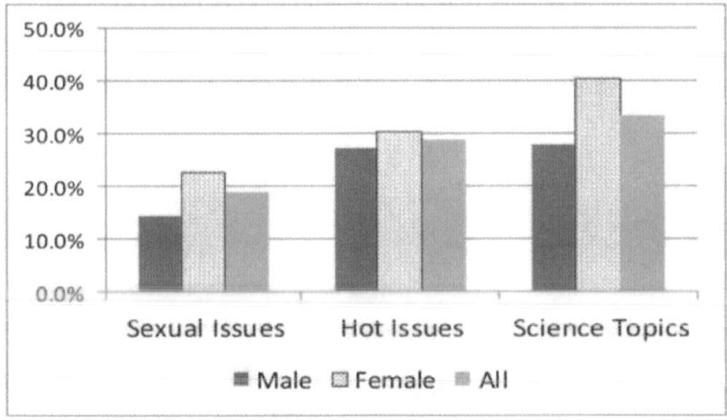

Figure 7-17 GSS Survey: Cultural Issues by Gender

Finally, let's return to look at the differences between the genders for these three cultural topics. For born-again, young adults, we find that women are more likely than men to espouse a biblical worldview toward these issues (60% more likely than men on Sexual Issues and 44% more likely on Science Topics). These differences between the genders persist for those who are not born-again, but the absolute levels are so small (generally less than 10% of the group), the differences are not as important.

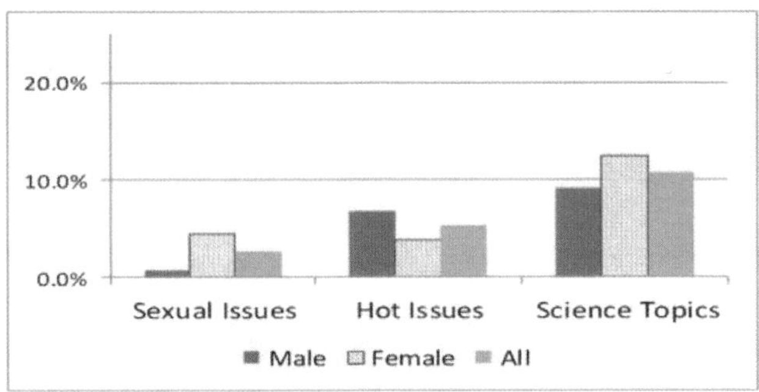

Figure 7-18 GSS Survey: Cultural Issues by Gender for Not Born-agains

Summary

The information presented in this chapter shows the significant differences existing among segments of the population relative to biblical worldview beliefs, religious practice and cultural beliefs addressed in the New Testament. Table 7-3 summarizes some of these key differences.

Table 7-3 Differences Due to Different Demographic Factors

Topic	Religious Belief and Practice	Cultural Beliefs
Ethnic Group	Blacks have a significantly lower percentage of biblical worldviews amongst born-agains than other ethnic groups. Hispanics vary widely between GSS and Probe survey questions.	Whites are much more likely to hold to a biblical view on Sexual Issues. Blacks/Hispanics much more likely on Hot Issues Blacks/Whites more likely on Science
Geography	Northeast has lowest and South has the highest percent of born-agains. Among born-agains, all areas are close in biblical worldview and practice.	Northeast is low on Hot Issues. Northeast and West are higher on Science topics.
Education	% of born-agains falls off significantly with age for non-college but are consistent at 25% of college graduates regardless of age. College graduates more likely to hold a biblical worldview and religious practices.	College graduates higher on Sexual Issues No high school diploma emerging adults are higher on Science topics.
Gender	Females are slightly more likely to be born-again. Born-again females are more likely to practice consistent religious practices. Both genders are equal when looking at combined worldview and practice.	Females are more likely to hold a biblical worldview on Sexual Issues. Females are more likely to hold a biblical worldview on Science topics.

These demographic differences clearly influence any response to the issues brought up here. However, in all cases, the vast majority of born-again, young adults regardless of race, education, region of the country or gender do not confess a belief in a consistent set of biblically influenced positions.

Chapter 8 Troubling Aspects of Emerging Adult Beliefs

In earlier chapters, we looked at disturbing information on the beliefs of emerging adults in America from five different surveys. In them, we found clear evidence of accelerating erosion in accepting and adhering to basic biblical truths for living; even among those who were born-again or Evangelical. Our emerging cultural milieu of pop post-modernism is clearly taking many young adult Christians captive to the 'philosophies of men'. It seems the new standard for worldviews is 1) for each person to adopt their own unique mixture of beliefs and practices and 2) to fully accept everyone else's contrary beliefs as being valid for them if not for me. What are the implications of this type of belief system?

Christian Smith and his fellow researchers at Notre Dame published an initial book, *Souls in Transition*, covering the results of their 2008 survey of the religious beliefs and actions of emerging adults from ages 18 through 23. Their deep distress over some of the results of their surveys and interviews led them to publish a follow up book in 2011 entitled *Lost in Transition: The Dark Side of Emerging Adulthood.* In this book, they focus on five specific areas of concern identified by their earlier research:

1. moral aimlessness,
2. materialistic consumerism,
3. intoxicated living,
4. deep troubles from sexually liberated behavior, and
5. lack of interest in civic and political life.

In this chapter, we will consider four of these concerns (excluding intoxicated living) and several other outcomes of the disconnected belief systems of today's emerging adults. In particular, we will also look at cheating, pluralism and the lack of meaningful spiritual activity as additional indicators of a disconnect we need to come to grips with.

The troubling characteristics of emerging adult life in America in the early years of the 21st century remind us of what Paul warned of in 2nd Timothy 3:1-5 when he wrote: ". . . *in the last days difficult times will come. For men will be lovers of self, lovers of money, . . . arrogant, . . . ungrateful, . . . without self-control, . . . reckless, conceited, lovers of pleasure rather than lovers of God, holding to a form of godliness, although they have denied its power;*"

Although the prime characteristics of this verse have been true throughout history, they are particularly true of the current cultural milieu of today's America. One major factor in the growth of these problems is the widespread acceptance of pop post-modernism throughout our culture. As Smith points out, the post-modern theory became "democratized and vulgarized in U.S. culture" becoming a "simple-minded ideology presupposing the cultural construction of everything, individualistic subjectivism, soft ontological antirealism and absolute moral relativism."[1]

This popularized post-modern view says there is no objective truth only the practical truth I choose to live by with my friends. This view leads to a basic disconnect with the teaching of Jesus who claimed His purpose was to "testify to the truth" [2] because He is the truth.

Dale Tackett, author of The Truth Project, put the problem this way, "When what is right is what's good for me, you will find all of the moral chaos that we see today."[3]

Moral Viewpoint – A Floating Standard

What is morality in the first place? Morality is defined as "a system of ideas of right and wrong conduct."[4] For Christians, this system is set out for us in the Bible; particularly in the Ten Commandments, the teachings of Jesus, and the New Testament epistles. The Bible makes it clear that God is the source of true morality. It is our responsibility to learn and apply His moral precepts. As Jesus said in the Sermon on the Mount, "*Let your light shine before men in such a way that they may see your good works and glorify your Father who is in heaven.*" (Matt 5:16) Or as Paul instructed in 1st Thessalonians, "*examine everything carefully; hold fast to that which is good; abstain from every form of evil.*" (1 Thess 5:21-22) Paul is saying hold fast to the morality taught by Christ.

In a Christian nation, how can there be any confusion about morality? Well, sixty percent of emerging adults say that "morality is a personal choice, entirely a matter of individual decision. Moral rights and wrongs are essentially matters of individual opinion, in their view."[5] And where do these opinions come from? One emerging adult put it this way, "Like just kinda things that I thought up, that I decided was right for me. So I don't know. I honestly don't. It just kinda came outta thin air."[6] So, we can either look to the Bible as the source of our morality or we can just create it out of thin air.

When faced with a moral choice, almost half said they would do what made them feel happy or would help them get ahead. Less than one out of five said they would "do what God or the scripture" says is right. Many of them said they would not really know if their choice was right or wrong until after it was done and they could evaluate how they felt about it.

Not only do they not look to the Bible or society for their moral compass, they believe that it is morally wrong to assume there is a common morality that applies to all. Because we must be tolerant and accept other's views as right for them, we must not apply our moral precepts to their actions. As Christian Smith put it, "*Giving voice to one's own moral views is itself nearly immoral.*" What they fail to realize is that complete moral relativism and tolerance actually dishonor the beliefs of others. With this view, they cannot accept new views which are superior to their own or act to correct views which are inferior. What someone else thinks about morality is immaterial to them.

This type of thinking will ultimately lead to disaster for the people embracing it. As Chuck Colson said, "So often, the great disasters (of the past) were caused by people disregarding God's standard of right and wrong and doing what was right in their own eyes. . . We've stopped moral teaching in our country and we are seeing the inevitable consequence of failing to teach moral values to a culture. We are seeing chaos."[7]

The whole topic of morality is not something most of them give much thought to. One third of them could not think of any moral dilemmas that they had faced in their lives. While another third of them offered examples that were not actually moral dilemmas. For example, one of them stated, "I guess renting the apartment thing, whether or not I would be able to afford it." That is a dilemma but it is not a moral dilemma. So through their education from their parents and schools, the vast majority of emerging adults really have not gained a good working knowledge of the concept of morality much less its importance to society. Yet it 1 Peter, Peter makes it clear that our moral actions are one of the most important ways that Christians can share the good news of Jesus Christ. As he said,

Keep your behavior excellent among the Gentiles, so that in the thing in which they slander you as evildoers, they may because of your good deeds, as they observe them, glorify God in the day of visitation. Submit yourselves for the Lord's sake to every human institution, whether to a king as the one in authority, or to governors as sent by him for the punishment of evildoers and the praise of those who do right. For such is the will of God that by doing right you may silence the ignorance of foolish men." (1 Pet 2:12-15)

As Paul points out, the principled life of conformance to Christ's commands is not going to align with the popular wisdom of pop behavioral standards. It is a morality based on an eternal, external standard of right behavior which all people will see to be true in the end. From Smith's research, it appears that today's emerging adults have no concept of such an objective morality.

Consumerism – The True Objective of Life

As Christians, our lives are called to be far more than how much we can consume. Jesus never gave his disciples instructions on how to increase their economic wealth. Instead, He sent his disciples out to minister with only the clothes on their backs. Similarly, Paul learned to be content with whatever the Lord provided. He states,

> "*I know how to get along with humble means, and I also know how to live in prosperity; in any and every circumstance I have learned the secret of being filled and going hungry, both of having abundance and suffering need. I can do all things through Him who strengthens me.*" (Phil 4:12-13)

To be fair, the Bible does teach us much about how to operate successfully in the business world. However, it is also clear that our purpose is to be focused on things with eternal value and not on how much we can accumulate and consume on this earth.

Yet, as a whole, the young, emerging adults in this nation have missed the call of Christ to focus our lives on the eternal rather than the temporal. Instead, not only have they bought into consumerism as the primary goal of life, but they appear to be unable to consider any shortcomings in a life focused on what they can consume. Smith reports, "Contemporary emerging adults are either *true believers* or *complacent conformists* when it comes to mass consumerism (emphasis added)."[8]

As one emerging adult put it, "It feels good to be able to get things that you want and you work for the money. If you want something, you go get it. It makes your life more comfortable and I guess it just makes you feel good about yourself as well."[9] That statement might not seem bad until you realize it is their sole method to feel good about themselves. The more you can consume the better. They miss the balanced view of material things taught in the Bible. In Proverbs we are told,

> *Give me neither poverty nor riches;*
> *Feed me with the food that is my portion,*
> *That I not be full and deny You and say, "Who is the LORD?"*
> *Or that I not be in want and steal,*
> *And profane the name of my God.* (Prov 30:8-9)

The idea of limiting ones consumption in order to have the resources to help others is foreign to most emerging adults. They would like to see the needs of the starving people met, "just not by me, not now." If they ever reach a state in life where all their consumer desires are met, they may consider using some resources for charitable causes. One obvious problem with this approach is that our consumer conscious society always has something new and better to purchase and experience.

This attitude is in contrast to that of the Macedonians Paul commends in his second letter to the Corinthian church,

> *". . . that in a great ordeal of affliction (the churches in Macedonia) abundance of joy and their deep poverty overflowed in the wealth of their liberality. For I testify that according to their ability, and beyond their ability, they gave of their own accord, begging us with much urging for the favor of participation in the support of the saints, and this, not*

> *as we had expected, but they first gave themselves to the Lord and to us by the will of God." (2 Cor 8:1-5)*

Rather than "seeking the kingdom of God and his righteousness"[10] and letting the material things be of secondary importance, most young American adults are seeking consumer nirvana and its false sense of wellbeing. With no external moral compass for guidance, they are unwilling to express concerns about the grossest forms of excessive consumerism. As most of them said when asked: "If someone wants it, who am I to say that they are wrong." When emerging adults refer to a good life, they talk about what they want to possess rather than the good that they can contribute to the world. I find it sad to think about being remembered for how much I consumed rather that how much I contributed. Unfortunately, this thought does not seem to bother most emerging adults.

Pre-marital Sex: Just How We Were Made

On the subject of sex, the Bible presents a clear consistent message notwithstanding those who would try to twist the Scriptures to say something else. Sexuality was created to be exercised by a man and a woman joined together in the life long bond of marriage. It is not a recreational activity, but rather a sacred union between a husband and wife. As we are told in Romans:

> *Let us behave properly as in the day, not in carousing and drunkenness, not in sexual promiscuity and sensuality, not in strife and jealousy.* (Rom 13:13)

And again in 1st Corinthians:

> *Do not be deceived; neither fornicators, . . ., nor adulterers, nor effeminate, nor homosexuals. . ., will inherit the kingdom of God.* (1 Cor 6:9-10)

However, for many emerging adults, this view is seen as outdated and unrealistic. For many years, entertainment media have been promoting the idea that sexual acts are a fun recreational activity not be confused with love and marriage. Every normal person is expected to be sexually active regardless of their marital state. In fact, 73% of never married 18-

to 23-year-olds have had sex with the average age for their first experience being 16.[11] Our analysis of three recent surveys[12] found that *sex outside of marriage is considered fine by two out of three young Evangelicals.* In addition, 45% of Evangelical, emerging adults believe it is perfectly fine to engage in homosexual activity. Almost half of young Evangelicals take a position which is directly counter to biblical teaching.

Through his extensive surveys and interviews, Christian Smith discovered that these beliefs are creating serious problems for many.

"Emerging adults can jump into intimate relationships assuming that sex is just another consumer item, recreational thrill, or lifestyle-commodity. But many of them soon discover the hard way that sex is much more profound and precious . . . . not far beneath the surface appearance of happy, liberated emerging adult sexual adventure and pleasure lies a world of hurt, insecurity, confusion, inequality, shame, and regret."[13]

As one young person put it, "God says not to have sex until you get married, and now I know why. . . Sex makes things a lot complicated."[14] Another one young woman shared, "Hooking up is the one thing in my life I would definitely take back if I could. Cause sleeping with someone you don't know is so sleazy, and it's just so not good."[15]

This misunderstanding of the role and purpose of sexual activity is going to take a high toll on our society. As a church, we need to take a stronger role in explaining why the New Testament writers knew what they were talking about and why television and movies are selling a dangerous lie.

Civic and Political Involvement – Not For Me

Consider emerging adults' perception of civic and political involvement. Smith summarizes their attitude saying, "The vast majority of the emerging adults we interviewed remain . . . politically disengaged, uninformed, and distrustful. Most in fact feel disempowered, apathetic, and sometimes even despairing when it comes to the larger social, civic, and political world beyond their own lives."[16] When we consider the polls and interviews driving this assessment occurred in the summer of 2008 during the perceived youth movement bringing President Obama into office, this result on political involvement is particularly surprising.

Some might say that being actively involved in politics is not the right course of action for Christians. And, thus, they may applaud this result. We certainly agree that our primary purpose as Christians will not and cannot be fulfilled through political action. However, what we are talking about here is not a lack of political activism, but rather a disengagement from active participation in the political process. As Paul instructed Timothy, "*I urge that entreaties, prayers, petitions and thanksgivings be made on behalf of all men, for kings and all who are in authority in order that we may lead a tranquil and quiet life in all godliness and dignity.*" (1 Tim 2:1-2) We are to be concerned about the impact of government on our lives. If the people Paul were writing to had the right to vote, I am confident he would have said pray for and exercise your right to vote.

Through his research, Smith identified six different attitudes toward civic involvement among emerging adults. These attitudes are:

1. The **apathetic** are completely uninterested in politics and make up 27% of emerging adults. Note that these individuals were not apathetic in general; just about this area of life.

2. The **uninformed** said their lack of interest was driven by their lack of knowledge about the issues and the players. The uninformed made up 13% of emerging adults.

3. The **distrustful (19% of emerging adults)** know a reasonable amount about political issues but do not participate because they distrust the political system and politicians. They believe exercising their right to vote will not make any difference.
4. The **disempowered** point to an inability to change the world (rather than distrust of the process) as their reason to be uninvolved. Around 10% of them fall into this category.
5. The **marginally political** represent those who expressed some interest in politics but whose interest did not appear to lead to actual involvement in the process. These marginally political emerging adults make up 27% of those interviewed.
6. That leaves 4% of emerging adults (all males) who appear to be **genuinely political**; that is interested and involved in the process.

In summary, their interviews found two thirds of the emerging adult population completely uninvolved and almost one third with a very limited involvement. This meant only 4% considered the process an important responsibility in life.

This seemingly fatalistic view of politics was found to carry over in other areas of civic involvement such as volunteering and charitable giving. Smith summarized their results saying, "Contrary to some of the stories told in the popular media, most emerging adults in America have extremely modest hopes, if any, that they can change society or the world for the better, whether by volunteering or anything else."[17] With that perception, providing help to others is not a requirement for righteousness, but simply an optional personal choice that most are not prepared to make.

Thinking back to our earlier discussion on the lack of a moral viewpoint, Smith's research found a significant association between those who believe all morality is relative and individualistic and an attitude of apathy, ignorance and distrust of the political process. In addition, Smith found a significant relationship between "enthusiasm for mass consumerism and lack of interest in political participation."[18] So these three attitudes (no moral standards, consumer consumption as our primary objective, and no real political or civic involvement) appear to be common elements of the emerging adult belief system. The attitude toward pre-marital sexual activity is also very consistent with a lack of moral standards and a consumption-oriented definition of success.

Cheating: Everyone Is Doing It

Today, popular culture is supplanting the message of Christ for most young Americans, including Evangelicals. This viewpoint can certainly be seen in their attitude toward cheating as a means to get ahead.

Cheating is not to be common behavior among followers of Christ. Cheating is defined to be the process of deceiving others by trickery; to swindle them. It's very definition indicates that it is not a good thing. Jesus was exposing this dangerous attitude when he chided his listeners,

> "*You are of your father the devil, and you want to do the desires of your father. . . He . . . does not stand in the truth because there is no truth in him. Whenever he speaks a lie, he speaks from his own nature, for he is a liar and the father of lies.*" (John 8:44-45)

According to Revelation chapter 22, "*everyone who loves and practices lying*" will not be able to enter into the new Jerusalem.

As a child growing up in the sixties, the people who cheated at school, were primarily trying to keep from failing. In the seventies, I went to a university where we signed an honor code with each test stating that "I did not give nor did I receive any unauthorized aid on this exam." Cheating was a temptation, but I knew that Jesus did not approve of cheaters. I am confident that most (but not all) of my classmates took this honor code to heart and avoided cheating on their exams.

Today, we find a different attitude toward cheating. One youth leader told me about a discussion with her church youth in a small city in the south. She asked them, "Do any of you have struggles with cheating?" They all told her, "No, I have no struggle with it, I just do it." They said that they needed to perform well to get top grades to get into good schools and the only way to do it was to cheat. Every single one of them told her that cheating was a mandatory skill to succeed in school. These students were "good kids" attending an Evangelical church in the heartland of the South. For them, cheating was the natural order of things.

Perhaps, cheating is not such a problem in college. Dr. Caroline Crocker, a university biology professor, wrote, "Possibly because the students thought I would not notice or care, some would try (cheating) at every opportunity. . ."[19] Speaking at a Probe event, she shared that her son encountered it in medical school as well. When he approached his professors about the rampant cheating going on in his classes, he was told, "We cannot punish the cheaters. They are our best students." Remember that the doctor you see may have learned nothing in medical school other than how to cheat effectively; a comforting thought no doubt.

If cheating is standard practice in academia, it will carry over to the work place. Cheating can be seen as a way to advance by 1) getting new business for your company, 2) covering up mistakes you have made, and 3) taking advantage of sick days and office supplies. As a co-worker once told me, "If you can't lie on a proposal, when can you lie."

Today's attitudes toward cheating are a natural extension of having no moral standards. In that mindset, there is no common moral standard to strive to obey. Instead, the individual is motivated to look primarily to their individual, short term good in evaluating these choices. As Christians, we should be striving to set an example of integrity in all areas of our lives. Instead, many have taken up the attitude that since everyone else is doing it, we had better do it too. Let us make it a point to encourage integrity over a "whatever it takes" mentality.

Pluralism: The Only Ethical Approach

Another disconnect of belief faced by today's emerging adults is pluralism. Pluralism views multiple religious beliefs with different teachings as equally true. Jesus did not agree, saying, "*I am the way, the truth and the life. No ones comes to the Father except through me.*" (John 14:6) When one does not want to bring others to share in their religious beliefs, it comes either from extreme ignorance or from an attitude of indifference. Extreme ignorance actually believes that all religions teach basically the same truths and are equally able to provide us a viable path to eternal life. Anyone who has studied different world religions at all knows that this is not the case. The major world religions present incompatible answers to questions of eternity. More often, I think it is an attitude of indifference. I actually believe my religion is correct and yours is wrong, but I don't want to upset the status quo and be branded a bigot by asking you to consider my religion over your current religious background.

They have years of diversity training without regard to the actual teaching of differing religions. Their attitudes are partially fueled by an indifference to religion. As Smith discovered, "For very many emerging adults, religion is mostly a matter of indifference. . . religion has a status on . . . their priority lists that is similar to, say, the oil refinery industry."[20]

While realizing religions claim to be different, most emerging adults believe that all share the same basic principles. Religion is about belief in God and learning to be a good person. One put it this way, "Faith is important to everybody, and it does the same thing for everybody, no matter what your religion is."[21]

Consequently, it is fine to select those aspects that feel right to you and mix in other faiths. Looking across similar data from four recent surveys[22] we find that more than two out of three Evangelical, emerging adults[23] do not believe you must trust in Jesus Christ to be reconciled to God. In fact, it is not really important to have the truth. As one of the interviewees stated, "What do you mean by religious truth? Because all religions pretty much have a good message that people can follow. . . . where they get their message from, is false, but the message itself is good."[24]

Most emerging adults have religious beliefs, but they don't impact their daily lives. One observed, "I don't think it's the basis of how I live, . . . I still kinda retain my own decision or at least a lot of it on situations I've had and experiences."[25] Perhaps the most chilling quote from Smith is his conclusion, "it was clear in many interviews that *emerging adults felt entirely comfortable describing various religious beliefs that they affirmed but that appeared to have no connection whatsoever to the living of their lives.*"[26]

When one affirms pluralism, one is affirming that their faith in not true. To counter this trend, we need to help our young people look at the inconsistencies in pluralistic thought. If Jesus is the truth, we are secure in him. If other religious teachings are true, we who are putting our trust in Christ are without hope in this world. As Paul pointed out in 1st Corinthians 15:17:

> *"and if Christ has not been raised, your faith is worthless; you are still in your sins"*

If Christ is not the unique Son of God raised from the dead for our sins, then Christianity is a total lie and we should flee from it. However, if Christ is indeed resurrected from the dead, we can trust His claim to be the only way to a restored relationship with our Creator.

Spiritual Activity: On the Back Burner

Historically, some key aspects of a committed, vibrant evangelical lifestyle have been:

1. Consistent prayer life
2. Regular, personal bible reading
3. Active involvement in the church
4. Vibrant personal witness to the gospel

These four activities are vital to any Christian as a representative of Christ and His eternal kingdom.

In America, these foundational tenets are being challenged by the need to spend more time playing Angry Birds, keeping up with Facebook and Twitter, and staying current on all the shows recorded on your DVR. Apparently, these activities are more important to a meaningful life than prayer, bible study and church involvement.

The four recent surveys of American religious beliefs and practices examined in this book clearly show the lack of interest in these important tenets of our faith. These surveys found that roughly two out of three Evangelical emerging adults do not pray, read the bible or gather together with other Christians on a regular basis. When we add holding a basic biblical worldview to these religious practices, we find that about 5 out of 6 of this group are not believing in and regularly practicing their faith.

For these emerging adults, the primary purpose of church attendance and bible reading was accomplished early in life. Kids learn right and wrong from church activities. As Christian Smith noted, "by the time a kid becomes a teenager or young adult, that person has pretty much learned his or her morals and so can effectively "graduate" and stop attending services at the congregation. What is the point, after all, of staying in school after you have been taught everything it has to teach?"[27]

What about being a vibrant personal witness? Less than 2% of Evangelical emerging adults witness to others during a typical month. As one put it, "You don't really want to push people away by making them feel like you're pushing your religion on them . . . I'm not going to be like, "So what do you think about . . .?" They'll be like, "Wait, are we having fun here? What are we doing?"[28] Smith summarized their feelings, ". . . many, if not most emerging adults do not even know the religious backgrounds or basic beliefs and commitments of their friends."[29]

Even though the number affiliated with an Evangelical church has remained between 25% and 30% of emerging adults for the last four decades, it appears that what it means to be affiliated with Evangelicals has changed dramatically.

Emerging Adults – Where Will They Take Us?

One root cause of the attitudes expressed by emerging adults is pop post-modern individualism. Each must decide what is true for him or her and must not accept a common truth. Therefore, most emerging adults cannot grasp the concept of an objective reality beyond their individual self that would have any bearing on their life. As seen already in this chapter, this concept undermines 1) their moral compass, 2) their attitudes about consumer consumption, 3) their involvement in society through politics, volunteering and charitable giving, 4) their attitude towards cheating to get ahead, 5) their acceptance of pluralism as a given for any belief system, and 6) their involvement in spiritual disciplines.

These dominant patterns of emerging adult thought in America should make us consider: "What does it mean?" and "How can we do something about it?" Some might say this is just the way young people are. We were that way when we were young. They will snap out of it. To that idea Smith would say, "It is a different world today. . . To think otherwise is to self-impose a blurred vision that cannot recognize real life as it is experienced today and so cannot take emerging adults seriously."[30]

Others may say that is not what I hear on the news. Our young adults are leading a new wave of service and public involvement. To which Smith would say, "The fact that anyone ever believed that idea simply tells us how flimsy the empirical evidence that so many journalistic media stories are based upon is and how unaccountable to empirical reality high-profile journalism can be. . . . we – without joy – can set the record straight here: almost all emerging adults today are either apathetic, uninformed, distrustful, disempowered, or at most marginally interested when it comes to politics and public life. Both the fact itself and the reasons for it speak poorly of the condition of our larger culture and society."[31]

So when we read news stories or view television highlights of emerging adults getting involved and making a difference, we must realize it is not the norm but rather the exception. Naturally, we want to believe that upcoming generations are going to be more involved in making the world a better place than preceding generations, but so far that is not the case. As Smith says, "One tendency is to claim that emerging adults are deeply committed to social justice, passionately engaged in political activism, actively volunteering in their local communities, devoting themselves to building a greener, more peaceful and just world. *Almost nothing could be further from the truth.*"[32] (emphasis added)

Although the vast majority of emerging adults is disengaged from involvement in the public sphere, they are quite engaged in a different way. As Smith points out, "they pursue these private-sphere emotional and relational investments with fervent devotion. . . . progressing yet further toward the nearly total submersion of self into fluidly constructed, private networks of technologically managed intimates and associates."[33] He is referring of course to their disconnected connections via Facebook, Twitter and other electronic social media.

Examining these areas of misguided belief uncovers a huge gap between Scriptural truth and actual behavior. Why are these differences so prevalent and what can we do to change the trend?

Among many, four incorrect beliefs stand out as primary causes of this widening disconnect:

1. Different times have different issues
2. Biblical views are no longer relevant
3. Jesus intention has been misstated
4. Religion is about the afterlife not this life

Some argue that the issues of our postmodern society are distinctly different from those addressed in the Bible. Our world of instant information access and globally connected populations is not addressed by the Bible. We must decide what is right for us now. This view is not based in reality. The issues discussed today are at their heart the same as they were 2,000 years ago.

Others take the position that biblical teaching is outdated. It needs to be updated especially in the light of the theory of evolution. Our scientific and societal advances cast new light on how we should live our lives. We may be trusting in Jesus for our eternal salvation, but we need to trust our culture on how to live right now. Once again, this viewpoint does not stand up to examination. In areas like cheating, pluralism and sexual misconduct, the biblical standards have been proven time and again.

Some think the Bible perverted through changes in the texts. Holding our mouth right, we can see that the teaching of Scripture is really consistent with the standards of our current culture, whether homosexuality, cheating or abandoning spiritual disciplines. Of course, this view does not stand up in the light of the intentional, careful promulgation of the biblical texts and the consistent teaching found therein.

Finally, some take the position that the Bible is all about where you go when you die. We need not concern ourselves with its positions dealing with our everyday lives. Instead we should look to our friends and our culture to set the standard. Of course, this view makes one wonder why well over two thirds of the New Testament deals with the way we should live on this earth at this time. Why waste all that time and paper writing down stuff that will be made obsolete by future cultural changes?

To counter these views, we need to address them head on and point out the inconsistency of thought associated with these delusions. We need to clearly discuss the shortcomings of popular culture versus the eternal truth of scripture. Finally, we need to pray the Holy Spirit will be active in our lives convicting the world of sin and righteousness and judgment.[34]

There are several positive actions that we can take as Christians to improve this situation.

First, we need to examine ourselves. Are we living our lives under the direction of the ultimate source of morality, Jesus Christ? Are we consumed by consumerism or are we living for eternity? Are we taking an active part in impacting our society so that we may live godly and peaceful lives for Christ?

Next, we need to recognize that emerging adults under the age of thirty are, for the most part, not taking on the full responsibilities of adulthood.

They are still emerging and, consequently, still need coaching. However, as Smith points out, "One of the striking social features of emerging adulthood is how structurally disconnected most emerging adults are from older adults. . . Most emerging adults live this crucial decade of life surrounded mostly by their peers . . . who have no more experience, insight, wisdom, perspective, or balance than they do."[35] As parents, pastors, co-workers, we should continue to actively engage them in a mentor role. It is important that they understand clearly

- We are looking to the Bible as the source for our moral decisions.
- We are living in this world as citizens of heaven and as such consumer consumption is not our purpose for living.
- We value the sexual relationship as something reserved for marriage.
- We have a responsibility to be engaged in our society, to keep our freedom, to lead godly lives serving the Lord.
- We are committed to living lives of integrity not attempting to further ourselves through cheating.
- We recognize that there can only be one religion that captures the actual truth of our situation and that religion is Christianity as put forth in the New Testament>
- We are committed to making our spiritual growth and behavior the most important part of our life.

The apostle Peter put it this way: "*Beloved, I urge you as aliens and strangers to abstain from fleshly lusts which wage war against the soul. Keep your behavior excellent among the Gentiles so that in the thing in which they slander you as evil doers, they may on account of your good deeds, as they observe them, glorify God in the day of visitation.*" (1 Pet 2:11-12)

Finally, we need to reach out to emerging adults who are already involved in Evangelical churches. We need to let them know that it is okay to engage others with their worldview and their source of truth, Jesus Christ. When they don't share their worldview with others as a gift from God, they are effectively consigning those others to hell. Probe Ministries is in the midst of preparing materials that you can use in your church to directly address these issues. The issues presented in this book are their reaction to what they understand about the world. Given a different understanding, we believe they would think and act differently.

Christian Smith captured the essence when he wrote, "Might it be true that the farthest boundary of sight that youth today can envision as real and being worth pursuit is entirely imminent, purely material, and completely mundane?"[36] As Christians, **our boundary** extends beyond this universe to the halls of heaven and puts our lives in a new perspective. Let that eternal perspective been seen in every area of your life.

As historian Christopher Lasch put it, "There is only one cure for the malady that afflicts our culture, and that is to speak the truth."

There are many conclusions that could be drawn from the data above. Two of the most important conclusions are as follows. First, the basic religious beliefs of emerging adults largely depart from the Bible. When religious practices and cultural beliefs and practices are added to the equation, we find that virtually no one maintains a distinctly biblical worldview. Second, there does not appear to be uniformity in the beliefs of emerging adults. Rather than having a subset of Evangelicals, say 15%, holding to a distinctly biblical worldview, what you actually find is basically none because they trip up in different areas.

As Christian Smith pointed out, ". . . emerging adults felt entirely comfortable describing various religious beliefs that they affirmed but that appeared to have no connection whatsoever to the living of their lives."[37] This is because religious teachings are not the authority on this world. Rather, it is what you choose to belief that is your authority for the "truth" in your life. As one emerging adult put it, "I think that what you believe depends on you. I don't think I could say that Hinduism is wrong or Catholicism is wrong . . . I think it just depends on what you believe . . ."[38] This concept results in a set of Evangelical, emerging adults who don't hold to a set of common beliefs about God, Jesus, religious practices and cultural practices, but instead hold to a wide variety of beliefs which are counter to the Bible. We must not infer that because they go to church that they believe the truth of the Bible. These surveys show that almost certainly they do not.

Chapter 9 Cultural Captivity Takes Many Forms

In Chapter 2, we examined a biblical perspective on different types of views that can take our minds captive and reduce our fruitfulness for Christ. At the close of the first part of this book, we return to this biblical discussion of cultural captivity. As seen in the preceding chapters, cultural captivity is the prevalent state of Evangelical, emerging adults. In this chapter, we will look at different types and levels of captivity described in the Bible. Hopefully, this perspective will better equip us to combat the incursion of cultural captivity in our own lives and in those of our emerging adult friends.

A common theme of many science fiction tales is mass delusion. From The Matrix to The Truman Show, we find fictional characters who think they are making decisions on their own volition based on an accurate perception of their situation. In each of these cases, the people are actually experiencing a false reality manipulated by outside forces which are using them for their own purposes.

Sadly, many of us are unwittingly being manipulated by distorted perceptions of reality. Moreover, just as in these fictional tales, these distortions are not an accident. They are promoted by the spiritual forces of darkness to keep us from being effective agents of light in this world.

As the apostle Peter explained, to fulfill our purpose of proclaiming Christ in a world of darkness, we must

> *Keep (our) behavior excellent . . . so that in the thing in which they slander you as evildoers, they may because of your good deeds, as they observe them, glorify God in the day of visitation (1* Peter 2:12).

Distinctive thoughts produce distinctive behavior. Only by applying Christ to every aspect of life will we be able to "keep our behavior excellent" even as we are being slandered by the world. This is why Paul commands us:

> *See to it that no one takes you captive through philosophy and empty deception, according to the tradition of men, according to*

> *the elementary principles of the world, rather than according to Christ* (Col. 2:8-9).

Paul is not talking about physical bars or chains. He is warning us about invisible chains constraining our minds to think like the world. Whenever we assume that the perspective of the world overrides the Truth of Christ in some aspect of life, we are allowing ourselves to be taken captive. Paul goes on to say that "*in Christ are hidden all the treasures of wisdom and knowledge*." Since that is true, we need to filter all truth claims through biblical revelation about the nature of God, man, and the universe.

Let us be honest. Most of us are oblivious to the invisible bars of cultural captivity. We think we are A-OK in balancing our spiritual beliefs with our everyday lives. However, most of us must be captive to some degree or the church would not be conforming to a degraded culture. As believers, we have the resources to escape from cultural captivity, but we need to make it a priority. We need to ask, "Are my eyes really open to the problem of cultural captivity so that I can avoid its mind numbing impact on my spiritual life?"

In this chapter, we will consider four types of captive believers:

1. Carnal
2. Confused
3. Compromised
4. Contented

As we consider these different manifestations of captivity, let's ask God to make us aware of areas of captivity in our own lives.

Carnal Christians

Just as there are different types of prisons, there are different ways that captivity can affect the lives of believers. Carnal Christians are believers who have misplaced priorities. As citizens of heaven,[1] they are living as if they are citizens of earth. The apostle Paul introduces us to these believers in his first letter to the Corinthians:

> *And I, brethren, could not speak to you as to spiritual people but as to carnal, as to babes in Christ. . . . For where there are envy, strife, and divisions among you, are you not carnal and behaving like mere men?* (1 Cor 3:1-3 NKJV)

The Greek word carnal literally means "fleshly". These people are believers who are focused on serving their flesh rather than on using their flesh to serve God. The carnal Christian looks upon salvation as an opportunity to cater to the flesh while avoiding eternal consequences.

For example, carnal Christians view marriage as a means to meet their needs. As one young husband told his pastor, "God wants me to be happy. I am not happy in my marriage. So, God must want me to get a divorce."[2] A 2008 survey found the divorce rate among "born-again" Christians was the same as the rate among the population as a whole about one in three (thirty-three percent).[3] However, the rate of divorce among those who regularly attend church is much lower, about one in four[4,5]. Beyond that, my personal observation among active, committed Christians is a rate of less than one in ten.

Another area where carnality is evident is in business practices. We all drop our heads when we read about a "respected" church member who has been caught applying unethical and sometimes illegal business practices. It is highly likely that these individuals viewed the Scriptures as supporting their unethical attempts for temporal riches.

As Paul points out, minds that view the world through a fleshly perspective often lead to division and strife within the church. In fact, if the church is dominated by carnal Christians it may be worse than the world as "cheap grace" turns into license.

Let us examine ourselves. Do we elevate the temporal above the eternal? What do our daily decisions reveal about our perspective? Is it carnal or spiritual?

A Christian struggling with a carnal perspective needs to start asking the question, "Which decision or course of action has the most positive benefits for eternity?" In Christ, we are no longer slaves to our flesh, so when we start turning control over to the Holy Spirit, the flesh cannot keep its control over us.

Confused Christians

Confused Christians desire to please God, but they are confused about what God wants. Unlike the carnal Christian, the confused Christian is concerned about their spiritual life. However, instead of being grounded in the Bible, they create their own spiritual truth from multiple sources.

Two thousand years ago, Paul warned believers that people will try to "*delude you with persuasive arguments*" (Col 2:5) based on "*the trickery of men, by craftiness and deceitful scheming*" (Eph 4:14). Today, believers are still bombarded with deceptive ideas designed to prevent them from living in a way that exalts Christ.

Recent surveys by the Barna Group show that this approach is prevalent among those between the ages of 18 and 25. According to their surveys, seventy-eight percent of emerging adults identify themselves as Christians, but more than half of them believe that the Koran and Book of Mormon offer the same spiritual truths as the Bible.[6] These 'holy' books only differ on issues such as the character of God, the nature of man, and the way to heaven. Is it any wonder that many sincere believers are confused?

Confused Christians are often influenced by those who offer to enhance their Christian experience with new insights. A few years ago, Oprah hosted a popular webinar with Eckhart Tolle. His repackaged Eastern mysticism is counter to the teachings of Christ on almost every topic. However, many of the participants were Christian women duped into believing that this false teaching was what Jesus was really trying to say all along.

One woman asked, "It's really opened my eyes up to a new way of thinking; . . . that doesn't always align with the teachings of Christianity. . . . Oprah, how have you reconciled these spiritual teachings with your Christian beliefs?"

In part, Oprah's reply was "I took God out of the box. . . I'm a free-thinking Christian who believes in my way, but I don't believe that it's the only way." In other words, "I am going to abandon the God of the Bible and create my own God who thinks like me."

Confused Christians often misapply God's character of love and compassion. We see this confusion in the debates on abortion, same sex marriage, and homosexual clergy. The level of impact is graphically displayed in Chapter 6 above. Many of them believe that loving others is not doing what is best for them and confronting them with their own harmful misunderstandings, but rather, it is mass acceptance of whatever anyone wants to believe or do.

The Bible is clear and our experience backs it up: there will be no shortage of false messages being preached in our society. Those false messages will take us captive if we unwittingly accept them as truth for our lives. Once again, we need to examine ourselves. Am I confident that my beliefs are based on the principles revealed in the Bible? Am I confusing the wisdom of the world with the wisdom of Christ?

The primary prescription for a confused Christian is a steady dose of God's word through personal study and trusted teachers who understand the Bible as the ultimate source of truth.

Compromised Christians

The third kind of captive Christian is a Compromised Christian. Compromised Christians profess a set of beliefs generally consistent with a biblical worldview, but compromise those beliefs by living like the world in one or more areas.

Jesus may have been referring to compromised Christians when He said,

> *And others are the ones on whom seed was sown among the thorns; these are the ones who have heard the word, but the worries of the world, and the deceitfulness of riches, and the desires for other things enter in and choke the word, and it becomes unfruitful* (Mark 4:18-19).

Knowing that they are called to a fruitful life, they allow the pressures and the temptations of the world to take precedence over the truth of Christ. They have allowed their concern for the things of the world to compromise their walk.

Some Christians are compromised by the desires of the flesh, such as addictions to alcohol, drugs or pornography. The high percentage of Christian men struggling with pornography is one sad example. Satan promotes the lie that this is a secret sin that can be kept from compromising ones public witness for Christ. Yet, anytime we consistently make provision for the flesh, it is going to result in a compromised walk. I distinctly remember the day my friend and fellow church leader who had been struggling with pornography had to confess to his wife that he had committed adultery. What a damaging thing to do to your spouse. Even with his sincere heart for restoration and reconciliation, the healing process was painful.

Other Christians are compromised by their pride or desire for earthly success. As Jesus warned the Jewish leaders,

How can you believe, when you receive glory from one another and you do not seek the glory that is from the one and only God? (John 5:44-45)

They rationalize unethical practices, questionable morals and the exploitation of others as worth the price to achieve success. These Christians embrace the sacred/secular split described by Nancy Pearcey in her book Total Truth. They partition their lives and their minds so that biblical truth only applies to their spiritual, church life while pragmatism determines what is true for every other aspect.

Let us examine our lives to see if we are rationalizing un-Christ-like behavior to satisfy our own selfish desires. Are we choosing to conform to the world because we think we will enjoy that more than conforming to Christ? Remember, we are citizens of heaven; living in eternity. When we lose that eternal perspective, we open ourselves up to a compromised life.

If you are struggling with compromise, look for others who can help hold you accountable. Find mature believers who can join with you in allowing God's Spirit to "*destroy fortresses and every lofty thing raised up against the knowledge of God*" (2 Cor. 10:4).

Contented Christians

We end this examination by looking at an insidious form of cultural captivity. Contented Christians are actively choosing the truth of Christ for their own lives, yet they are content to allow others to continue in cultural captivity. Either from fear of persecution or concern with hurting others or time pressures, these Christians avoid confronting others to unmask the deceptive, destructive ideas crippling their witness.

Although the apostle Paul was always content with his physical circumstances,[7] he was never satisfied with the spiritual condition of the world. Paul said:

> *We proclaim Him, admonishing every man and teaching every man with all wisdom, so that we may present every man complete in Christ. For this purpose also I labor, striving according to His power, which mightily works within me* (Col. 1:28-29).

Mature Christians are called to impart their understanding to others, particularly carnal, confused and compromised Christians. The fact that we have not been doing so in recent decades can been seen in the diminished influence of the church on public life.

For example, over eighty-seven percent of Congress members are affiliated with a Christian denomination. Yet, our Congress recently passed so-called hate crimes legislation which will limit the ability of Christians to speak biblical truth on sexuality. While abhorring any crimes, we realize that one of the most loving things we can do is to point out to others when they are engaged in destructive behavior. Yet contented Christians stood by as a nation with a nominally Christian majority of elected national leaders who seem to be carnal, confused, and compromised.

As contented Christians, we have let family hour on television move from *Father Knows Best* to *The Secret Life of Teenagers* feeding American youth a constant diet of promiscuity and disrespect for authority. As contented Christians, we have allowed pluralistic postmodernism to become the dominant voice within our public square.

As contented Christians, we have let carnal, confused, and compromised believers set the example for our younger generations. Is it any wonder that these generations are largely confused about their beliefs? As seen in the earlier chapters, although over one in three young adults can be identified as born-again, less than one in a hundred has beliefs consistent with a biblical worldview.

So let us examine ourselves. Do I sit on the sidelines watching other believers conforming to the world without attempting to intervene?

We are not spectators seeking to keep from getting stains on our white, linen knickers. Instead, we are called to be warriors in the battle for the fate of our fellows. If we do not stand firm and confront error, we are just as much captives of our culture as the others. Our response to the cultural captivity of today will be discussed further in the last chapter of this book.

Part 2: Restoring Captives To Freedom

Chapter 10 How Did We Get This Way? A Survey of Young Adult Born-agains

If you find your child trapped inside the dryer at home, your first objective is to get them out of the dryer. Once they are out and recovered from their ordeal, you also want to understand how they got into that mess so you can prevent them and other children from ending up as captives in the future. In the same vein, we have had generations of young adults taken captive by popular cultural views on life. Unfortunately, we have made little progress in preventing succeeding generations from following them in even greater numbers. As seen in Part 1 of this book, we are on a path rapidly leading to a society where true Christians are a small, minority group with little influence on society.

Motivated by this imminent danger, Probe undertook an in-depth survey to help us understand how seemingly born-again believers in Christ are so often taken captive by the thoughts of men rather than Christ. Of course, we are interested in all young adults. But if we can understand how to reach those who already claim to be born-again, we will make a great start on reaching an entire generation. As seen above, we have a large amount of data on what they believe. We wanted to get data on why they believe the things they believe **and** what caused them to accept those beliefs rather than others.

To delve into this topic, we worked with the Barna group to design and carry out a survey that would provide meaningful information on these questions. We chose to limit our survey to 18 – 40 year olds who self-classified as born-again using the two Barna qualifying questions. Those questions are

1. *Have you ever made a personal commitment to Jesus Christ that is still important in your life today*? and
2. *After I die, I will go to heaven because I confessed my sins and accepted Jesus as my savior.*

Those respondents meeting these criteria were given the opportunity to respond to approximately 160 questions. The questions covered:

- Their use of and reliance on various types of media (looking at internet, broadcast media, books, and social media for purposes such as entertainment, information, connecting with others, work, school and spirituality/faith)
- The people or things that influenced their religious beliefs
- Their preferred method of learning about new topics and faith related topics (e.g. class or workshop, book, video or DVD, online, etc.)
- Their sources for moral and ethical decision making in different environments (i.e. personal life, work or public life, religious beliefs)
- Alignment of beliefs and behavior with the Bible
- Areas of struggle in their behavior covering areas such as anger, lust, temper, selfishness, jealousy, homosexuality, pornography, etc.
- Challenges faced in five general categories: 1) marriage and family, 2) health and fitness, 3) sexuality, 4) work, money and finances, and 5) moral and ethical issues
- Agreement with Biblical truths ranging from the six biblical worldview questions to topics such as 1) valid ways to God, 2) the Bible and science, 3) sharing my religious experience, etc.
- Impact of significant life events on their relationship with God
- Demographics (age, area of country, education, income, race, etc.)

This survey looks at the beliefs of respondents who self-identified as born-again according to the Barna criteria. The group may not be representative of the distribution of born-again individuals as a part of society as a whole. To check that out, we compared it with other surveys that asked respondents if they considered themselves to be born-again. As you can see in Table 10-1, we included a column for the distribution across all 18 – 40 year olds as well as the columns for born-again, 18 – 40 year olds.

Demographics of Our Survey

Table 10-1 Demographic Data on American Born-agains Age 18 - 40

		% of Total by Source		
Race		GSS 2008	GSS 2008 BA	Probe BA
	White	70%	60%	58%
	Black	12%	13%	19%
	Hispanic	14%	20%	18%
	Asian & others	4%	7%	5%
Region		GSS 2008	GSS 2008 BA	Probe BA
	Northeast	17%	11%	17%
	Midwest	21%	15%	23%
	South	37%	48%	41%
	West	30%	30%	19%
Education		GSS 2008	GSS 2008 BA	Probe BA
	Less than HS	14%	16%	3%
	HS graduate	58%	61%	49%
	College grad +	28%	23%	48%
Religion		Baylor 2005	Baylor 2005 BA	Probe BA
	Evangelical	37%	75%	63%
	Mainline	19%	13%	24%
	Catholic	18%	4%	5%
	Other	26%	8%	8%

As shown in the table above, the distribution of born-again, young adults used in the Probe survey roughly tracks the distribution found for born-agains in surveys of all young adults. There are some significant differences in the percentages by region of the country and by education level, but not of a magnitude to impact our analysis of born-again, young adults using the Probe survey.

Before moving on to look at the details of what shapes their religious beliefs, consider one other division of the data from our surveys. By looking at the church attendance frequency of born-agains, one can obtain a feel for where born-again, 18 to 40 year olds can be touched with the truth of Christ and His teaching. Now look at the correlation between church attendance and biblical worldview across multiple surveys as shown in Figure 10-1 and Figure 10-2.

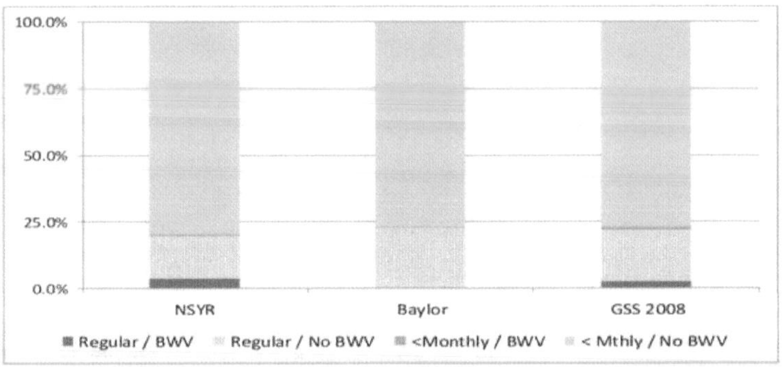

Figure 10-1 Multiple Surveys: Biblical Worldview & Attendance for Not Born-again Young Adults

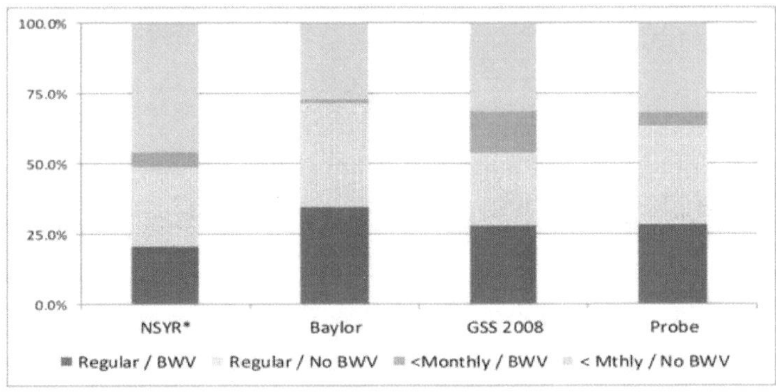

Figure 10-2 Multiple Surveys: Biblical Worldview & Church Attendance for Born-again Young Adults

Note 1: NSYR data does not identify born-agains so evangelicals were used instead
Note 2: BWV – biblical worldview as defined by the six Barna questions

The four categories covered in each survey are 1) regular church attenders (more than twice a month) with a biblical worldview, 2) regular church attenders without a biblical worldview, 3) irregular church attenders with a biblical worldview, and 4) irregular church attenders without a biblical worldview. As shown, almost no person who is not born-again has a biblical worldview and the vast majority are not regular church attenders. For born-again individuals, our survey found they fall into three nearly equally sized categories:

1. Free Ones: those *with* a biblical worldview who *attend* church regularly (about 26%),
2. Partially Captive: those *without* a biblical worldview who *attend* church regularly (about 33%), and
3. Captive Ones: those *without* a biblical worldview who *do **not** attend* church regularly (about 33%).

And one significantly smaller category:

4. Partially Free: those *with* a biblical worldview who *do **not** attend* church regularly (less than 8%).

The summary names of these categories, e.g. Free Ones, are used in the remainder of the book to refer to these categories. So, we can reach almost two thirds of the young born-agains through their church which also includes about half of the young born-agains without a biblical worldview. To reach the other half of young adults without a biblical worldview will require communicating with them outside of the context of their local church. Although the Free Ones appear to be on the right track, keep in mind that when asked an additional six worldview questions on religious topics[1] only half of the Free Ones expressed a biblical point of view on those questions.

Broad Take Aways on Beliefs of Young Born-agains

Another take away from our survey was a difference in attitude as a function of age. Those between 30 and 40 were almost 30% more likely to subscribe to a biblical worldview than those between 18 and 24. Similarly, Christian Smith's data shows that over one third of all 18- to 24-year-olds are no longer affiliated with any Christian religion today as compared to about one in five thirty-somethings.[2] If this is a precursor to permanent erosion in the number of people with a biblical worldview, we need to address it now.

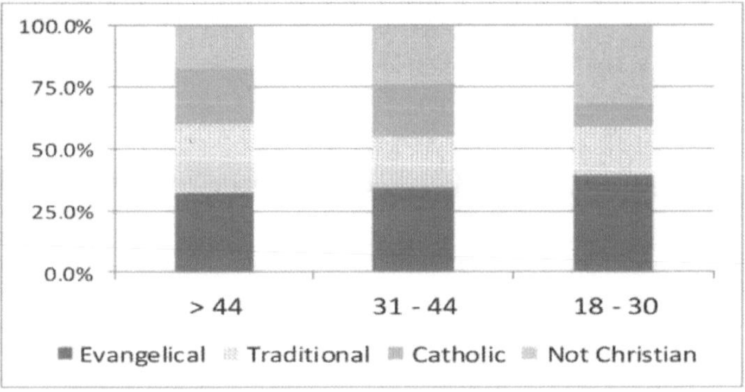

Figure 10-3 Baylor 2005: Denominational Distribution

Not all of the 817 born-agains questioned in our survey are affiliated with Evangelical churches. Let us take a look at how their distribution relates to the population in general. Figure 10-3 shows the distribution for different age ranges of Evangelicals, Mainline Protestants, Catholics and those who are not affiliated with a Christian church. As we move down in age, the percentage of non-believers increases and the percentage of Protestants decreases. Roughly, one third of Americans under age 44 are affiliated with an Evangelical church.

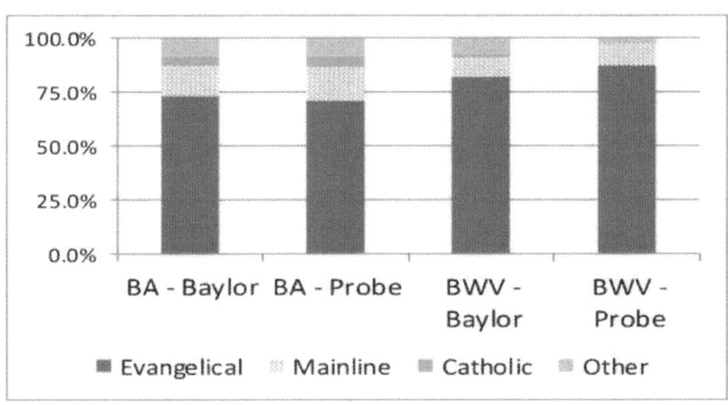

Figure 10-4 Baylor 2005/Probe: Denominational Distribution for Born-again Young Adults

The next figure, Figure 10-4, looks at the same distribution for those who are born-again and those born-again with a biblical worldview. Evangelicals comprise about three fourths of born-again young adults and close to 85% of born-agains with a biblical worldview. Clearly, the vast majority of born-again Americans are affiliated with an Evangelical church. However, over a quarter of them are associated with other faith traditions and should not be ignored in considering how they may be reached with a message promoting authentic biblical beliefs and practices.

In this pluralistic society, one area of questioning which gives insight into whether Christ or the culture is controlling our thinking is on the uniqueness of Jesus as our way to heaven. The Bible is very clear that if there were other ways to restore our relationship with our Creator, God would have chosen them over the agony of the cross. Faith in Jesus Christ's death and resurrection for us is the only way to become reconciled to God. In our survey, we asked two questions on this topic dealing with:

1. Mohammed, Buddha, and Jesus are all valid ways to God.
2. Jesus Christ is the only path to God.

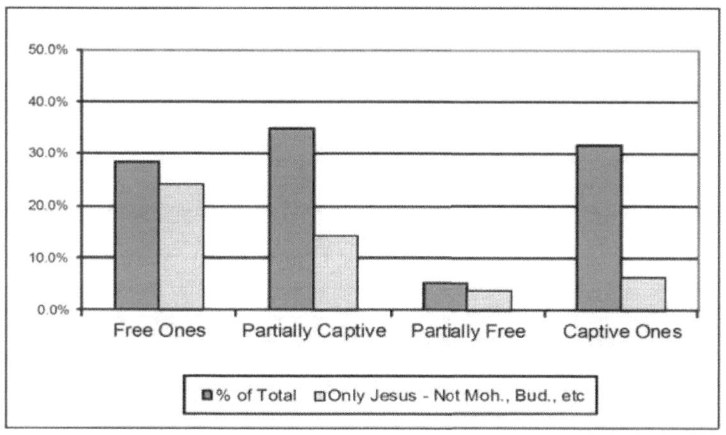

Figure 10-5 Probe Survey: Jesus is the Only Way to Heaven

One would expect that born-again, young adults would agree that the first statement is false and the second is true. But, that does not turn out to be the case. In Figure 10-5, we see that almost all (> 80%) of the Free Ones agree with this conclusion. However, only 40% of the Partially Captives agree and only 20% of the Captive Ones agree with this conclusion. On the whole, over half of born-again, young Americans believe that Jesus is not the only path to God; that Mohammed or others are equally valid.

This false belief highlights a major disconnect between biblical truth and the thinking of young, American adults who claim to be born-again.

Let take this analysis to a deeper level of religious belief. Figure 10-6 below shows the percent of born-again, young adults who apply a biblical worldview to the questions below:

- Share Truth - I should present my truth to others without judging them.
- Share Truth - I should share my religious experience with others.
- Bible and Science - The Bible and science are essentially consistent.
- Bible and Science - Bible is right and I try to follow its teachings.
- Small group – I attend Bible or small group study in a typical month.
- Witness - I witness to others in a typical month.

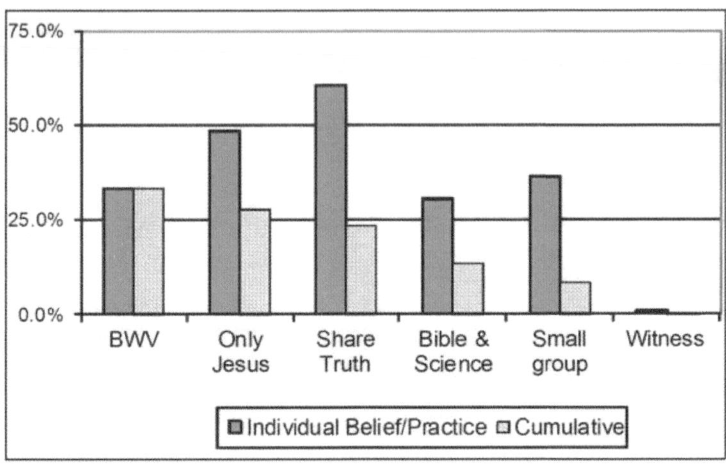

Figure 10-6 Probe Survey: Combined Biblical Beliefs and Practice by Young Adults Both Independent and Cumulative[3]

As shown, close to 60% say they present their view of truth and share their religious experience with others. At the same time, these young adults admit that less than one in a hundred actually witness to their faith in a typical month. Only one out of four believe that the Bible and science are essentially consistent and they should try to follow the teaching of the

Bible. The cumulative number who combine a biblical worldview with these other basic beliefs drops to about 14%. If we add in the number who attend a small group in a typical month, it drops to 8%. Clearly professing to be born-again per the Barna questions does not imply a consistent set of biblical beliefs or a practice of studying the Bible to develop those biblical beliefs.

If their beliefs do not come from the Bible, where do they come from? We will examine that question in the next chapter.

Chapter 11 Family - The Primary Source for Beliefs

Recapping: The State of Born-again Emerging Adults

In the preceding chapters, we examined the dramatic differences between the most common beliefs of American Evangelical emerging adults and a biblically informed position. It certainly appears that we are sliding into an era of cultural captivity where ones identification with Christ and an Evangelical church does not keep one from holding a set of beliefs consistent with the culture and counter to biblical truth. Now consider

1. the role that parents had in establishing these inconsistent belief systems of their children
2. some ways today's parents may be able to counter these destructive patterns in the future.

Before looking at the roles parents do and should play in establishing these belief systems, recall from Part 1 of this book, some of the key trends that are driving our concern.

Foremost among our concerns is the dramatic change in the number of emerging adults who hold to no Christian religious beliefs or espouse a liberal, non-Evangelical view of Christianity. Looking at data from 1976 to the present collected in the GSS surveys, we reported a disturbing new trend in the first chapter. From 1976 through 1990, the number of 18- to 25-year-old Americans who professed no Christian belief was constant at about 20% of the population. In 2000, this non-Christian group had grown to about 30% of this young generation and by 2010 the numbers had continued to grow to around 36%. If this trend continues, less than half of emerging adults will consider themselves Christians by the year 2020. When we add in the emerging adults who profess to being "weak Christians", the number having no or weak beliefs grows from about 60% of American emerging adults to over 72% from 1990 to 2010.

Our concern over the future of the American church is heightened by the conflicted beliefs of young born-agains. Among young adults, who consider themselves born-again believers, only about one third of them ascribe to a basic set of biblical beliefs, i.e. a biblical worldview. These beliefs include a creator God, a sinless Jesus, salvation through grace, a real Satan, an accurate Bible and the existence of absolute moral truths. This statistic means that over two thirds of these born-agains do not ascribe to one or more of these beliefs. Overall, this means that less than 10% of young American adults profess to being born-again and hold to a basic set of biblical worldview beliefs as compared to the 72% who hold to no Christian beliefs or profess to being a "weak Christian".

When we delve further into young adult beliefs, we find their beliefs appear to be a hodgepodge of cultural concepts and what's going on in their life with little or no connection to their religious upbringing. Even though emerging adults looked to religion as a place to learn good morals, in his study Christian Smith discovered a chilling paradox, "it was clear . . . that emerging adults felt entirely comfortable describing various religious beliefs that they affirmed but that appeared to have no connection whatsoever to the living of their lives."[1] One emerging adult observed, "I don't think it's the basis of how I live, it's just, I guess I'm just learning about my religion and my beliefs. But I still kinda retain my own decision or at least a lot of it on situations I've had and experiences."[2] In fact, when we look at how many have a consistent biblical worldview that carries over into their view on sexuality, science, a concern for the poor, and basic religious practices, the survey data indicates that less than 2% of Evangelical emerging adults would qualify. Therefore, the overwhelming majority of young Evangelicals are not carrying their basic religious beliefs into the realm of everyday thought or decision making.

The Impact of Parents on Spiritual Beliefs

Suzie strongly believed that sex outside of marriage was wrong before God. It had a detrimental effect on the individuals caught up in it and on society which promoted it. However, she felt that many of her friends did not view it in the same way she did. To get along, she never said much about it. What she did not realize was that her children were watching what she said. Even though she had told them she hoped they would remain pure until marriage, they did not hear her standing up for sexual purity among her friends. Without thinking about it, her children relegated sexual purity to a nice ideal but not an important belief for their lives. Suzie was instrumental in establishing their thinking on this topic.

Their thinking lined up with what Suzie demonstrated was important even though it did not really line up with what she truly believed.

To what extent have parents' played a role in shaping the spiritual views of young adults? Is the culture swamping the voice of reason expressed by their parents? Or, are their parents communicating the same mixed up beliefs as professed by their young adult children?

In 2010, we commissioned a survey to help us examine the causes and identify potential opportunities to change the marked shift in the thinking of young adults away from a consistent biblical worldview. We surveyed over 800 born-again, young adults across America to get an understanding for what they thought about spiritual and cultural issues AND how they felt about their beliefs and actions. One area of questioning was "When you think about how you developed the religious beliefs you hold today, who do you feel had the greatest influence on you?" Did your beliefs come from your family, your friends, your church, your independent studies, your college professors, or others?

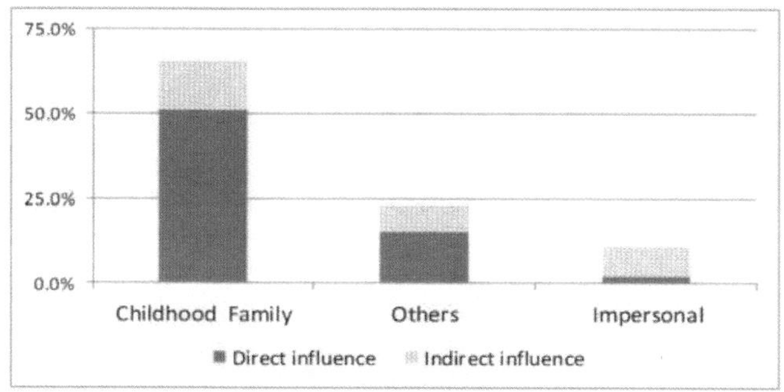

Figure 11-1 Probe Survey: Primary Source Influencing Faith of Born-again Young Adults

The answers we received to this question were not shocking but still sobering as seen in Figure 11-1. Over 65% of the respondents reported that the source that had the greatest influence on their religious beliefs was a family member. With the vast majority of those saying it was parents or grandparents. Over 20% of the respondents pointed to another influential individual such as a pastor, youth leader or college professor. Only about 11% stated that something less personal such as a youth group or the Bible was the greatest influencer of their religious beliefs. In the chart, Direct

Influence refers to things such as "they taught me what to believe" or "they read the Bible to me". Indirect Influence includes less direct methods such as "encouraged me", "took me to church" or "showed me love".

As Christian Smith noted, "what the best empirical evidence shows . . . is that . . . when it comes to religion, parents are in fact *hugely* important."[3] In fact, "religious commitments, practices, and investments made during childhood and the teenage years, by parents and others in families and religious communities, matter – they make a difference."[4]

Of those who stated that a family member was the primary influence, over 7 out of 10 stated it was their mother/grandmother while less than 3 out of 10 said it was their father/grandfather. Amongst born-again young adults, the female side of the family has a greater influence in passing down religious beliefs than do the males. One can postulate this may be due to a combination of greater spiritual involvement on the female side of the family and a higher level of communication with their children. However, the rate of fatherly influence almost doubles for young adults with a biblical worldview compared to those without it. So it appears that fathers who hold a biblical worldview are much more likely to be involved in establishing the spiritual beliefs of their children. Perhaps, when a mother and father are both communicating a biblical worldview perspective, it heightens the transmission of that perspective to their children. When mother and father are communicating different perspectives, it must increase uncertainty in the minds of their children.

Less than 1 out of 10 of the respondents listed a pastor as the primary source of influence and only 3% listed a youth group. These church related functions may have an important role in helping to shape our religious beliefs, but our survey shows that it is at best a secondary role for the vast majority of people. We are mistaken if we are relying on the church to pass on the right type of beliefs to our children. *Parents, what you communicate through your lives is picked up by your children. What are you communicating to them concerning religious beliefs?*

I think a common scenario is as follows. When a pastor instructs them on how a Christian should view the world and make decisions that reflect

Christ, it is only natural that they should look somewhere to see how this instruction is actually lived out. Perhaps they look to their parents to see if their lives are actualizing the pastor's message or not. If not, it is not important for them to worry about trying to actualize it in their own lives. If parents appear to be ignoring the pastor's message, either overtly or through a lack of emphasis in communicating with their children, it would be very unusual for the child to actively and consistently apply the pastor's instruction to their life. Conversely, if as seen by their child, the parent's lives are attempting to directly apply the truths of the message, the child is very likely to see the need to apply it in their own life.

The Translation of our Beliefs Across Time

Our survey indicated that over two thirds of today's young adults state that a parent or grandparent was the dominant factor in establishing their current religious beliefs. Are the beliefs of today's young adults dramatically different from the dominant beliefs of 40 years ago? Have older adults changed their beliefs as well or have the beliefs been translated by the younger culture into something different? Refer back to the GSS survey data to see how the beliefs and religious practices correlate between 18- to 29-year-olds and their parents who are roughly 45- to 59-year-olds. In the figures to follow, we have three columns for each level of belief. The first column reflects todays parents of emerging adults when they were young adults back in 1988. The second column reflects people who are now 45 to 59 representing those young adults grown up. The third column reflects current emerging adults age 18 to 29.

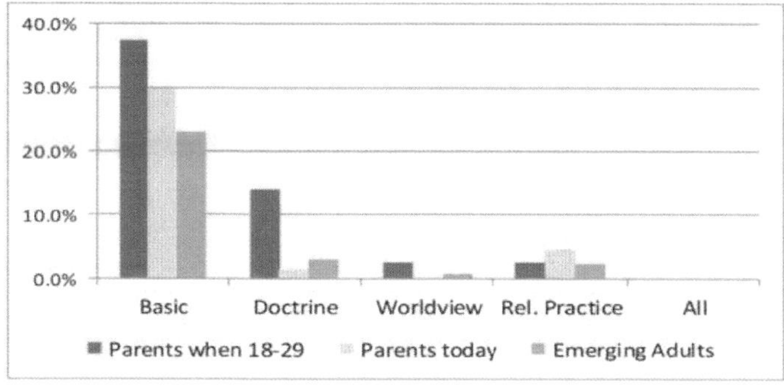

Figure 11-2 GSS Survey: Religious Beliefs & Practice for Three Different Groups

For those not born-again (Figure 11-2), a degradation exists in a basic belief in God and the Bible moving from parents during their young adult years to those same parents as 45 to 59 year olds today to today's emerging adults. This is followed by a significant drop in basic belief in doctrine for both the parents and the emerging adults relative to the low level of 14% when today's parents were emerging adults. The combined worldview, the religious practices and the combination of the preceding elements is extremely low for all.

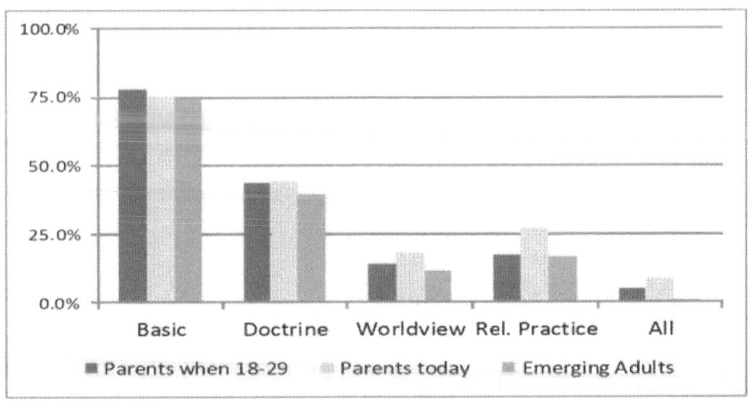

Figure 11-3 GSS Survey: Religious Beliefs and Practice for Born-agains Across Three Groups

Looking at the same elements for born-again believers in Figure 11-3 paints a somewhat different picture. Here we see a slight increase as the parents age from young adulthood to middle age, but only a slight difference. Generally, we see consistent levels across all three types. As noted before, the composite levels (i.e. columns labeled All) of 5%, 9% and 1% for the three different groups are extremely disappointing, but they certainly show a relationship between the beliefs of the parents and their emerging adult children.

Both the 1988 and 2008 GSS surveys had similar questions on sexual behavior and attitudes. The questions could be divided into four areas, abortion, fornication, homosexuality, and pornography. All of which are clearly identified in the Bible as behaviors which are harmful to us as individuals and as a society. How do these questions compare across the generations?

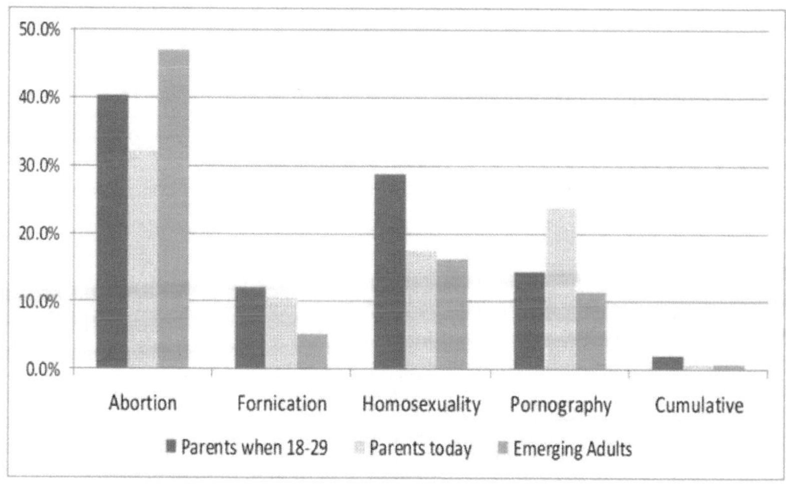

Figure 11-4 GSS Surveys: Cultural Beliefs for Not Born-again Young Adults Aligning with the Bible

Looking at Figure 11-4 for those who are not born-again, there appear to be a number of different issues at play. On abortion, we see that the parents are somewhat more accepting of abortion now than when they were young. At the same time, the emerging adults are significantly more likely to be against abortion than their parents, almost 50% more likely to oppose abortion. However, still over half of emerging adults do not oppose abortion. This clearly reflects a growing concern among emerging adults regarding the morality of abortion on demand.

On the question of sex outside of marriage almost no one opposes it regardless of age and time period. Still, todays emerging adults are 95% in favor of fornication versus 90% of their parents' generation. Homosexuality paints an interesting picture where 30% of not born-again 45 to 59 year olds opposed it as young adults versus only 18% opposing it as middle agers. This result is not surprising given the massive campaign to legitimize homosexual relations over the last twenty years. The emerging adults have a similar view as their parents do today. The questions on pornography look a little strange with the middle agers increasing the percentage against it from 14% to 24%. This growth is probably not due to a change in opinions about the acceptance of pornography, but rather is a result of the nature of the question. One of the questions used asks whether you have viewed a pornographic X-rated movie in the last year. As middle aged, married parents they are less likely to have the opportunity to view such material without drawing the scorn and hurt of their spouse. Finally, the percentage who oppose all four areas of sexual sin is very small for all three groups.

Looking at the same sexual areas for born-agains produces a somewhat different picture of attitudes and behaviors. In Figure 11-5, we see the same general trends as found for those not born-again but they are significantly muted in scale. There is a slight increase of emerging adults who oppose abortion relative to their parents. Similar to the previous chart, there is a declining number of people who oppose homosexuality as we move to the younger, emerging adult generation. In addition, we see the same spike in the area of pornography by the parents of emerging adults, for the same reason as was discussed for those who are not born-again. Although, it is significantly improved over those who are not born-again, the percentage of born-again emerging adults who stand against all four areas of sexual sin is a disappointing, disheartening 3%. So 97% of born-again emerging adults do not hold a biblically consistent view of these important life areas. However, we also find that 85% of born-again, middle aged adults fall in the same category.

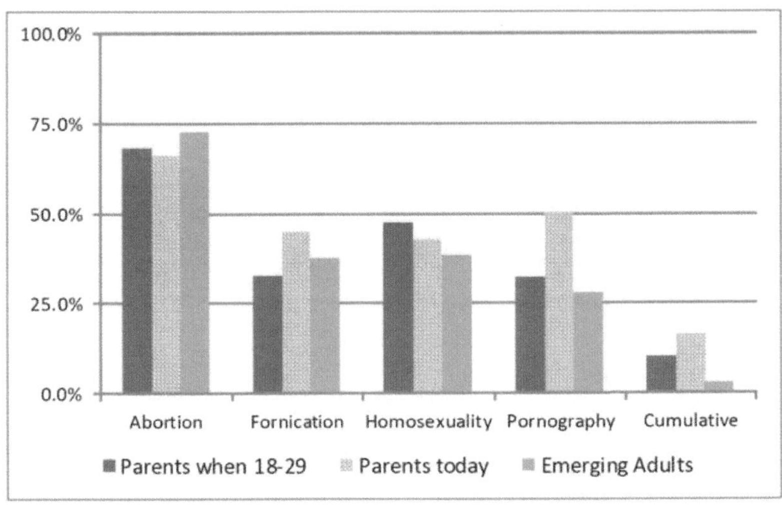

Figure 11-5 GSS Surveys: Cultural Beliefs for Born-again Young Adults Which Align with the Bible

From this data, it appears to be safe to conclude that today's born-again, emerging adults follow along with the beliefs of their parents with some minor degradation probably caused by the continuing degradation found in the population as a whole.

The Disturbing Result

Importantly, the most significant source of our religious beliefs was almost identical regardless of racial background or levels of church attendance. In other areas of consideration such as biblical worldview, views on cultural behavioral issues, and church involvement, we found significant differences based on racial background, education, etc. as we will see in Chapter 13. Nevertheless, it appears clear that no matter our race, economic level, or religious beliefs, our mothers are the primary sources that pass down those beliefs to the next generation. In other words, if born-again believers have degraded views on worldview and cultural issues, it appears that their parents are communicating (or at least not contradicting) similar views.

As we look at the mixed up religious and cultural beliefs held in our society, we can see the results of what Christian Smith referred to as Moralistic Therapeutic Deism. The baby boomers and their children are captives of our societies focus on pluralism and tolerance as the only acceptable views. With this view, I can hold to certain religious beliefs that are strictly private in their application. But, when those religious views begin to move into areas which may imply someone elses belief is wrong, then I need to modify my beliefs to be more accepting. To believe in God as creator and Jesus as his sinless Son is probably ok. But when I say that Jesus is the only way we can be reconciled to God, I am starting to step on other's toes; making it inherently wrong.

On the one hand, baby boomers have bought into the cultural distaste for absolute beliefs making them loathe to state their beliefs too strongly. This viewpoint has been interpreted by the younger generation as an indication that those beliefs are not firm, but rather culturally determined. So living in a more multi-ethnic, culturally diverse and sexually liberated generation, these young adults pick and choose amongst biblical beliefs and distinctly non-biblical beliefs with no apparent concern for the discontinuity in their belief systems.

The culture is winning the battle on two fronts: first the older generation is buying into the importance of not being too forthright with their views and secondly, the younger generation, given no clear direction from their parents, is buying into a disjointed set of views that avoids any conflict with others. According to Smith's research, the result is the vast majority of emerging adult Americans holding to some form of mainline protestant philosophy. This philosophy states that Jesus is a worthwhile model of ethical behavior but our focus should be on getting along and not making waves rather than promoting faith in Christ.

Countering Parents with a Truth Experience

The data suggests that the parents of today's young adults have passed on a stunted set of religious views. Have the baby boomers, the parents and grandparents of our society, so flummoxed up the works that we have started a downward spiral of disconnected beliefs from which we cannot recover? Of course, time will tell, but if we hold to a consistent set of biblical worldview beliefs, we should not sit back and wait patiently for the end of Christianity as we know it. We are called to "*proclaim Him, admonishing every man and teaching every man so that we might present every man complete in Christ.*" (Col 1:28)

Interestingly, of those respondents who graduated from college and have a biblical worldview, a much greater percentage of them pointed to a source other than a family member as the most influential source. As shown in Figure 11-6 below, a college graduate influenced by a source other than their family (middle column, bottom area) is 33% more likely to be a regular church attender with a biblical worldview than a college graduate whose primary influence is their family (left column, bottom area) and 110% more likely than a young adult who did not graduate from college (right column, bottom area). This factor is probably the result of college students having their faith challenged and looking for answers from pastors, bibles and books. In other words, the direct challenge to their faith presented by some professors and many of their young peers caused some to fall away, but caused others to examine the reasons for their belief in Christ. We do not need to fear this examination. Our Lord's case is more than capable of standing up to examination. In fact, it is the only religion that has a consistent, viable explanation for the complexities and challenges of life, as we know it.

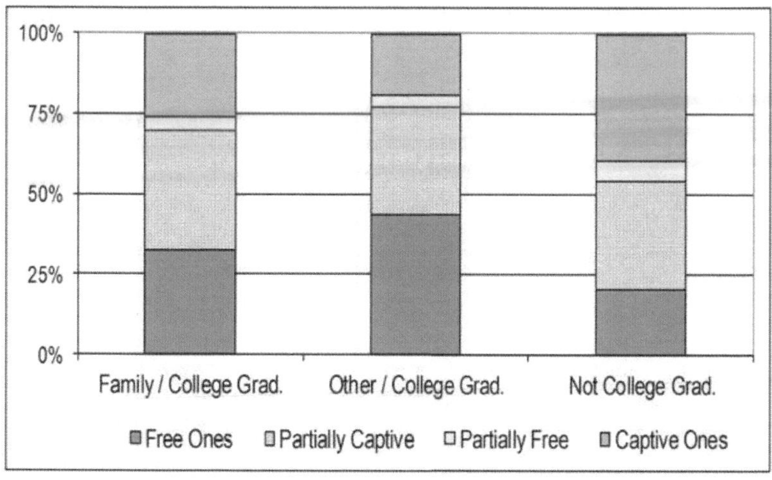

Figure 11-6 Probe Survey: Impact of College on Source of Religious Influence Across Four Categories

If a hostile, or at least a highly skeptical, attack on the basis of their faith caused some to examine their reasons for belief and come out with a stronger, more biblical faith, perhaps a friendly encouragement to examine their faith could produce similar results. If the parents are passing on a watered down, inconsistent set of beliefs, perhaps we can change those beliefs by causing the young adults to run them through a consistency and credibility filter. Probe has been doing this for years through our Mind Games camps for high school seniors. We have seen that this approach makes a difference. Some of the comments from the campers at our 2011 camp:

"I am getting a lot out of it. It is directly applicable. The speakers really know what they are talking about and explain it clearly."

"We connect with the other campers here very quickly which is not my normal experience. I was able to share my experience with others. The best part was the staff hanging around to answer questions; any questions we might have."

"I would recommend this for everybody. It is something we all need."

Is it too late to make a difference in the lives of our young adults? When Viggo Olsen was in his mid-twenties, beginning his residency to become a doctor, his wife's parents had a change in their belief system becoming followers of Jesus Christ. Viggo wanted to restore his wife's parents to sanity so he began an intense study to show the obvious failure of Christianity to address the real world. What he discovered was that a biblical worldview was the only viable answer to understanding our lives and our future. He went from a mission to disprove Christianity to accepting Jesus not only as his savior but as his purpose in life as a medical missionary to Bangladesh.[5]

In a similar way, we need to encourage, or better yet force, our younger church goers to examine their beliefs and compare them with the teachings of Christ. Ask them not to live an unexamined life conforming to the culture, but rather to examine their beliefs and see if they stand up to close examination.

One take away from this study is disturbing but not very surprising. Most American born-agains between the ages of 18 and 40 received their spiritual beliefs (and most of their other beliefs) from their parents or grandparents. In other words, their hodgepodge of inconsistent beliefs covering everything from God to gossip they essentially obtained from the prior generation. What the surveys show is that people in their 40s and 50s have viewpoints that are more conformed to the culture than to Christ just as their children do. It is not quite as dramatic but it is very pronounced. If we parents are holding beliefs that are captive to the traditions of men and the elementary principles of this world, then it is not surprising to see that thinking expanded in our children.

It is very interesting to note that 42% of church-going young adults with a biblical worldview (the Free Ones) stated that their spiritual beliefs were driven by sources other than immediate family members versus only 30% for other born-agains (an increase of 40%). Interestingly, this difference also coincides with the higher percentage of college graduates among the Free Ones relative to other young born-agains. In fact, college graduates influenced by sources outside their family are more than twice as likely to be church attendees with a biblical worldview than are those who did not graduate from college. Therefore, it appears that this committed group of church going young adults with a biblical worldview had to deal with challenges to their faith in college leading them to delve into the questions and develop a solid biblical worldview, drawing from sources outside their families. Is it possible that we could introduce this process into our churches for young adults and teenagers?

Consistent Worldview Parents are Best

We have been looking at the pervasive influence parents have on the religious beliefs of their children. Unfortunately, many parents have not been passing on a clear view of faith in Christ from generation to generation. Instead, our belief system, even among those who believe they are going to heaven when they die because of their faith in Jesus, has been eroding into a mishmash of popular cultural beliefs mixed in with some variation of beliefs taught in the Bible.

We have seen ways in which parental "wishy-washy-ness" can be overcome when young adults are challenged to consider the validity of their views. Confronting young adults with the disconnects and shortcomings created by their mixture of beliefs as compared to a consistent Christian worldview can get their attention and bring about changes in their thinking. This confrontation with truth has been a major focus of Probe throughout the years.

A major take away from these studies should be for the young adults who are parents of our future generations. Listen up young adults! If you do not communicate a clear set of biblical worldviews through your words and through your actions, your children are going to pick up on the worldview you do communicate. Your desire to fit in with the culture and not make too many waves will result in children who believe that the culture is the ultimate authority on truth and right living. Why? Because that is what your life is saying to them; loud and clear.

As parents, our beliefs have the greatest impact on our children's views. Things that you may not believe, but grit your teeth and say nothing about, will become core beliefs of your children. The society is saying they are true; they don't see a consistent disagreement from your words or your life. Thus, it must be the right value to hold. This process of gradually turning over our core beliefs to be reset by the culture is at least partially the reason for the tremendous shift in our cultural morality over the last 60 years.

Parents can make a difference in the belief systems of future generations. We need to hold fast to the truths taught by Jesus Christ, speak them with our tongues, and live them through our actions. Our children are still looking to us for truth in this area. Let us commit not to let them down by deferring to the norms of the culture.

Chapter 12 What Parents Are Passing On

As we saw in the previous chapter, many of the beliefs of young adults discussed in Part 1 are passed down from their parents. How do born-again young adults relate to these beliefs in their performance and their perceptions of their performance? Are there different ways of viewing non-biblical thinking among these young adults?

To gain an understanding of how young born-agains felt about their behavior, Probe Ministries included questions in our surveys on this topic. We surveyed their attitudes and actions on a number of unbiblical areas of behavior including sexual activity, self-centeredness (such as judging others and not being generous), unethical use of the tongue, greed, cheating, etc. Rather than simply asking them if they thought these behaviors were right or wrong, they were asked if they sometimes face difficulties or challenges related to these unbiblical behaviors. They could select from the following responses:

1. "Yes, a great deal,"
2. "Yes, to some extent,"
3. "No, I do it but have no problem with it", and
4. "Does not apply to me".

Not surprisingly, the Free Ones tended to have the same level of participation in each area as other born-agains, but had a significantly lower percentage who said the behavior wasn't wrong or did it without feeling guilty or embarrassed. On the other hand, amongst the one third with irregular church attendance and no biblical worldview (the Captive Ones), about one third had no guilt with their sexual indiscretions and over one half felt no guilt associated with issues of internal attitudes and external attitudes, and other negative actions.

Sexual Attitudes and Activity

Let us look into these results in greater detail. One area of disconnect relates to sexual activity outside of marriage and our attitudes toward it.

First, let us set the context by looking at the beliefs and practices of born-again, emerging adults ages 18 through 29 in this area. Figure 12-1 shows the average across three external surveys (NSYR, GSS and Baylor) of the percent of born-again, emerging adults who do **NOT** believe the listed behavior is wrong. The first bar shows the percentage for the listed topic and the third bar in each group shows the cumulative probability for that topic and those preceding it. For example, the first bar above Living Together shows that 57% of born-again, emerging adults do not believe that living together before marriage is wrong. The third bar in the same set shows that 79% do not belief that pornography, <u>and</u> casual sex outside of marriage, <u>and</u> living together are wrong.

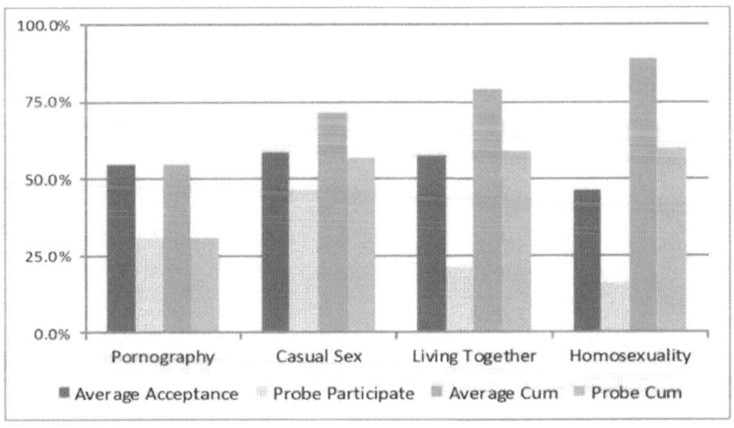

Figure 12-1 Multiple Surveys: Belief & Practice on Sex Related Issues for Born-again Young Adults

The second and fourth bars in each set are from the Probe survey. Recall that the Probe survey does not ask them what they think about a behavior unless they actually participate in the behavior. So for example, although over 50% of these born-again, emerging adults do not believe that living together is wrong, only about 20% of them have actually lived with someone in a carnal way before marriage. The bars above homosexuality show beliefs about homosexual activity and marriage in contrast to participating in homosexual ***thoughts or activities***. These two areas are similar but do not match up fully since there is a big difference between having thoughts of homosexual activities and actually participating in them. Looking at the cumulative[1] probabilities for all four activities, we see that 90% of born-again, emerging adults find at least one of these four activities acceptable. At the same time, almost 60% of born-again, emerging adults have participated in or struggled with one or more of these activities.

As noted above, the Probe survey went on to ask these born-again, young adults ages 18 to 40, who participated in one or more of these behaviors, how they felt about their participation as shown in the figure. In Figure 12-2, the solid section at the bottom of each bar indicates those who participated in the activity and said "no, I do it and have no problem with it". The hatched section at the top of each bar indicates those who stated they considered their participation in the activity a difficulty to a great deal or at least to some extent. Ideally, one would like to see all columns less than 1%. Realistically, one would expect born-agains to admit to participating in some of these sinful behaviors, but with none of them saying it was okay.

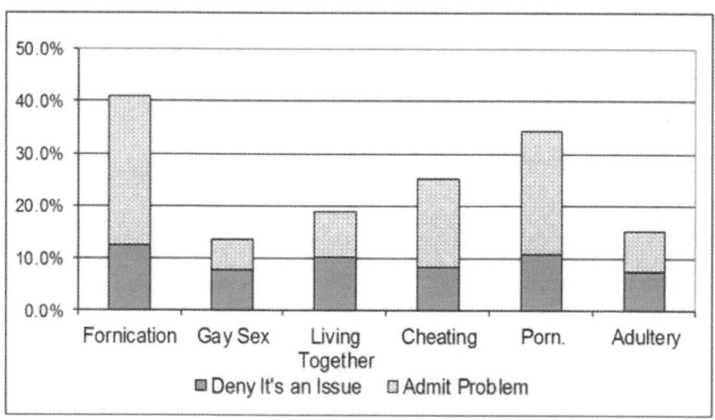

Figure 12-2 Probe Survey: Born-again Young Adults Who Participate in Sexual Sin and Their Attitude Toward It

Over half of those who participated in homosexual thoughts or behavior, living together with a sex partner, or adultery claimed that they had no problem with the activity. In other words, even though the Bible clearly states that this behavior is harmful to their life and testimony, they say it is fine for them. All of these six areas of sin had at least one third of the participants say it was not a problem for them.

Over a quarter of these born-again, young adults admit to being involved in fornication, pornography or cheating on their partner. Of course from the prior chart, one can see that close to 60% of them admit to being involved in one or more of those three areas of sexual sin. When we look at all of the categories shown, we find that 60% are involved in one or more of these activities and 30% of those involved do not believe it is a problem for them. Interestingly, when we consider that 90% of the born-again emerging adults in the other surveys considered at least one of these areas not a problem, finding that 70% of those actually involved considered it a problem creates somewhat of a conundrum. Most likely it shows that the area one does not believe is sin may not be the area that the person is actually involved in.

How do these issues align with our four categories of born-again, young adults? Figure 12-3 shows us the relationship as we look from the Free Ones to the Captive Ones. First, one can see that the Free Ones are much less likely than the other groups to be involved in a sexual sin (about 45% to 70% meaning they are 40% less likely than others). Similarly, they are 50% less likely to consider it "no problem" (about 10% compared to 20% for the others). For the Partially Captive and the Captive Ones, the attitudes are almost identical. So, it appears that having a biblical worldview is more important than going to church in impacting your susceptibility for and attitude toward sexual sin.

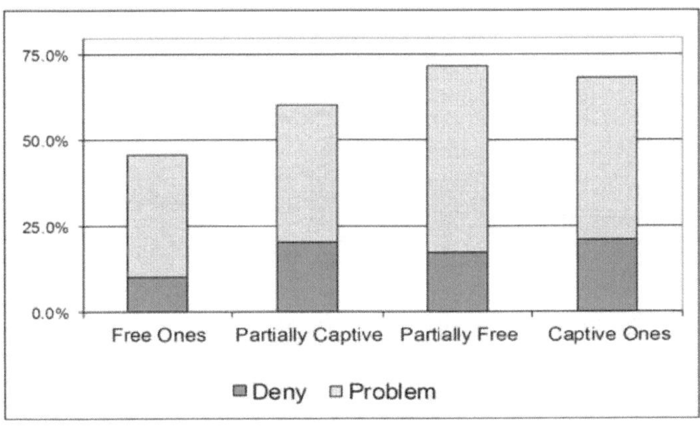

Figure 12-3 Probe Survey: Those Participating in a Sexual Sin Across Our Four Categories

Moral Attitudes and Behavior

Another area of questioning involved their attitudes toward things such as gossiping, lying, judging, greed, etc. First, the participants were asked for various areas of thought and behavior if they sometimes face difficulties or challenges in each area. The participants could select one of the four responses laid out at the beginning of this chapter.

For sake of brevity, these issues have been grouped into four different categories of behavior as follows:

- Self Centered – not being generous or giving to those in need, judging others, not loving
- Tongue – not keeping your word, lying or being dishonest, gossiping
- Greed – not having everything I want in terms of possessions, excessive consumer or credit card debt, gambling
- Larceny – cheating, stealing

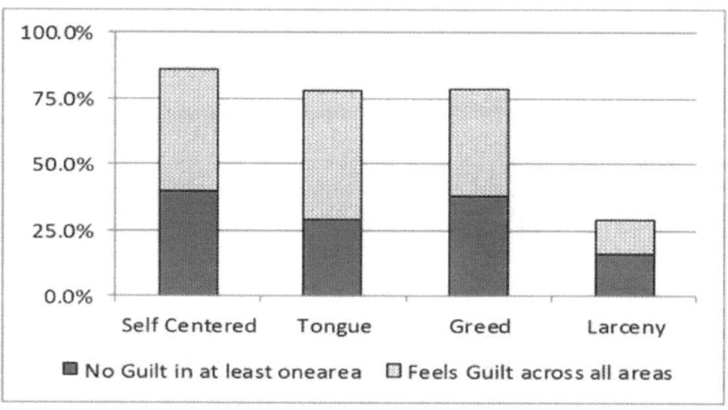

Figure 12-4 Probe Survey: Attitude Toward Behavioral Sins

As shown in Figure 12-4, over three fourths of these 18- to 40-year-old, born-agains find Self Centered, the Tongue, and Greed as a challenge in their lives. The other areas grouped under Larceny are reported to be a challenge for only about a third of those responding. These results are somewhat surprising until we realize that for those over age 22 the opportunities for cheating on tests are much less than when they were younger. Of those who find an area as a personal challenge, the solid shaded area indicates those who engage in it without any remorse. In the areas of Self Centered, Greed and Larceny about half of those challenged in that area fall into this category. For the other area of the Tongue, it is close to 40% of those challenged who engage in lying or gossiping without any remorse. It is probably not surprising to find these types of attitudes and behaviors creating problems for these young adults.

How do these responses map into our breakdown of Free Ones, Partially Free, Partially Captive, and Captive Ones? First, in Figure 12-5, consider the areas which are primarily internally expressed: Tongue and Greed. Interestingly, about 90% of the respondents struggle in one or more of these areas regardless of their worldview or church attendance. We find some difference in the portion of those who engage in these negative behaviors and consider it not a problem. About 44% of Free Ones who have an issue in these areas say it is not a problem for them. In contrast 45% of the Partially Free and 52% of the Captive Ones report that these negative behaviors are not wrong or if they are wrong they have no guilt about their behavior. Those who apply a biblical worldview to their approach to life do not appear to have a significantly different view of their internal thoughts and actions.

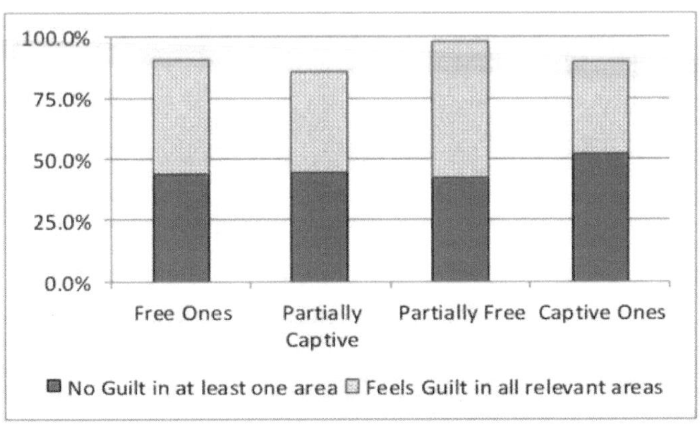

Figure 12-5 Probe Survey: Attitude Toward Behavioral Sins Related to the Tongue and Greed for Born-again Young Adults

Do we see a similar trend for areas which are more externally expressed: Self Centered and Larceny? As shown in Figure 12-6, the answer is yes to a small degree. Once again, we see close to 90% that are challenged by these areas across all four types of individuals. In addition, we find that 41% of Free Ones say it is not a problem versus 47% of the Captive Ones, an increase of about 13%. Once again, the data shows that nearly half of these young adults are unwilling to admit that these behaviors are counter to God's desire for our lives. Those without a biblical worldview are somewhat more likely to decide that there is nothing wrong with adopting these behaviors specifically discussed as problems for Christians in the New Testament.

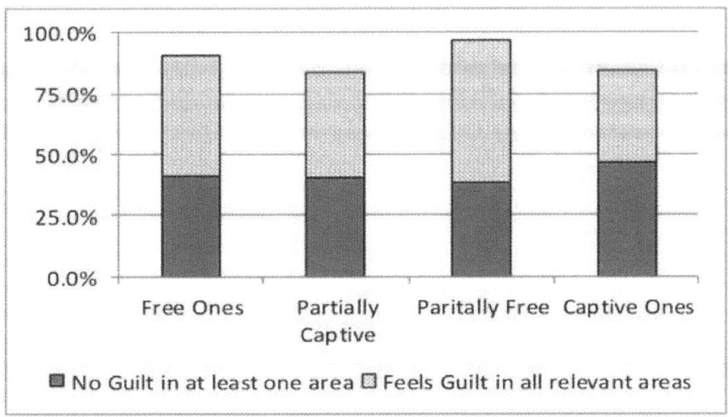

Figure 12-6 Probe Survey: Attitude Toward Behavioral Sins Related to Self Centered Behavior and Larceny for Born-again Young Adults

In these areas, in which sin is more common and oftentimes not as evident to others as sexual sins, we see a much higher rate of participation which a probably to be expected. However, we also see a much higher level of denial. When over half of those who admit to struggling with these types of sins state that they have no reason to feel any guilt, the message of Jesus Christ is not getting through. Of course, when we confess our sins, He promises full forgiveness (1 John 1:9), but the same book also tells us "*these things I have written to you so that you may not sin*" (1 John 2:1).

Attitude Toward Money and Work

Another area of significant interest in the lives of these born-again young adults is one related to their money and jobs. For this area, once again, we looked at answers to the question: Do you sometimes face difficulties or challenges in: ____? The specific areas considered were:

- Manage money - excessive consumer or credit card debt, mismanaging money
- Giving to Others - not being generous or giving to those in need, not giving regularly or tithing to a church
- Work Attitude - seeing my job as service to God rather than just trying to get by
- Employer - giving my boss the proper respect

The potential answers were the same as those listed for the behavioral attitudes above. In Figure 12-7 for the first three areas, we have over 70% admitting to a problem and over a third of those seeing no problem in their behavior. They do not see their work as part of their service to God as prescribed in Colossians 3:23-25:

Whatever you do, do your work heartily, as for the Lord rather than for men, knowing that from the Lord you will receive the reward of the inheritance. It is the Lord Christ whom you serve.

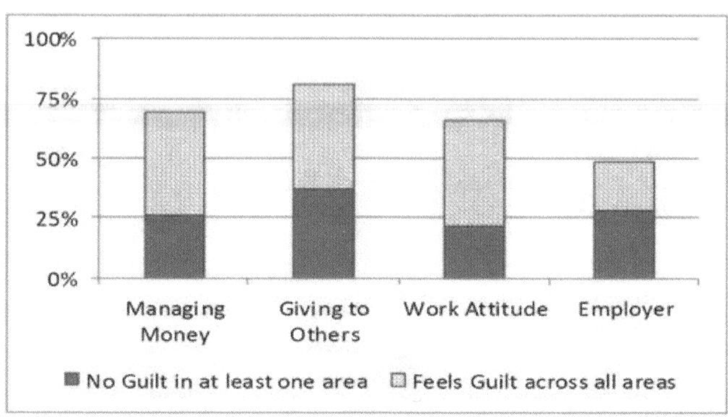

Figure 12-7 Probe Survey: Attitudes Toward Sinful Behavior Related to Money or Work

In addition, the money they earn is hard for them to give cheerfully as requested by God. Clearly, there are a large number of born-again, young adults who do not have the attitude of the Macedonians as Paul described in 2nd Corinthians 8:1-4:

Now, brethren, we wish to make known to you the grace of God which has been given in the churches of Macedonia, that in a great ordeal of affliction their abundance of joy and their deep poverty overflowed in the wealth of their liberality. For I testify that according to their ability, and beyond their ability, they gave of their own accord, begging us with much urging for the favor of participation in the support of the saints,

While just under half indicate they have a problem giving their boss respect, well over half of them do not consider it a problem to disrespect their boss. Once again they are clearly struggling with the admonitions in Scripture, for example in 1 Peter 2:18-19:

Servants, be submissive to your masters with all respect, not only to those who are good and gentle, but also to those who are unreasonable. For this finds favor, if for the sake of conscience toward God a person bears up under sorrows when suffering unjustly.

How are these areas of work and money distributed across our four categories of born-again, young adults. The data in Figure 12-8 clearly shows almost no distinction between the types of people. Unlike other areas considered above, in this area, the Free Ones are basically the same as the Captive Ones. Although this is not a problem unique to the current blend of postmodernism and Christianity, it certainly appears that many born-again, young adults choose to hold much tighter to their money and position than they hold to the commands of Jesus Christ.

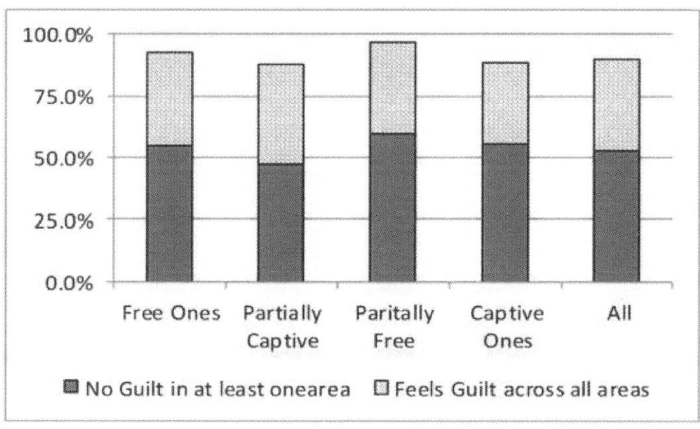

Figure 12-8 Probe Survey: Attitude Toward Sinful Behavior Related to Money & Work for Our Four Categories

Source for Making Decisions

In the prior chapter, we looked at where born-again, young adults believe they got their religious beliefs. Now we want to consider two additional aspects:

1. how they assess their current beliefs in regard to the Bible
2. how they choose to apply those beliefs to decisions regarding culturally relevant attitudes and actions as identified earlier in this chapter.

In our survey, we asked them three questions related to their current beliefs. First, we asked about the Bible as a source of truth in the following way:

> Which of the statements listed below comes closest to what you believe about the Bible?

1. Bible is my source of truth; applies to all situations and all people
2. Bible is my source of truth; others may have another source
3. Bible is source of truth for some situations, not for all
4. Bible is a religious history book, doesn't apply to my life
5. none of the above

Then they were asked two additional questions:

- On a scale from 0 to 100 - where "100" means complete alignment and "0" means not at all aligned, how would you rate your attitudes and beliefs about things in general compared to what the Bible says about the same topics?
- Similarly, on a scale from 0 to 100 - where "100" means complete alignment and "0" means not at all aligned, how would you rate your personal behaviors compared to what the Bible says?

Using these questions, we can obtain an idea of the difference between their stated beliefs and their actual beliefs and behavior. The chart in Figure 12-9 compares their stated level of beliefs with three of the measures of belief reported on earlier in this book. First, consider their self-assessment. The first solid bar shows that fully three fourths of these born-again, emerging adults stated that their attitudes and beliefs are at least 75% aligned with what the Bible says about various topics.

Whereas, the first solid bar in the last group of bars indicates that just under 25% of them believe their attitudes and beliefs are completely aligned with the Bible, i.e. 100%. The second bar in each group shows their responses on biblical worldview (1st group), basic religious practice and biblical worldview (2nd group), and cultural beliefs combined with other two (3rd group).

These figures demonstrate a significant disconnect between their level of confidence in their alignment with the Bible and their actual alignment. Although half of these born-again young adults claim to align with the Bible on 90% of topics, only about 20% actually align on basic religious beliefs and practices. In the same vein, we see that about one out of four state that their beliefs are completely aligned with the Bible and yet only about one out of forty really affirm the religious and cultural teaching of the Bible.

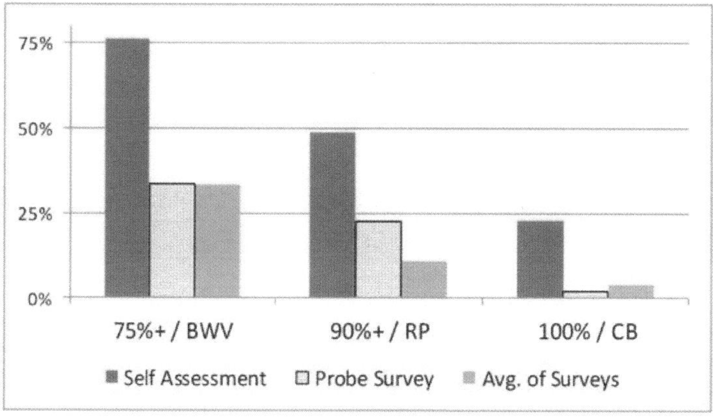

Figure 12-9 Probe Survey: Relationship Between Self-Assessment of Biblical Beliefs and Actual Level of Biblical Beliefs Among Born-again Young Adults

Another insight into their self-assessment is shown in Figure 12-10 below. In this figure, we look at the difference in their self-assessment of their beliefs for the four different categories of belief and church participation. For this chart, the data from the first question and the second question are combined and the responses are divided into four groups as follows:

Table 12-1 Definition of Four Categories Used in Figure 12-10

High belief / action	Bible is the source of truth for all situations and people AND Believe 90% or more of beliefs align with the Bible AND Believe 75% or more of personal behaviors are in alignment with the Bible
Moderate belief / action	All combinations not in the other three categories; primarily: Believe between 76% and 89% of beliefs align with Bible OR Believe between 66% and 74% of personal behaviors align with the Bible
Low belief / action	Bible is the source of truth for all situations/people AND Believe 75% or less of beliefs align with the Bible AND Believe 65% or less of personal behaviors align with the Bible
Very Low belief / action	Bible is NOT the source of truth for all situations/people AND Believe 75% or less of beliefs align with the Bible AND Believe 65% or less of personal behaviors are in alignment with the Bible

As shown, there is a major difference in self-assessment between the Free Ones and the Captive Ones. The Free Ones report almost 60% with a High level of belief and action and less than 10% with a Low or Very Low level. In contrast, the Partially Captives report slightly more than 25% with a High level of belief and action and almost 20% with a Low or Very Low level. The Captive Ones are almost the inverse of the Free Ones with only 10% reporting a High level and over 40% reporting a Low or Very Low level of biblical belief and action.

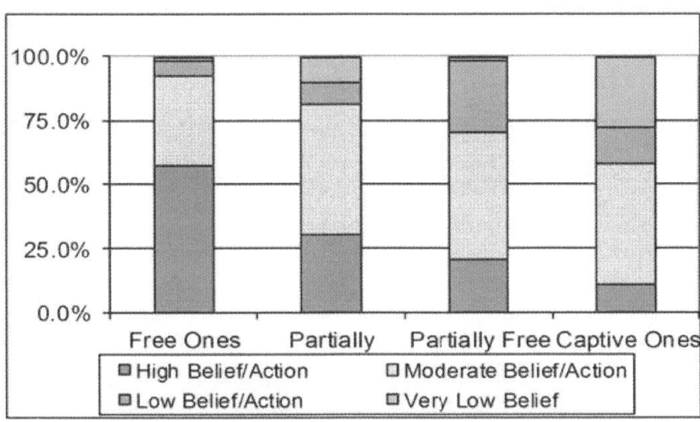

Figure 12-10 Probe Survey: Self Assessed Belief and Behavior Among Born-again Young Adults Across Our Four Categories

Clearly the minds of young, born-again adults exhibit a significant range of views toward the Bible and their ability to follow it's teachings. Less than a quarter of these young adults have a confident view of their desire and ability to follow the teachings of the New Testament. While a quarter of them have low or very low correlation between their actions and the teachings of the New Testament.

We asked these born-again, young adults, "What is the primary basis or source of those principals and standards that you take into consideration?" in making decisions associated with family, business, and religious matters. As shown in Figure 12-11, there was a huge difference between Free Ones and the remainder. In fact, 75% of the Free Ones looked to a biblical source in making those decisions about family and business while only 33% of the Partially Captive and 10% of the Captive Ones considered a biblical source.

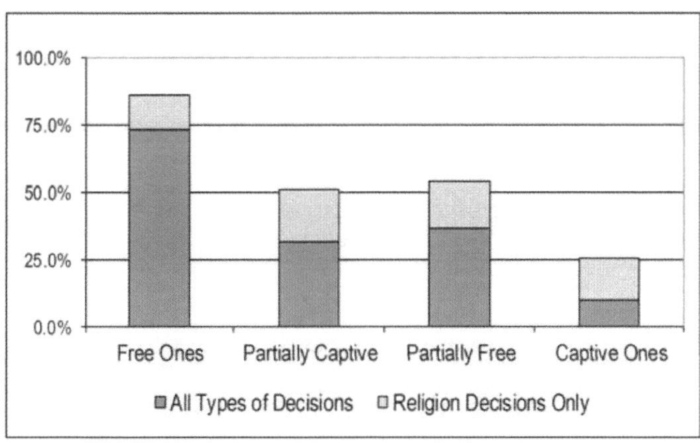

Figure 12-11 Probe Survey: Those Relying on a Biblical Source for Making Decisions Among Born-again Young Adults

It is clear from the analysis above that

1. Born-again, young adults demonstrate a disconnect between their self-assessment of their biblical belief and their actual beliefs when compared to the teaching of the New Testament.
2. Even so, those who attend church and profess a biblical worldview are the only ones where a majority gives themselves a high self-assessment of their biblical beliefs and actions.

3. Those who attend church and profess a biblical worldview are likely to say they rely on a biblical source to help them make decisions in life. Those not doing both of these things are unlikely to look to biblical sources to aid them in making decisions about family or business matters.

The Free Ones do a better job in some areas of relying on the bible as their guidebook for living and in owning up to their sin. But on the whole, these born-again young adults fall far short of knowing and living according to the instructions of the New Testament.

Chapter 13 Different Groups Highlight Different Issues

In Chapter 7, some of the variations across demographic groups were considered looking at the GSS 2008 Survey and the Probe Survey data from 2010. Now we will take a deeper look at these differences focusing on key survey data from our Probe Survey of born-again, young adults. In particular, we will look at how these demographic groups are distributed across the four types of born-agains identified in Chapter 10 above: Free Ones, Partially Free, Partially Captive, and Captive Ones. Clearly, these four types may require different methods and media to impact their thoughts on what it means to live a Christian life. It may be that some of the other distinctives, e.g. race, education, location, etc., are also important in understanding how best to get a message across to each group.

Racial Background and Religious Belief/Practice

Using the Probe survey results, consider how racial background impacts their religious views. As shown in Figure 13-1 and Figure 13-2, there are significant differences based on these ethnic backgrounds. In Figure 13-1, the Probe survey portion of the chart on biblical worldview and religious practice are repeated here from Figure 7-2. It clearly highlights a significant difference in the worldviews of the different ethnic groups. In general, it shows that born-again whites and Asians have one set of worldviews and religious practice, while born-again blacks and Hispanics are less likely to hold to those beliefs and practices. Don't forget, that even among the born-again whites and Asians, only one out of five hold a biblical worldview and have a minimally active set of religious practices.

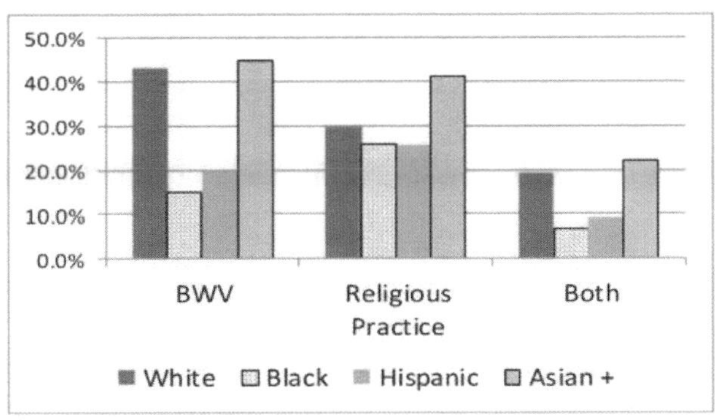

Figure 13-1 Probe Survey: Religious Beliefs & Practice vs. Ethnic Background for Born-again Young Adults

Now, let us look at how each ethnic group distributes across the four types of people. The bottom two categories (Free Ones and Partially Captives) are the ones who attend church more than twice a month. Looking at the percent of these born-again, young adults who attend church regularly, we see it is fairly consistent across all ethnic groups ranging from 58% to 66%. But, looking at the percent who attend church regularly and have a biblical worldview (i.e. the bottom category – Free Ones), we see large differences ranging from about 15% of the blacks and Hispanics to about 35% of the whites and Asians. In fact, a white born-again, young adult is almost three times as likely to hold to a biblical worldview as is a born-again, young black adult. Looking at the top category, i.e. those who don't go to church regularly and do not hold a biblical worldview, about 40% of the black and Hispanic believers fall into this category versus only about 25% of the white and Asian.

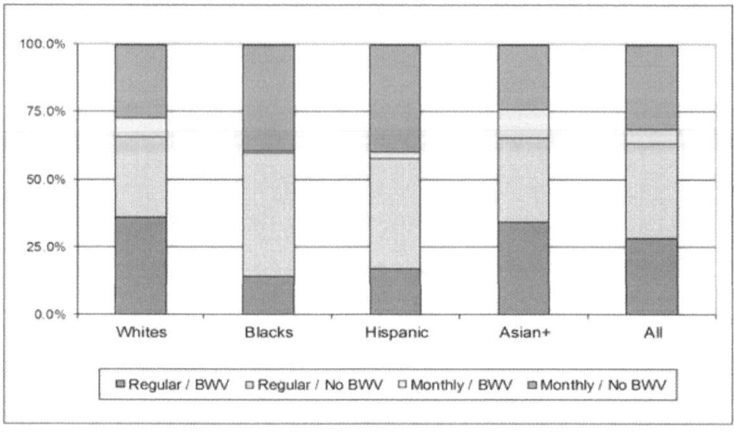

Figure 13-2 Probe Survey: Our Four Categories by Ethnic Group for Born-again Young Adults

Perhaps, their church affiliations more than their ethnic backgrounds are the primary drivers of these differences. What is the breakdown of denominations across the born-again, young adults in the Probe survey? There are 37 different denominations identified in the responses to the question: "What is the denomination or affiliation of the church you attend most often?"[1] Using the Classification of Protestant Denominations from the Pew Forum on Religion and Public Life, we classified those denominations into four categories: Evangelical, Mainline, Catholic and

No Answer. The breakout shown in Figure 13-3 also includes a similar analysis of data from the Baylor 2005 survey. The data from the two surveys is almost identical as should be expected. As shown, approximately 72% of our born-again, young adults are associated with an Evangelical church. While the Mainline Protestant, Catholic and No Answer groups represent approximately 15%, 5% and 8% respectively. When we consider those with a biblical worldview, our break out now becomes about 90% Evangelical and 10% Mainline Protestant.

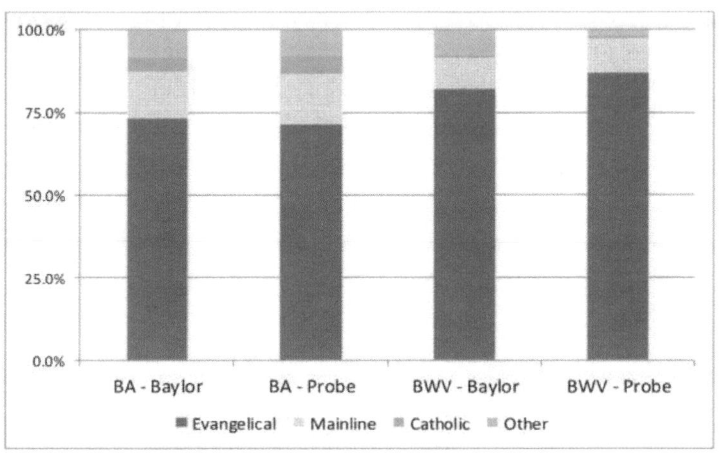

Figure 13-3 Baylor 2005/Probe Surveys: Denominational Distribution of Born-agains and Biblical Worldview Holders for Born-again Young Adults

How do these different denominational groups map out against our four different types of people? As shown in Figure 13-4, each denominational group is very different. Evangelicals are pretty evenly distributed with about 40% holding a biblical worldview (i.e. sum of Free Ones and Partially Free Ones). For those without a biblical worldview, they are evenly divided with 30% regular church attenders and 30% irregular in church attendance. For born-again Mainlines, only about 20% hold a biblical worldview while almost 50% are regular church attenders without a biblical worldview. The few born-again Catholics who participated in our survey had only 5% with a biblical worldview and 65% who attended church without a biblical worldview. Remember that all respondents in this survey are born-again so this is not a direct comparison of the denominations which is far more skewed across these three religious traditions than this data shows for only born-agains.

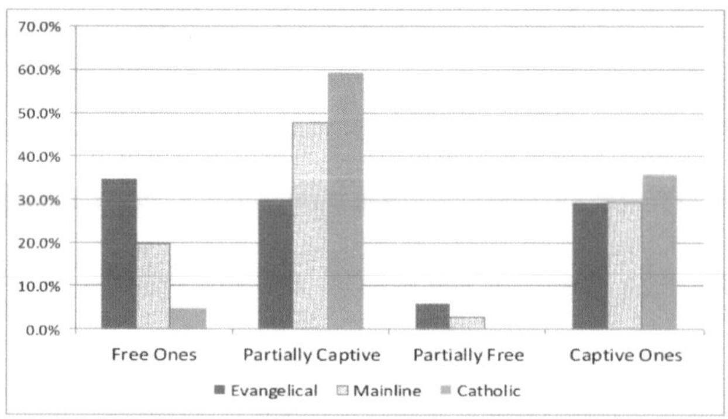

Figure 13-4 Probe Survey: Denominational Alignment Across Our Four Categorys for Born-again Young Adults

Look at each of these four ethnic groups in more detail considering their denominational affiliations. First consider the breakdown of white, born-again, young adults as shown in Figure 13-5. By adding across each group, we can see that there are about 72% Evangelical, 16% Mainline, 6% Catholic, and 5% No Answer. Compared to the entire group of respondents (see Figure 10-5), we have 43% who hold a biblical worldview (i.e. sum of Free Ones and Partially Free) versus 33% for those across all ethnic groups. We also see that of those who attend church regularly and have a biblical worldview (Free Ones), 85% are affiliated with an Evangelical denomination and 15% are affiliated with a Mainline Protestant denomination. Looking across the four columns, those white, born-agains attending a Mainline Protestant church are about one third Free Ones, one third Partially Captive and one third Captive Ones.

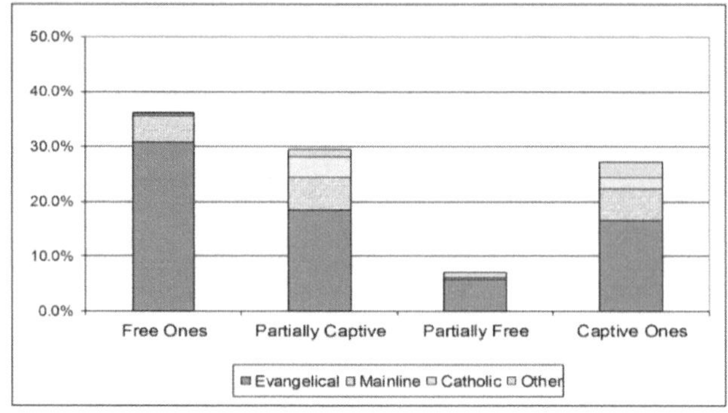

Figure 13-5 Probe Survey: Denominational Affiliation Across Our Four Categories for Born-again, White Young Adults

Let us compare these results with those for black respondents as shown in Figure 13-6. Once again, looking across the groups, we see that there are about 72% Evangelical, 15% Mainline, 2% Catholic, and 11% No Answer; almost identical with the breakdown of whites. But, those with a biblical worldview drops from 43% of whites to 15% of blacks. Similarly, the portion with no biblical worldview who do not attend church regularly grows from 28% to 40% between these two groups. The distribution of Mainline Protestants is much different for blacks with over two thirds of them regular church attenders with no biblical worldview.

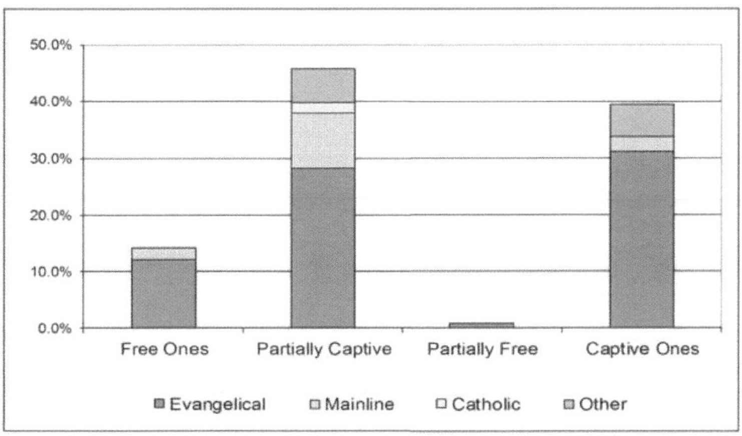

Figure 13-6 Probe Survey: Denominational Affiliation Across Our Four Categories for Born-again, Black Young Adults

How do Hispanics compare with the other ethnic groups? Figure 13-7 shows 70% are Evangelical, 11% are Mainline, 6% are Catholic and 13% are No Response. When we consider that 65% of emerging adult Hispanics are identified with a Catholic church, this chart highlights that Hispanic Catholicism does not teach an evangelical biblical worldview. Similar to black born-agains, less that 20% of Hispanic born-agains hold to a biblical worldview. Note that all of those with a biblical worldview are affiliated with an Evangelical church. Those without a biblical worldview have over 35% who are affiliated with a non-Evangelical church.

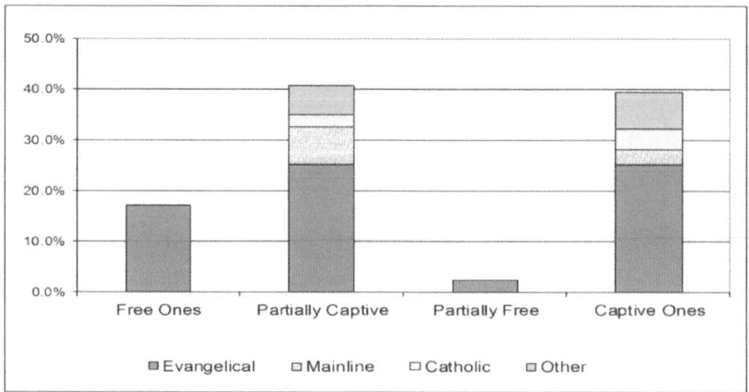

Figure 13-7 Probe Survey: Denominational Affiliation Across Our Four Categories for Born-again, Hispanic Young Adults

Finally, how do Asian born-again, young adults compare with these first three ethnic groups? Figure 13-8 shows that 72% are Evangelical, 16% are Mainline, 6% are Catholic and 6% are No Answer. The Asian born-again, young adults have a distribution across denominations and belief systems that are virtually identical with whites (Fig. 13-5). However, the uncertainty of the breakdown of Asians into categories is much higher than for whites due to the relatively small number of Asian respondents.

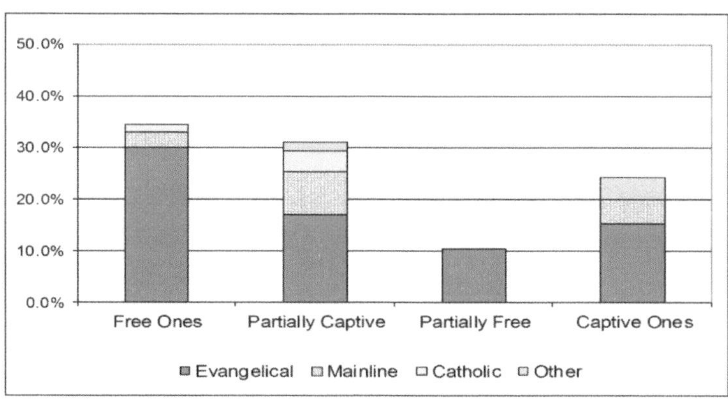

Figure 13-8 Probe Survey: Denominational Affiliation Across Our Four Categories for Born-again, Asian Young Adults

Geographic Location and Religious Belief/Practice

In Chapter 7, we saw that the percentage of born-again or Evangelical believers varied significantly by geographic region; from 43% in the

South to 22% in the Northeast. However, of those who were born-again, the percent with a biblical worldview and at least a nominal set of religious practices were about equal across the regions at the disappointing figure of 15%.

Let us look at how this data maps across the four types of born-again, young adults. As shown in Figure 13-9, the break out between Free Ones, Partially Captive, Partially Free and Captive Ones are reasonably consistent across born-again, young adults regardless of their geographic location. Although reasonably consistent, it should be noted that the percentage of Captive Ones in the Northeast exceeds that in the Midwest and West by about 25%. This appears to indicate a decreased interest in church attendance in the Northeast even among born-agains. Also, the percentage of Free Ones in the Midwest and West exceeds that found in the Northeast and South by almost 40%. So, born-again, young adults appear to be more engaged in those areas of the country. When making these percentage comparisons, keep in mind that there are almost 50% more born-agains in the South than in the Midwest and West. Therefore, as an absolute number, the number of Free Ones in the South exceeds the number in the Midwest and West. On a percentage basis, it is the other way around.

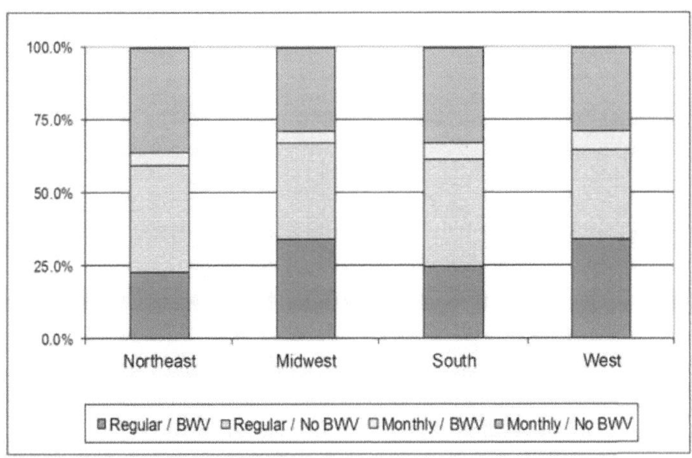

Figure 13-9 Probe Survey: Region of the Country Across Our Four Categories for Born-again Young Adults

Education and Religious Belief and Practice

In Chapter 7, we saw that among those who had not graduated from college, the percent of born-agains declined from almost 50% of those 45 and over down to only 30% of those age 18 – 29. While for those who had graduated from college, it remained a constant 25% across all ages. Even though there were a greater percentage of non-college graduates, among those who were born-again those with a college degree were much more likely to have a biblical worldview and participate in at least a nominal level in basic religious practices (see Figure 7-6 and 7-8).

In this chapter, we will consider how education relates to the four types of born-again individuals as shown in Figure 13-10. This figure highlights a significant difference between college graduates and others. College graduates are 75% more likely to be regular church attenders with a biblical worldview than those with a high school degree or less. In fact, those with a college degree make up a strong majority of these regular attenders. Apparently, those with a college degree believe that attending church is more important and adding a biblical worldview increases the importance of church attendance in their minds. In fact, much fewer than 50% of those without a college degree attend church on a regular basis.

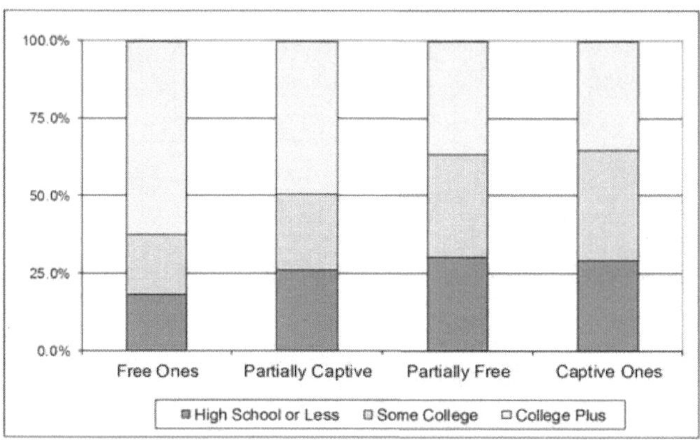

Figure 13-10 Probe Survey: Educational Level Achieved Across Our Four Categories for Born-again Young Adults

Another way to look at the same effect is to map the four types of people against household income as shown in Figure 13-11. Looking at the boundary between those making more than $50,000 per year in this figure and those with a college degree in the previous figure, we see they are almost identical. Those with the higher income are much more likely to be regular attenders with a biblical worldview. Although, we cannot be certain, it seems logical that it is the education level that impacts their religious beliefs and practice rather than their economic income. Those with the higher levels of education tend to have higher levels of income.

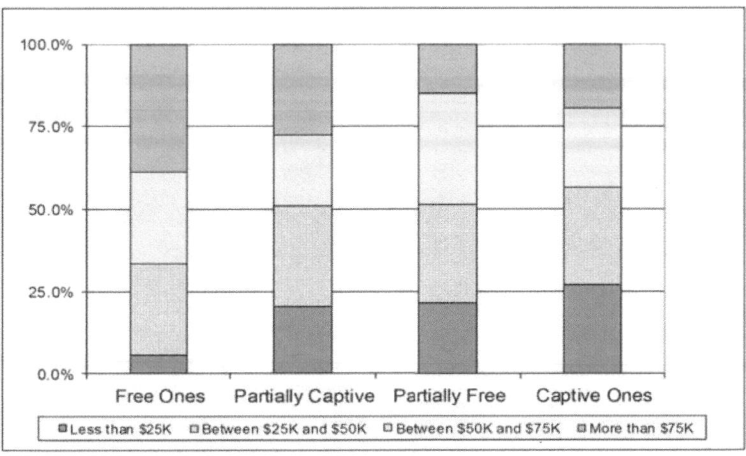

Figure 13-11 Probe Survey: Income Level Across Our Four Categories for Born-again Young Adults

Gender and Religious Belief and Practice

Finally, consider the impact of gender on the four types of born-agains. In Chapter 7, we saw that males and females were very consistent in their biblical worldview and religious practice both coming in at a disappointing 15% of all born-again, emerging adults. Dividing them into the four types as shown in Figure 13-12, we see some differences between the two genders. The males are somewhat more likely to have a biblical worldview and the females are more likely to attend church regularly without ascribing to a biblical worldview. In fact, 40% of these males profess a biblical worldview as compared to only 28% of the females.

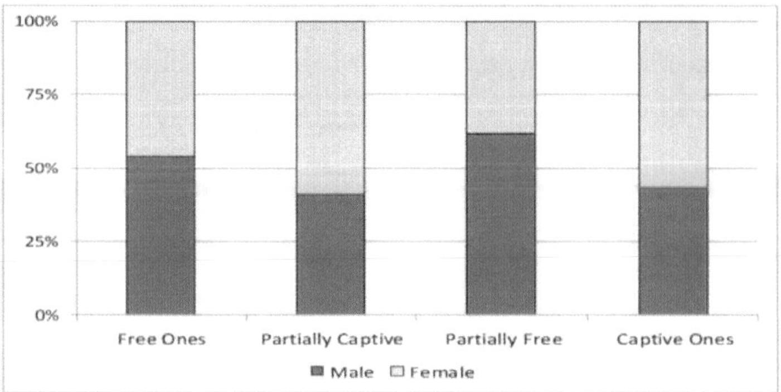

Figure 13-12 Probe: Gender Across Categories for Born-agains

Demographics and Cultural Actions

The Probe Survey did not ask the respondents how they felt about a list of cultural applications of biblical teaching. Instead, it asked them if they participated in an activity and, if so, how they felt about their participation. It is informative to look at how different groups of born-again, young adults responded to the questions relating to sexual behavior.

Racial Background and Cultural Actions

Just as we saw some significant differences in biblical beliefs and religious practices across different ethnic backgrounds, we find differences in their attitudes toward sexual behavior.

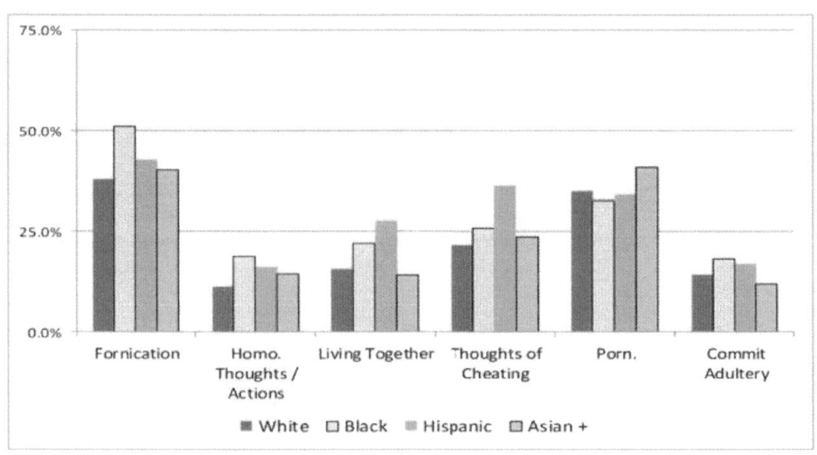

Figure 13-13 Probe Survey: Experience Difficulty with Sexual Sin Across Ethnic Backgrounds for Born-again Young Adults

The figure above (Figure 13-13) shows the percent of the born-again young adults who indicated they face difficulties or challenges with the behaviors shown. As shown, minor variations exist across the ethnic groups, but nothing major. The figure below (Figure 13-14) shows the percent of those who reported having a difficulty who said "no, I do it, but have no problem with it". Here we see a significant difference with our white respondents much more likely so indicate that they have no problem and presumably feel no guilt about these various activities. The majority of the other ethnic groups appear to have been taught to believe that their behavior is wrong. In contrast, many of the whites participating in these activities appear to feel justified in doing them.

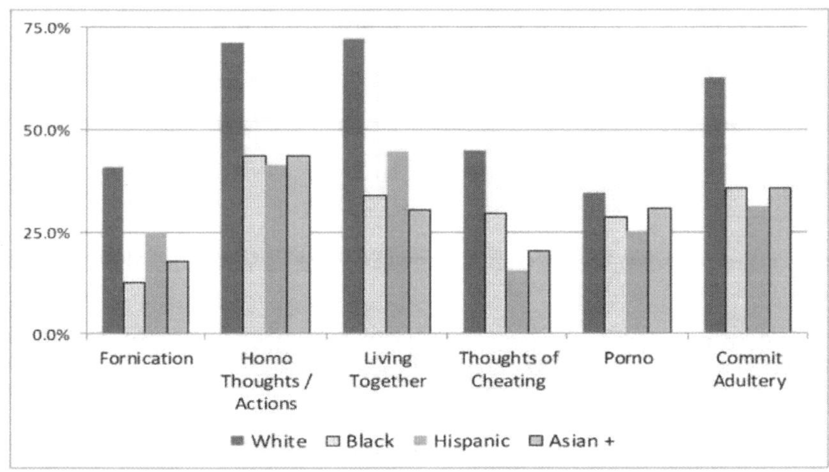

Figure 13-14 Probe Survey: Deny Difficulty is a Problem Across Ethnic Backgrounds for Born-again Young Adults

Education and Cultural Actions

There do not appear to be any significant differences in sexually related actions and feelings toward them across different levels of education.

Gender/Age and Cultural Actions

Let's look at the same data on sexually related issues across gender and age.

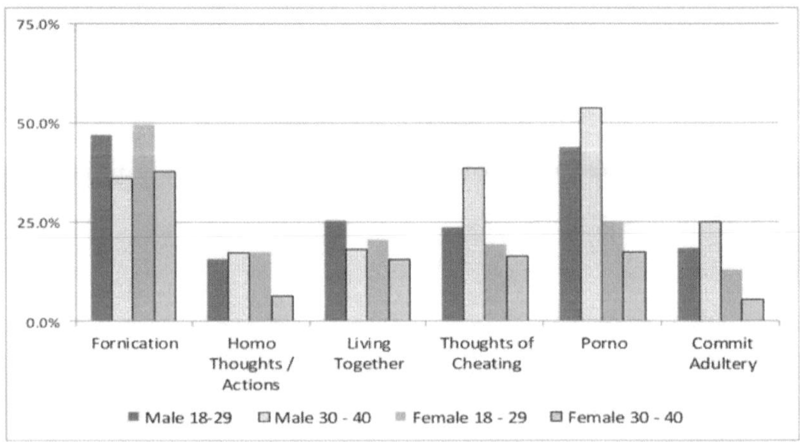

Figure 13-15 Probe Survey: Experience Difficulties with Sexual Sin Across Gender/Age for Born-again Young Adults

As shown in Figure 13-15, the primary differences based on gender are participation in pornography and thoughts of cheating on a spouse. As far as age matters, it appears that participating in fornication is more prevalent in the younger age group. This result may be caused by some in the over 30 group only applying the question to recent years and not thinking back to before they were married. Once again the next chart (Figure 13-16) shows the percent of those participating in the activity who do not think it is wrong. Interestingly, although females are much less likely to participate in viewing pornography than males, those who view it are almost twice as likely to say it is not a problem as are their male counterparts. We find a similar result on the issue of adultery. On the other hand, women are somewhat less likely to believe that fornication or living together are ok even though they have participated in those behaviors. Finally, over 50% of all groups who have participated in homosexual thoughts and actions say they are perfectly fine while only 25% of those in engaged in fornication or thoughts of cheating. This discrepancy in thought toward essentially equivalent sins appears to reflect the tremendous push to make homosexual behavior mainstream in our society.

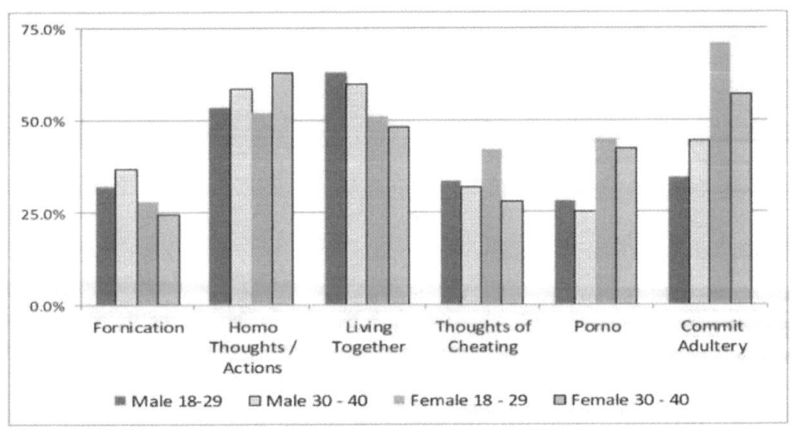

Figure 13-16 Probe Survey: Deny Difficulties are a Problem Across Gender/Age for Born-again Young Adults

Summary of Demographic Results Among Born-again, Young Adults

What, if any, difference is evident in our survey results based on demographic factors? The key results of the analysis of this chapter are summarized in Table 13-1.

Table 13-1 Summary Results of Demographic Analysis

Demographic Factor	Key Results
Ethnicity	• Although equal in church attendance, blacks and Hispanics were much less likely to ascribe to a biblical worldview than whites and Asians. This result probably reflects a difference in the teaching and terminology among those ethnic churches. • Whites are significantly more likely to profess no guilt for their sexual sins.
Denomination	• Those who identified with an Evangelical church were evenly distributed across Free Ones, Partially Captives and Captive Ones. • Those who identified with a Mainline Protestant Church were almost 80% without a biblical worldview.

Demographic Factor	Key Results
Ethnicity & Denomination	• Regardless of their church affiliation, over 80% of born-again blacks and Hispanics do not profess a biblical worldview as defined by Barna. • Among whites, the majority of Evangelicals profess a biblical worldview.
Geographic Location	• Only minor differences exist among born-again, young adults across location of the country.
Education Level	• Free Ones are much more likely to be college graduates.
Income Level	• Free Ones are much more likely to have a higher income level.
Gender	• Males are somewhat more likely to profess a biblical worldview. • Females are somewhat more likely to attend church regularly. • Females who commit adultery or look at pornography are much less likely to feel any guilt for their actions. Females are less likely to commit adultery or partake of pornographic material.

As shown, only Ethnicity and Denominational background had a significant impact of the reported results. The Ethnicity certainly appears to reflect some differences in the teaching and emphasis of white/Asian churches vs. black/Hispanic churches. In approaching black and Hispanic churches, it may be worthwhile to consider these differences in formulating the best approach to communicating a biblical worldview.

Chapter 14 From Captives to Conquerors

Diving into the data on how the American church is faring today, we started with something that looked like a pure, white sand Caribbean beach but turned out upon further evaluation to be a trash filled swamp of putrid, stale water. The data leads us to ask the question, "Can the church continue on this trajectory of scattered beliefs and split personalities for long?" I think the answer has to be no. Either the Evangelical church will follow the path of other Protestant denominations into shrinking, irrelevant entities or something will bring it back to the truth found in Christ Jesus.

In the data examined herein, a clear difference exists between those who claim to be born-again and those who do not. Clearly in our society, those who are not born-again typically hold to a set of beliefs and practices that are far removed from the lifestyle taught by Christ and His apostles. However, the difference when measured against the example of born-again, emerging adults is much less than one would hope. Whether looking at religious truths, religious practice or cultural truths clearly addressed in Scripture, time and again, we have seen that born-again Christians are more likely to side with their culture than with Christ.

We have raised multiple generations of people who claim to be born-again, but who turn their back on the teaching of the one whom they claim is God Almighty in the flesh. They are living as if Christ's teaching was irrelevant to our postmodern situation. Through our in depth survey, we took a closer look at the causes and outcomes of this mindset. In summary, we found the **majority** of born-again, young adults:

- Do not profess a basic biblical worldview
- Have a set of beliefs that appear to have been selected by a blindfolded person randomly picking items from a cafeteria line, i.e. they are inconsistent
- Caught their inconsistent, unbiblical beliefs from their parents (or grandparents)
- Make important decisions without considering biblical truth
- Don't consider sinful behavior much of a problem.

If they follow the example of their parents, they will do an excellent job of supporting the next cultural trend to come along and a poor job of passing down a unique Christian perspective of everything going on in their lives. So, what should we do? Should we give up on trying to impact the practical faith of today's young adults and, instead, focus on changing the minds of their children? Of course, we should focus efforts on intersecting the lives of today's teenagers with the clear message of the gospel. However, the data we have seen here tells us that strategy may work for a few, but most will continue to follow in their parent's footsteps.

An interesting factor in the data we have examined is that the thoughts of baby boomers have changed over the last 30 years; primarily in the wrong direction. Perhaps we can get the attention of these born-again, young adults by putting them into an immersive environment like college where some of them took on stronger beliefs than those held by their parents. Then, it may be possible to begin a change of mind from a hodgepodge of culturally acceptable beliefs to a consistent set of God honoring beliefs. Beliefs that God promises us are the bedrock of truth.

An encouraging note in this discouraging journey of discovery is our status is not new. The apostle Paul expressed concern about a similar loss of the Truth impacting the genuine believers of Colossae. He warns them, "*I say this so that no one will delude you with persuasive argument*" (Col 2:4) with the intent of taking you captive "*through philosophy and empty deception, ... rather than according to Christ*" (Col 2:8).

We find in the New Testament, a clear strategy of Satan is to offer up watered down and distorted views of what it means to live in Christ. This strategy can effectively prevent Christians from bringing more people into eternal life through faith in Jesus. Clearly, from the data we have looked at for American evangelicals, this strategy is having a powerful effect in America today.

In this second chapter of Colossians, Paul goes on to highlight four different types of arguments that could lead us astray: Naturalism, Legalism, Mysticism and Asceticism. All four of these false views are alive and well in our world today. Naturalism (e.g. neo-Darwinism) and Mysticism (e.g. the forms presented by Eckhart Tolle and Oprah Winfrey[1]

) are the most prevalent in our society, but Legalism (i.e. religious rituals and performance over grace) still has a strong influence. Asceticism (i.e. denying the body through severe treatment) is very strong in other parts of the world and a version where we worship the body above all else is certainly prevalent in our society.

Just as it was true for the Colossians, it is true for us: we don't have to fall for these traps that are out to delude our minds. Note that Paul does not say that they are going to become captive to poor worldview thinking. Rather, he is warning them of the danger and giving them instructions on how to avoid this fate. Christ gives us the freedom and Paul gives us clear directions on how to escape from delusional thinking. Paul's advice can be summarized in five key areas:

1. BE FILLED WITH TRUTH: Ask God to fill us with the knowledge of His will (of the truth) with all spiritual wisdom and understanding (Col. 1:9-10; 2:2-3). We cannot be free from the traps of the world without having a handle on the truth to which we are called to cling.

2. CHRIST IS THE SOURCE OF TRUTH: Recognize that Christ is the maker and the sustainer of all and therefore every truth in this world is Christ's truth (Col. 1:15-20). Don't for a moment assume that accepting Christ's truth is an excuse to turn off our brains and accept as true that which is clearly false. Christ's knowledge of truth is perfect far exceeding our attempts to gain truth about the universe. Embracing that fact prepares us to better understand the intricacies of this universe in whatever field we study.

3. THE WORLD CANNOT ADD TO THAT TRUTH: Accept that in Christ, I have been made complete and the acceptance of men and accolades of this world cannot add to that completeness (Col. 2:9-10). The world, the flesh and the devil are going to try to take us captive through our egos. When we put the acceptance of men ahead of the truth of Christ, we are chasing after fleeting accolades and accomplishments. These worldly things cannot make us complete; only in Christ can we find completeness.

4. WALK IN THE TRUTH OF CHRIST: In the same way I received Christ Jesus for eternal life, I am to walk in His Truth in this life. Jesus is not just my insurance when I die; He is my life and I need to be "firmly rooted and grounded in Him" (Col. 2:6-7). I cannot be fulfilling Christ's purpose for my life and at the same time be ignoring His directions for living contained in the New Testament. If I am not firmly rooted in the truth of Scripture, I am choosing to live as if Christ were some guy who lived in a different age who is not up to speed on today's "truth". Remember that Christ lives in eternity outside of the creation of time and His truth is eternal and consistent.

5. I AM A CITIZEN OF HEAVEN: Realize that I am now living in eternity with Christ and am assigned for a brief time to this temporal world (Col. 3:1-3). If we keep in mind that our time on this earth is a temporary assignment albeit with eternal implications, we will take a different view of the culture around us. We are citizens of heaven called to live in ways that glorify Jesus Christ; lifting Him up before a world that desperately needs to turn to Him. (Phil 2:17-21)

Probe Ministries has prepared material available through a variety of delivery mechanisms intended to help you incorporate and disseminate the truth of Christ. Check out the latest material at www.probe.org and www.OnceCaptive.com . Don't fall for Satan's trap that some man-made concept has a better grip on truth than Jesus our creator and sustainer. Regardless of your current age, we have seen that coming generations are looking to you to define their beliefs. Are you going to show them an active belief in Christ as your Truth? If you do, it can make a difference!

Appendix A: Survey Questions Employed from Different Surveys

Biblical Worldview Related Questions:

Topic	Barna & Kinnaman and Probe Survey[1]	Smith (NSYR)[2]	Johnson & Stark (Baylor)[3]	Wright (GSS)[4]
God	God is the all-knowing, all-powerful creator of the world who still rules the universe today.	God is a personal being involved in the lives of people today.	I have no doubt that God exists.	I know God really exists and I have no doubts about it.
Heaven	A person cannot earn their way into Heaven by trying to be good or do good works.	Only people whose sins are forgiven through faith in Jesus Christ go to heaven.	My religion is the one true faith that will lead to salvation and only a few or none non-Christians will go to heaven.[5]	*I definitely believe in life after death, and I definitely believe in heaven.*
Jesus	*Jesus lived a sinless life on earth.*	Jesus was the Son of God who was raised from the dead.	Jesus is the Son of God.	**No question asked on Jesus.**
Bible	Is totally accurate in all of the principles it teaches. (strongly agree or agree)	No question asked on the Bible.	The Bible means exactly what it says & should be taken literally and/or it is perfectly true but should not be taken literally.	The Bible is the actual word of God and is to be taken literally, word for word OR is the inspired word of God but not everything should be taken literally, word for word.

Topic	Barna & Kinnaman and Probe Survey[1]	Smith (NSYR)[2]	Johnson & Stark (Baylor)[3]	Wright (GSS)[4]
Satan / Demons	The devil, or Satan, is not a living being but is a symbol of evil. **Disagree Strongly**	Believe in the existence of demons or evil spirits?	Satan does exist.	I definitely believe in hell.
Morality	Do you believe that there are moral absolutes that are unchanging, or that moral truth always depends upon the circumstances? **Unchanging**	Some people say that morals are relative, that there are no definite rights and wrongs for everybody. **Disagree / Strongly Disagree**	No similar question asked.	Morality is a personal matter and society should not force everyone to follow one standard. **Disagree Somewhat Or Disagree Strongly**
Life Change	No similar question asked.	How important or unimportant is religious faith in shaping how you live your daily life? **Extremely And Very**	No similar question asked.	Have you ever have a religious or spiritual experience that changed your life? **Yes**
Personal God	No similar question asked.	No similar question asked.	God is concerned with the well-being of the world.	There is a God who concerns Himself with every human being personally.

Topic	Barna & Kinnaman and Probe Survey[1]	Smith (NSYR)[2]	Johnson & Stark (Baylor)[3]	Wright (GSS)[4]
One True Religion	No similar question asked.	Only one religion is true.	How many non-Christians will get into heaven? **None Or A Few**[6]	No similar question asked.

Religious Practices Related Questions

Topic	Probe Survey	Smith (NSYR)	Johnson & Stark (Baylor)	Wright (GSS)
Pray	Pray regularly in a typical month.	I pray alone daily and have experienced a specific answer to prayer in the last two years.	Pray at least daily outside of worship services.	About how often do you pray? **At Least Daily**
Read the Bible	Read Bible at least Weekly.	I read from the Bible at least once a week.	Outside of attending religious services, about how often do you read the Bible? **At Least Weekly**	No similar question asked.

Topic	Probe Survey	Smith (NSYR)	Johnson & Stark (Baylor)	Wright (GSS)
Attend church services	Attend church in a typical month.	Attend at least 2-3 times per month.	Attend religious services 2-3 times per month or more.	How often do you attend religious services? 2 to 3 times a month or more.
Involved in church activities	Attend Small Group at least monthly.	Attend SS or other religious group during the week.	How often did you participate in religious education programs, such as Bible study or Sunday school? **At Least Monthly**	How often do you take part in the activities and organizations of a church or place of worship other than attending services? **At Least Monthly**
Share their faith with others	Believe I should share my religious experience with others.	In the last year, I have shared my faith with someone else not of my fait.h	How often did you witness/share your faith with your friends during the last month? **At Least Once**	No similar question asked.
Giving	No related question asked.	No related question asked.	During the last year, contributed more than $500 to your current place of worship.	I try hard to carry my religious beliefs over into all my other dealings in life. **Strongly Agree**

Biblically Informed Cultural Beliefs and Actions

Topic	Probe Survey	Smith (NSYR)	Johnson & Stark (Baylor)	Wright (GSS)
Abortion	No related question asked.	No related question asked.	Abortion because the woman does not want the child is wrong.	Possible for a pregnant woman to obtain a legal abortion if she is married and does not want more children or not married and does not want to marry.
Sex before marriage	1) I do not face difficulties or challenges in: having sex prior to marriage. 2) I do not face difficulties or challenges in: living with someone who I'm not married to.	1) People should wait to have sex until they are married. 2) Two unmarried people who are not in love should not have sex. 3) How important is it to live with the person you are thinking of marrying before getting married? **Not Important**	Sex before marriage and living together before marriage is always wrong.	If a man and woman have sex relations before marriage, I think it is always wrong.
Adultery	I do not face difficulties or challenges in: having sex with someone other than my spouse.	No related question asked.	No related question asked.	A married person should not have sexual relations with someone other than the marriage partner.
Divorce	No related question asked.	A couple without children should stick with it even if they are not happy.	Divorce is almost always wrong.	No related question asked.

Topic	Probe Survey	Smith (NSYR)	Johnson & Stark (Baylor)	Wright (GSS)
Gay sex	I do not face difficulties or challenges in: homosexual thoughts or actions.	No related question asked.	Sex between two adults of the same sex is always wrong.	Sexual relations between two adults of the same sex is always wrong.
Gay marriage	No related question asked.	No related question asked.	Gay marriage is always wrong.	Homosexual couples should have the right to marry one another. **Wrong**
Porno-graphy	I do not face difficulties or challenges in: watching pornography..	About how many X-rated movies, videos, or cable programs have you watched in the last year? **Zero**	Viewing of porn is always wrong.	I have not seen an X-rated movie in the last year **and** there should be laws against the distribution of porn, whatever the age.
Suicide	No related question asked.	No related question asked.	Physician assisted suicide always wrong.	No related question asked.
Material-ism	I do not face difficulties in: not being generous or giving to those in need and/or not having everything I want in terms of possessions.	I would be happier if I could afford to buy more things. **Disagree**	No related question asked.	No related question asked.
Lying / Cheating	I do not face difficulties in: lying or being dishonest or in cheating.	No related question asked.	No related question asked.	No related question asked.

Topic	Probe Survey	Smith (NSYR)	Johnson & Stark (Baylor)	Wright (GSS)
Evolution	No related question asked.	Do you believe it is possible that God may have used evolution to create the world over a long period of time, or not? **Not**	Humans evolved from other primates over millions of years **Disgagree** Creationism should be taught in public schools **Agree**	Human beings, as we know them today, developed from earlier species of animals. **False**
Science	The Bible and science are essentially consistent.	The teachings of science and religion often ultimately conflict with each other. **Disagree**	Science and religion are incompatible **Disagree** Science helps to reveal God's glory. **Agree**	We trust too much in science and not enough in religious faith. **Agree**
Research	No related question asked.	Scientists should be free to do any research, even on controversial subjects like human cloning, without interference from religious morals or teachings. **Disagree**	Embryonic stem cell research is almost always wrong.	No related question asked.

Items in italics are significantly different from the questions from other surveys

Appendix B: Denominations Used in Different Surveys

Denomination	Probe	Baylor 2005
Evangelical/Pentacostal Denominations		
Adventist (7th Day or other)	X	X
African Methodist Episcopal	X	X
Anabaptist		X
Assembly of God	X	X
Baptist		X
Baptist, Southern	X	
Baptist, Other	X	
Bible Church		X
Brethren	X	X
Christian	X	X
Church of Christ – other	X	
Church of God		X
Congregational	X	X
Evangelical Free	X	
Foursquare	X	
Holiness		X
Lutheran – Missouri Synod	X	
Lutheran – other	X	
Mennonite	X	X
Nazarene	X	X
Non-denominational/independent	X	X
Pentecostal	X	X
Presbyterian – other	X	
Reformed	X	X
Wesleyan	X	
Other	X	
Mainline Protestant Denominations		
Baptist – American	X	
Church of Christ – United COC	X	X
Disciples of Christ	X	X
Episcopal	X	X
Lutheran		X
Lutheran – ELCA	X	
Methodist	X	X
Orthodox	X	X
Presbyterian		X
Presbyterian – PCUSA	X	
Protestant – not specified	X	
Quaker/Friends		X
Not sure	X	

Notes

Introduction

[1] The data was downloaded from the Association of Religion Data Archives, www.TheARDA.com, and were collected by the principal investigators named in the referenced endnotes.

[2] NSYR The National Study of Youth and Religion, http://www.youthandreligion.org, whose data were used by permission here, was generously funded by Lilly Endowment Inc., under the direction of Christian Smith, of the Department of Sociology at the University of Notre Dame

[3] Baylor University. 2005. *The Baylor Religion Survey*. Waco, TX: Baylor Institute for Studies of Religion

[4] General Social Survey 2008 Cross Section and Panel Combined, National Opinion Research Center, 2008

[5] David Kinnaman, *The Buster Report – A New Generation of Adults Describes Their Life and Spirituality*, The Barna Group, 2007

[6] Probe Ministries, *Culturally Captive Christian Study 2010*, 2010, Barna Group

Chapter 1 Living as Captives of our Culture

[1] Christian Smith and Patricia Snell, *Souls in Transition, The Religious & Spiritual Lives of Emerging Adults*, 2009, Oxford University Press

[2] Ibid p. 5

[3] Colossians 2:8 NASU

[4] Smith and Snell, *Souls in Transition*, p. 101

[5] Ibid p. 46

[6] Ibid p. 51

[7] Ibid p. 47

[8] Ibid p. 49

[9] Ibid p. 68

[10] Ibid p. 72

[11] Ibid p. 67

[12] Ibid p. 62-63

[13] Ibid p. 252

[14] Ibid p. 296

[15] David Kinnaman, *unchristian: What a New Generation Really Thinks About Christianity . . . And Why It Matters*, Baker Books, 2007, p. 11

[16] Smith and Snell, p. 133 Table 4.15

[17] Ibid p. 296

[18] Ibid p. 286

[19] Ibid p. 297

Chapter 2 A Clear Warning Against Cultural Captivity

[1] Vine's Expository Dictionary of New Testament Words, Thomas Nelson Publishers

[2] Dr. Ray Bohlin, *Redeeming Darwin: The Intelligent Design Controversy*, 2007, http://www.probe.org/site/c.fdKEIMNsEoG/b.4218231/k.DC2E/Redeeming_Darwin_The_Intelligent_Design_Controversy.htm

[3] http://www.thearda.com/Archive/Files/Descriptions/NSYRW3.asp. "The National Study of Youth and Religion," http://www.youthandreligion.org, whose data were used by permission here, was generously funded by Lilly Endowment Inc., under the direction of Christian Smith of the Department of Sociology at the University of Notre Dame.

[4] Eckhart Tolle, *A New Earth: Awakening to Your Life's Purpose*, Penguin Group, New York, 2006

[5] For more information on Eckhart Tolle's brand of new age mysticism see the article on the Probe website, Steve Cable, "Oprah's Spirituality: Exploring "A New Earth", 2008, http://www.probe.org/site/c.fdKEIMNsEoG/b.4217681/k.E59/Oprahs_Spirituality_Exploring_A_New_Earth

[6] Colossians 2:10

Chapter 3 The Confusing Clamor of Statistical Studies

[1] Bradley Wright, PhD, *Christians are Hate Filled Hypocrites . . . and Other Lies You've Been Told*, Minneapolis, Minn., Bethany House, 2010, p. 75.

[2] Ibid p. 66.

[3] Ibid p. 41.

[4] Baylor University. 2005. The Baylor Religion Survey. Waco, TX: Baylor Institute for Studies of Religion.

[5] Bradley Johnson, PhD, *The Good News About Evangelicalism*, *First Things* online edition, February 2011, http://www.firstthings.com/article/2011/01/the-good-news-about-evangelicalism.

[6] Ibid

[7] Rodney Stark, *What Americans Really Believe*, Baylor University Press, 2008

[8] Smith and Snell, You can find two extensive articles on the Christian Smith book and data by Steve Cable at the Probe web site (www.probe.org) www.probe.org/site/c.fdKEIMNsEoG/b.6213441/k.DC74/Emerging_Adults_and _the_Future_of_Faith_in_America and ww.probe.org/site/c.fdKEIMNsEoG/b.6417481/k.D4EB/Emerging_Adults_Part_ 2_Distinctly_Different_Faiths

[9] Ibid p. 101.

[10] Ibid p. 286.

[11] Ibid. p. 286.

[12] Ibid. p. 288.

[13] Christian Smith, *Lost in Transition: The Dark Side of Emerging Adulthood*, Oxford University Press, 2011, p. 3

[14] Barna Group, Barna Survey Examines Changes in Worldview Among Christians over the Past 13 Years, http://www.barna.org/barna-update/article/21-transformation/252-barna-survey-examines-changes-in-worldview-among-christians-over-the-past-13-years, 2009

[15]. For the purposes of the survey, a "biblical worldview" was defined as believing that absolute moral truth exists; the Bible is totally accurate in all of the principles it teaches; Satan is considered to be a real being or force, not merely symbolic; a person cannot earn their way into Heaven by trying to be good or do good works; Jesus Christ lived a sinless life on earth; and God is the all-knowing, all-powerful creator of the world who still rules the universe today. In the research, anyone who held all of those beliefs was said to have a biblical worldview.

[16] David Kinnaman, *The Buster Report – A New Generation of Adults Describes Their Life and Spirituality*, The Barna Group, 2007

[17] Kinnaman, *unchristian*, p. 11

[18] Ibid, p. 28

Chapter 4 Sorting Out the Confusion

[1] Barna and Kinnaman data used consistently in assessing biblical worldview

[2] NSYR data from ARDA

[3] Baylor data from ARDA

[4] GSS data from ARDA

[5] We selected to consider the case where a few non-Christians will go to heaven to cover those who would consider Moses, David, Abraham and the like as non-Christians who will be in heaven. Of course some people who say at there will be

a few Non-Christians in heaven may be relying on good works or other schemes as another way to heaven.

[6] See endnote 15 from Chapter 3 above

[7] See endnote 5 from Chapter 4 above

[8] Nancy Pearcey, *Total Truth: Liberating Christianity from Its Cultural Captivity,* Wheaton, IL: Crossway Books, 2004

Chapter 5 Disconnected Religious Beliefs and Behaviors

[1] Smith and Snell, p. 145

[2] Ibid p. 146

[3] See endnote 5 from Chapter 4 above

[4] Ibid p. 148

[5] Ibid p. 149

[6] Ibid p. 149

[7] Ibid p. 154

[8] Ibid p. 154

[9] Pearcy, page 33

[10] Ibid p. 109

[11] Smith and Snell, p. 153

[12] Ibid p. 158

[13] Ibid p. 158

[14] Ibid p. 158

[15] Ibid p. 158

[16] Ibid p. 157

[17] Ibid p. 157

[18] Ibid p. 285 emphasis added

[19] Ibid p. 284

[20] Ibid p. 249

Chapter 6 Combined with Inconsistent Practices

[1] Kerby Anderson, *Divorce*, 1997, www.probe.org/Divorce . See also Rusty Wright, *Divorce and You*, 2005, www.probe.org/divorce_and_you

[2] Kerby Anderson, *Pornography*, 2008, www.probe.org/pornography

[3] The Big Bang Theory, CBS

[4] Kerby Anderson, Cohabitation, 2003, www.probe.org/cohabitation . See also

Kerby Anderson, Love Myths, 2002, www.probe.org/love_myths

[5] The cumulative format is explained in the text immediately preceding Figure 5-4

[6] Kerby Anderson, *Arguments Against Abortion*, 1997, www.probe.org/arguments_against_abortion . See also Sue Bohlin, *Abortion*, 1992, www.probe.org/abortion

[7] Kerby Anderson, *Homosexual Theology*, 1997, www.probe.org/Homosexual_Theology . See also Sue Bohlin, *Homosexual Myths*, 1996, www.probe.org/Homosexual_Myths

[8] Kerby Anderson, *Heterosexual and Homosexual Marriages*, 2008, www.probe.org/HandH_Marriages

[9] Dr. Ray Bohlin, *Euthanasia: The Battle for Life*, 1996, www.probe.org/battle_for_life . See also Kerby Anderson, *Euthanasia*, 1998, www.probe.org/Euthanasia

[10] Dr. Ray Bohlin and Richard Milne, *Christian Views of Science and Earth History*, 1998, www.probe.org/Earth_History . Dr. Ray Bohlin, *Redeeming Darwin: The Intelligent Design Controversy*, 2007, www.probe.org/Redeeming_Darwin

[11] Dr. Ray Bohlin, *Human Cloning*, 1994, www.probe.org/Human_Cloning . See also Dr. Ray Bohlin, *Stem Cells and the Controversy Over Therapeutic Cloning*, 2001, www.probe.org/Stem_Cells_and_Cloning . See also Heather Zieger, *What Do We Make of the Stem Cell Debate*?, 2009, www.probe.org/Stem_Cell_Debate

Chapter 7 Belief and Behavior Vary by Demographic

[1] Data exists in the Baylor survey which could be used to augment the GSS data, but it has not been analyzed.

[2] The lowest rated question among black Americans is "There is a God who concerns Himself with every human being personally."

[3] Smith and Snell, p. 248-250

Chapter 8 Troubling Aspects of Emerging Adult Beliefs

[1] Smith, Lost in Transition, p. 15

[2] John 18:37 NASU

[3] Del Tackett and Chuck Colson, *The Way Out: God's Solution to Moral Chaos in America*, 2011, www.truthinaction.org/index.php/landing-doing-the-right-thing-full-episode/

[4] American Heritage Dictionary

[5] Smith, p. 21

[6] Ibid p. 22

[7] Del Tackett and Chuck Colson

[8] Smith, p. 72

[9] Ibid p. 73

[10] Matthew 6:33 NASU

[11] National Study of Youth and Religion

[12] National Study on Youth and Religion (NSYR), Baylor Religious Survey 2005, GSS 2008

[13] Smith, p. 193

[14] Smith and Snell, p. 169

[15] Ibid, p. 174

[16] Smith p. 196

[17] Smith, p. 211

[18] Smith, p. 218

[19] Dr. Caroline Crocker, *Free to Think: Why Scientific Integrity Matters,* Leafcutter Press, 2010, page 79

[20] Smith and Snell, p. 145

[21] Ibid p. 146

[22] National Study of Youth and Religion (NSYR), Baylor Religious Survey 2005, GSS 2008, Probe Ministries Culturally Captive Christian Study 2010

[23] Or born-again

[24]Smith and Snell, p. 149

[25] Ibid p. 154

[26] Ibid p. 154

[27] Ibid, p. 149

[28] Ibid, p. 153

[29] Ibid, p. 153

[30] Ibid, p. 227

[31] Ibid, p. 224-5

[32] Ibid, p. 228

[33] Ibid, p. 223

[34] John 16:8 NASU

[35] Ibid, p. 234

[36] Ibid p. 236

[37] Ibid p. 155

[38] Ibid p. 156

Chapter 9 Cultural Captivity Takes Many Forms

[1] Philippians 3:20 NASU

[2] Al Janssen, *The Marriage Masterpiece,* Tyndale House Publishers, 2001.

[3] Barna Group, "New Marriage and Divorce Statistics Released," March 31, 2008.

[4] Ibid.

[5] Bradley Wright, "Divorce Rates Among Christians by Church Attendance," December 4, 2006

[6] Barna Group, "Most Twentysomethings Put Christianity on the Shelf Following Spiritually Active Teen Years"; "New Research Shows How Different Generations View and Use the Bible", October 19, 2009.

[7] Philippians 4:11-13 NASU

Chapter 10 How Did We Get This Way

[1] These questions are as follows: Life Purpose - any answer with God or Jesus as the center, Jesus Christ is the only path to God, Mohammed, Buddha and Jesus are not all valid ways to God, I should present my truth to others without judging them., the Bible and science are essentially consistent, and everything the Bible says is true when interpreted correctly

[2] From GSS survey data.

[3] The cumulative format is explained in the text immediately preceding Figure 5-4

Chapter 11 Family – The Primary Source for Beliefs

[1] Smith and Snell, p. 154

[2] Ibid p. 154

[3] Ibid p. 285

[4] Ibid p. 256

[5] Viggo Olsen, *Daktar: Diplomat in Bangladesh*, The Moody Bible Institute, 1973

Chapter 12 What Parents Are Passing On

[1] The cumulative format is explained in the text immediately preceding Figure 5-4

Chapter 13 Different Groups Highlight Different Issues

[1] Denominations are listed in Appendix B

Chapter 14 From Captives to Conquerors

[1] Steve Cable, *Oprah's Spirituality: Exploring* A New Earth, www.probe.org/site/c.fdKEIMNsEoG/b.4217681/k.E59/Oprahs_Spirituality_Exploring_A_New_Earth

Appendix A: Survey Questions Employed from Different Surveys

[1] Barna and Kinnaman data used consistently in assessing biblical worldview

[2] NSYR data from ARDA

[3] Baylor data from ARDA

[4] GSS data from ARDA

[5] We selected to consider the case where a few non-Christians will go to heaven to cover those who would consider Moses, David, Abraham and the like as non-Christians who will be in heaven. Of course some people who say at there will be a few Non-Christians in heaven may be relying on good works or other schemes as another way to heaven.

[6] See endnote 5 from Chapter 4 above